WITHDRAWN

BUREAUCRACY AND
SOCIAL JUSTICE

Kennikat Press

National University Publications

Interdisciplinary Urban Series

General Editor

Raymond A. Mohl

Florida Atlantic University

JOSEPH P. VITERITTI

BUREAUCRACY AND SOCIAL JUSTICE

THE ALLOCATION OF JOBS AND SERVICES TO MINORITY GROUPS

National University Publications
KENNIKAT PRESS // 1979
Port Washington, N. Y. // London

Manufactured in the United States of America

Published by
Kennikat Press Corp.
Port Washington, N.Y. / London

Library of Congress Cataloging in Publication Data

Viteritti, Joseph P   1946–
    Bureaucracy and social justice.

    (National university publications) (Interdisciplinary
urban series)
    Bibliography: p.
    Includes index.
    1. Civil service—New York (City)—Minority
employment. 2. Municipal services—New York (City)
I. Title.
JS1234.A4 1979   352.0474'1   79-10707
ISBN 0-8046-9244-0

TO
MY PARENTS

CONTENTS

TABLES

GRAPHS

PREFACE

My work on the present subject began about seven years ago. Its first product appeared in 1973 in the form of a case study on policy making in the New York City Police Department.[1] The purpose of the first study was twofold. On the one hand, it was a critique of the "ideology of participation" which emerged from the federal anti-poverty program and was embraced by many local government reformers, including the then incumbent mayor of New York, John Lindsay. On the other hand, it was designed to evaluate the normative conclusions which appeared in Sayre and Kaufman's classic study of power and politics in New York.[2]

Urban reformers in the mid-sixties and throughout the seventies, who have now become identified in the professional literature with the "New Public Administration," had denounced traditional administrative institutions as unrepresentative and unresponsive.[3] They advocated the decentralization of local government bureaucracies in a way which would provide citizen groups with direct access to the decision making process. To the contrary, Sayre and Kaufman, in the fashion of the pluralist thinking which had dominated the political science literature of their time, praised the political and governmental system of New York as one which was open, responsive, and receptive to new groups. In his final years the late Wallace Sayre emerged as one of the most articulate critics of decentralized government in New York, and his colleague Herbert Kaufman responded to the idea with something less than enthusiasm.[4]

Despite the points of difference which existed between the decentralists and the pluralists, they did have some important common ground. Both worked according to the assumption that the political systems in American cities were capable of accommodating the wants, needs, and interests of all urban residents. It was this type of thinking which gave birth to the ideology of participation. Thereby many well-meaning reformers were advocating the political mobilization of the poor as an antidote to the many social maladies by which they were victimized.

I found the assumptions of these reformers rather disturbing, for they had run contrary to the conventional wisdom that had evolved from several decades of political science research. Most evidence on the subject of American political behavior had demonstrated that the poor, by nature, do not participate in public affairs, they do not possess the social requisites for successful political action, and therefore it was not very likely that they would emerge as a viable force for change either in their own interest or for the benefit of the system as a whole.

The first part of my case study seemed to illustrate the point once more that the poor, particularly racial minorities in New York, are at a significant disadvantage when they find themselves advocating a policy which is contrary to the preferences of older, more established interest groups in the city. Yet the conclusions of the study were not entirely pessimistic. The second part proceeded on the notion that while politics and government are closely interrelated, the two are not the same. Perhaps, therefore, there is an aspect of the governmental system which is capable of working to the advantage of the poor despite their political deficiencies. It was the latter idea which led me to an investigation of bureaucratic decision making.

It was my concern that, in decentralizing our local bureaucracies, the reformers of the day might be dismantling those very institutions which were responding to the needs of the poor. In the meantime, through the advocacy of citizen and group participation in the administrative process, they might be widening the scope of that aspect of public decision making which was least responsive to the poor, the political.

Needless to say, my curiosities ran contrary to the predispositions of many of my contemporary colleagues. However, these queries led to a number of interesting questions, which were far from novel in our profession. Was there any validity to the politics-administration dichotomy once believed to exist by classical public administration theorists? Did bureaucracy really work towards the rational and efficient accomplishment of social ends? Did the impersonal, objective, and procedural activities of career civil servants really lead to an equality of treatment among clientele? These older questions led to some newer ones. Could the politically neutral activities of bureaucratic decision makers be transformed into a distribution of public goods which benefits all citizens regardless of social influence? Is there any logical and empirical relationship between the traditional administrative goal of neutral efficiency and the capability of our bureaucratic institutions to serve the needs of the citizenry in an equitable manner? What impact did the recent demands for a more "scientific" approach to public management have on this relationship?

The second part of my case study focused upon the application of modern management techniques for the deployment of resources in the Police Department. It demonstrated that there is an aspect of bureaucratic decision making which is objective, seemingly rational, and, for the most part, removed from the realm of political activity. The outcome of this process proved to be both operationally efficient and especially favorable to the nonwhite poor of the city.

Of course, it was not my intention at the time to propose that bureaucracy would ever serve as a panacea to our existing social ills, or that the administration of government could ever be divorced from its politics. As I stated then and explained further in a complementary essay on the subject, it was not my understanding that the business of government could ever proceed along a wholly objective course, or that the efficient management of government would ever work to offset the political impotence of the poor.[5] However, the positive findings were still intriguing, and they gave rise to more questions of the type which are indigenous to the case study approach. How typical were the policy outcomes which had been observed? What were the conditions which set the stage for their development? Obviously, more research was needed before these questions could be addressed. It was for this reason that the present study was begun.

The present study is greater in both scope and depth than the original one. It is not meant as either an attack upon the New Public Administration or as a defense of bureaucracy. Instead, it is an attempt to integrate the traditional principles of the old public administration with contemporary concerns over normative issues and the modern techniques of policy analysis. It may be said that the present book takes the New Public Administration as a starting point and then looks back upon the past to discover what in our intellectual heritage is worthy of being salvaged.

The ongoing discussions in the professional literature concerning the representativeness of our bureaucratic institutions and the equity with which they distribute their services are fundamental to the proper study of government. Such issues suffered from too much neglect during the brief period when the social sciences were going through their "behavioral revolution." However, a good part of this recent discussion has been clouded by an almost casual reference to the ideals enunciated with no clear definition of what they mean, how they are related, or how they might be operationalized for use in empirical analysis. Therefore, my first purpose in the present book is to add clarity to the discussions by focusing on the concepts of representativeness and social equity, incorporating them into a single definition of justice, and then applying them to research on the bureaucracy of a particular city, New York. In so doing I have borrowed much from the valuable works of John Rawls and Hanna Pitkin.[6]

These normative concerns notwithstanding, the fiscal crisis which has struck New York City and continues to threaten other municipalities across the nation serves to demonstrate that local governments must cultivate a capability to go about their business in a more efficient and effective manner. This troubling fact of urban life brings to mind once again the traditional goals of our own profession. While these pragmatic concerns are perhaps less esoteric than our contemporary normative ones, they are still basic to the survival of our urban centers. American cities will not survive unless they pursue the goals of social justice and operational efficiency simultaneously. It is my intention to show that these goals are not only achievable within our bureaucratic institutions, but that they are also complementary.

ACKNOWLEDGMENTS

The acknowledgment of one's debts is the most pleasant part in the preparation of a manuscript. It is usually the last page written, and therefore signifies the completion of the task undertaken. It also provides the writer with an opportunity to thank some of those who have been helpful along the way. I have been most fortunate in the amount and the caliber of assistance with which I was provided.

Ned Schneier was one of the first individuals to take an interest in the present project. His advice and support have been instrumental in its development from a research proposal to a finished product. If I have herein demonstrated any facility in the treatment of theoretical issues and conceptual analysis, much of it is due to Melvin Richter, from whom I have learned much. Richard Halverson's contributions of time and constructive criticism have been both helpful and generous. Blanche Blank stimulated my interest in the present subject and guided the original case study.

I am also grateful for the access, information, and insights provided me by several individuals who were directly involved in the events to be described. Among them are the former Rand analysts Warren Walker and Ed Ignall, the former New York City Budget Director David Grossman, the former Civil Service Commissioner Frank Arricale II, and Mitchell Sviridoff of the Ford Foundation. Other friends and colleagues have read earlier drafts of the manuscript. Among them are Raymond Horton, Ron Edmonds, and Carol Brownell.

My greatest debt is to Frank Macchiarola, who, more than anyone else, has played the role of mentor. He served as a helpful critic and supportive friend. While he was not always in agreement with my ideas or conclusions, he always demonstrated a concern that they be expressed in a clear and professional manner. In a three-year interval, when he was faced with demanding responsibilities as deputy director of the New York State Emergency Financial Control Board, as vice president of a graduate school in a period of crisis, and as Chancellor of the nation's largest school system, he always found time to make himself available. That was not only a feat in the efficient management of personal time, but also an expression of genuine interest. For that commitment, I will always remain grateful.

Finally, a note of gratitude is in order for my proofreader Allyson Kleinman, my secretary Audrey Smith, ánd my typist Marcy Shain, all of whom proved to be unusually reliable.

BUREAUCRACY AND SOCIAL JUSTICE

ABOUT THE AUTHOR

Joseph P. Viteritti is Assistant to the Chancellor of the New York City school system where he specializes in the areas of management and policy analysis. He is also an Adjunct Professor of Political Science at Bernard Baruch College. Dr. Viteritti is formerly Assistant Director of the CUNY Urban Academy for Management which was created in 1974 as a cooperative effort between the City University of New York and the City of New York to provide management training and technical assistance to local government agencies. He has served as a management consultant to eight New York City agencies including the Sanitation and Fire departments. Dr. Viteritti received his Ph.D. in Political Science from the City University of New York. He is the author of *Police, Politics and Pluralism in New York City* (1973) and has written a number of articles and technical papers in the fields of government and politics.

1

INTRODUCTION

It has been more than two decades since Herbert Kaufman's article on the doctrines of public administration appeared in the *American Political Science Review*.[1] In that article Kaufman proposed that throughout the history of this nation our administrative institutions have been organized and operated in pursuit of three values, which he designated as representativeness, neutral competence, and executive leadership. According to his analysis, each of these values has been dominant in different periods of history. However, he also emphasized that at no time was one value supported to the point of a total suppression of the others. To the contrary, each had been framed in terms of the advancement of that which preceded it. Thus, Kaufman writes, "The story is one of changing balance among the values, not of total displacement."[2]

Kaufman traced the origins of the representative doctrine to colonial times, and its prominent rise in administrative matters to the election of President Andrew Jackson. He observed the simultaneous growth of political neutrality and executive leadership as twentieth-century phenomena which emerged in response to the abuses brought about by the spoils system and the dominance of corrupt legislators in public affairs.

By the early part of the twentieth century, the merit system had begun to replace patronage as the prevailing method of official recruitment, and efficiency succeeded influence as a standard for administrative decision making. The merit system was designed to provide each qualified individual with an equal opportunity to serve in an official capacity and at the same time was meant to insure a minimum level of competence within the public workforce. The pursuit of increased efficiency in government, which grew out of the scientific management movement, represented a public sector response to the need for a better quality of service at a lower cost to the taxpayer. It was based on the idea that the objective pursuit of administrative goals by politically neutral professionals would eventually allow government to be run in a businesslike fashion for the better interest of the general public.

We have now come full circle. Just prior to the last two decades most prescriptive analysis in the professional literature emphasized the need to segregate administration from the forces of politics. Neutrality was the behavioral guideline for the public administrator. Now contemporary students are advocating institutional reforms which would increase the role politics plays in the administration of government.

In September of 1968 a group of young social scientists met at the Minnowbrook Conference Center near Syracuse University to set down the precepts for what is now commonly known as the New Public Administration. The participants at that event were motivated by a strong determination to accentuate the important part which normative issues should play in the study and practice of public administration. They enunciated a demand for "social equity" in the provision of government services and outlined an agenda for reform which was anti-bureaucratic in its orientation. Thus, H. George Frederickson, one of the major organizers of the conference, has written: "The rationale for Public Administration is almost always better (more efficient or economical) management. New Public Administration adds social equity to the classic objectives and rationale."[3]

The New Public Administration calls for the decentralization of our administrative institutions in a way which permits citizen groups and community residents to participate in, or at least influence, the decision making process of those government agencies by which they are served. It is based upon the assumption that decentralization and public participation in administration will bring about greater representation of the citizenry in our government institutions and a more equitable distribution of services. The major beneficiaries of this client-responsive system, it is believed, would be the socially disadvantaged, who allegedly enjoy neither adequate accessibility to our traditional institutions nor a fair share of the services provided.

Since decentralization has already been implemented in a number of American cities, a good deal of research has been performed concerning its impact upon citizens, local services, and the distribution of government resources. However, the evidence emerging from this work is of a rather mixed and incomplete nature. There are some indications that decentralization has a positive impact upon public opinion regarding feelings of political efficacy and satisfaction with services.[4] However, at the same time other research has shown that decentralization has had a minor impact upon the distribution of power and influence in local communities.[5] In a most comprehensive review of the current research literature, Yin and Yates have found that, while decentralization tends to improve the flow of public information and actual service delivery, it has little effect upon the attitudes of service officials and has not increased client control.[6] Despite the broad scope of this work, which covers 269 separate studies, the authors concluded that much of the existing research is opinion-based and that the findings are rather uncertain. Thus, they have written:

... by strictly scientific standards it is for several reasons an unarguably weak literature. The studies rarely contain careful experimental designs and procedures. Often the evaluators were themselves active participants in the innovations. In addition, the criteria for success and failure varied and were vague and ambiguous. Many of the studies covered brief time periods and therefore did not present a persuasive account of the innovation's changing character over time.[7]

It appears that racial minorities continue to have a more favorable attitude towards the idea of decentralization than do whites.[8] However, there is no convincing evidence that they have gained better representation or a more equitable share of public goods as a result of decentralization experiments.

The ongoing debate over the relative merits of our traditional bureaucratic structures and the decentralized institutions proposed by contemporary reformers might easily be misconstrued as a conflict over values. One side demands direct citizen representation in administrative decision making, while the other defends a standard of political neutrality which is supposedly protected by a merit system of recruitment and a dedication to the efficient performance of governmental operations. However, there is no necessary reason why the two doctrines are incompatible. As Kaufman has explained, our traditional institutions, which were born in an era when the ideal of efficient neutrality had dominated administrative thinking, were never meant to undermine the democratic features of our governmental system.

What is at issue today is the proficiency with which bureaucratic institutions have represented the needs and the interests of the entire citizenry, particularly the disadvantaged. The following study will evaluate that capability. It will examine the compatibility between the traditional institutional arrangement and the concerns for representativeness and social equity voiced by present-day reformers. It will proceed in the form of a case study of New York City, which will focus on the relationship that existed between local government agencies and black and Puerto Rican minority groups during the mayoralty of John V. Lindsay.

The empirical research to be presented will address two distinct, though closely related, issues. The first will examine the degree of representation under a recruitment policy governed by the merit system. This analysis will cover all New York City agencies for which data are available. The second will investigate the allocation of essential services among racial communities by three traditionally organized local government agencies. These will include the Police, Fire, and Sanitation departments of the city.

New York City has long been the scene of a wide variety of administrative reforms. Historically, it was the birthplace of both the merit system and the bureau movement. During the turbulent sixties it provided a testing ground for several federally sponsored and locally initiated experiments in decentralized government and community control. In 1972 the City bureaucracy became the target for a major effort to improve productivity in the delivery of local services. In its eight-year stay in City Hall beginning in 1965, the Lindsay administration implemented a variety of managerial and organizational reforms which epitomized the principles of both the old and the new public administrations. Under the leadership of a strong yet controversial chief executive, it attempted to increase the representation of the city's poor in the administrative process and at the same time called upon the skills of professional technicians to improve the efficiency of the city government.

While New York is currently in the midst of several financial and managerial reforms designed to increase the accountability and efficiency of its local service organizations, the city also stands at the threshold of a major organizational innovation which displays an obvious affinity to the goals commonly identified with the New Public Administration. In November of 1975 the voters of the city approved a new Charter which by 1981 will decentralize several local government agencies into coterminous administrative districts.[9] Those services affected include police patrol, street cleaning and refuse collection, parks and recreation, social services, housing code enforcement, neighborhood preservation and rehabilitation, highway and street maintenance, and health services. Each district will contain a local community board representing the population of the area, a district service manager chosen by the board, and a service cabinet composed of delegates from operating agencies in the district. The local boards will be granted advisory power on matters concerning land use, budgeting, and service monitoring. While the new plan does not provide local communities with any direct decision making authority, it does represent one of the most ambitious steps taken by a major American city in the direction of a decentralized, client-responsive service delivery system.

It is not possible to estimate with any degree of certainty the eventual impact of the stated reforms upon New York City. We do not know if the future will bring a more representative government, a more equitable distribution of services, or a highly volatile politicized environment which will unravel the fabric of a now operable system. At best, any assessment about what remains before us is merely an act of informed speculation. However, it is presently possible, and indeed appropriate, to evaluate the assumptions of some reformers that the current institutional arrangement is neither representative of certain groups nor equitable in the distribution of services. It is time to reassess the impact of the old civil service and managerial reforms as we prepare to take a step in another direction.

It goes without saying that any major change from the established way of doing things involves a certain amount of risk. However, only by a comprehensive evaluation of the current state of affairs can we hope to define the magnitude of the risk. While at this point the matter may be merely "academic" insofar as New York is concerned, perhaps there is something to be learned from the New York experience by other cities which are contemplating reforms similar to those in the new charter.

In going about our work here, however, we must also be conscious of the limitations of the present study. I do not mean to claim that if racial minorities are well represented in New York, or if they do receive an equitable share of public service, the same is necessarily the case in other local areas. It should also be emphasized that it is not my purpose here to undermine the normative concerns of well-intentioned reformers, nor to minimize the inherent value of active participation in public life. Instead, I would like to issue a note of caution, that perhaps in some American cities bureaucratic institutions may provide a more effective means to the ideal of social equity than would the participatory devices brought about by some of the proposed reforms.

PUBLIC ADMINISTRATION: OLD AND NEW

Before discussing the research in greater detail it is essential, for the sake of analytical clarity, to begin defining more precisely what is meant here by the old and new public administrations. One might say in a cursory manner that the New Public Administration represents all that the Minnowbrook group stood for, and the old all with which it found fault. In fact, however, there is no one model for the old public administration any more than there is a singular prescription for decentralized government.

In its most orthodox form the traditional model of administrative organization is found in Max Weber's ideal type definition of bureaucracy.[10] Despite the serious misgivings Weber had concerning the impact of a bureaucratic society upon the human spirit, he believed that bureaucratic organization represented the most rational and efficient form of human activity for the accomplishment of a given social end.

Woodrow Wilson eventually adapted a version of this classical model to his normative studies on administrative institutions within the United States.[11] Hence, it is for good reason that the former chief executive is sometimes referred to as one of the founders of American public administration. Wilson's model was later revised, perhaps refined, by behaviorally oriented social scientists such as Herbert Simon.[12] Simon and his followers, while raising some basic questions about the limits of rationality and objectivity in human organizations, continued to identify efficiency as a defendable administrative goal.

In the latter half of the twentieth century, the human and organizational components of the traditional model underwent yet another change. This resulted from the influx of non-career managerial technicians into public agencies, called technocrats by some, who were brought into government service for the purpose of applying more "scientific" methods to administrative and policy-related problems.

In spite of several aberrations from the original classical form which evolved over a period of some fifty years, the variety of institutions which we would include under the old public administration type are still commonly referred to in the literature as "bureaucratic." While most proponents of the traditional model or models supported the politics-administration dichotomy as a normative ideal, few, including Weber, believed the separation was ever fully attainable. This apparent contradiction would finally become an important point of contention between defenders and opponents of the older institutions.

Criticisms of the traditional model which finally culminated in a demand for a New Public Administration can usually be traced to two distinct places of origin. On the one side were those directed by organization theorists who challenged the conceptual premises upon which it stood, particularly its claims of operational superiority and political neutrality. On the other side were those political activists who participated in the civil rights and black power movements, who challenged the legitimacy of those institutions, which they believed were inherently undemocratic and non-representative.

Decentralization, as we know it today, exists in at least two general forms. Alan Altshuler draws the distinction between what he calls "administrative decentralization" and "political decentralization."[13] The first involves the delegation of authority from superior to subordinate officials within a particular administrative organization. The second refers to the transfer of authority to officials who are dependent upon a subjurisdictional electorate or clientele outside the administrative organization. It is the latter with which we are most concerned here when contrasting the New Public Administration with the bureaucratic approach.[14]

Political decentralization may vary in form from an institutional arrangement which merely provides citizen groups with advisory powers and an opportunity to voice their policy preferences, as is the case under the recently adopted New York City charter, to the granting of actual decision making power to citizen groups, as in the New York City school system. In its most extreme form political decentralization has been associated with the demand for "community control" of local service agencies.[15]

We will discuss more explicitly in the next two chapters the historical development and significance of the various types of institutions which fall under the traditional and decentralized categories. At this time, in order to provide a clearer basis for distinguishing between the two broader classifications of the old and the New, let us focus upon some of their more general characteristics.

At the risk of oversimplification, and cognizant of existing aberrations from the general forms, one may designate three principal criteria by which traditional administrative institutions can be distinguished from the newer forms. These include organizational structure, the manner in which officials are selected, and the conditions of tenure.

Organizational Structure. The organizational structure of most bureaucratic institutions is hierarchic in nature, with decision making authority decreasing as one descends the formal chain of command. It is believed by most proponents of this type that a hierarchic structure establishes a mechanism for order, uniform cooperative action, and the means for accomplishing goals in the most efficient manner.[16]

In the decentralized institution, as the name implies, authority and discretion are more widely shared among individuals at all levels of the organizational structure. Under political decentralization this dispersion of the decision making prerogative actually extends outside the formal structure of the organization to client and citizen groups. The major virtue of this institutional arrangement is believed to be its democratic features, which protect against the concentration of power in the hands of one individual or group.

Manner of Selection. With some exceptions, which will be explained later, most officials within the traditional bureaucratic institution are selected according to a uniform standard of merit. The rationale for this system of recruitment is consistent with the operational goal of maximized efficiency. It is assumed that selecting personnel with the appropriate technical qualifications and skills will provide for a certain minimum level of job performance.

One of the most distinguishing features of a politically decentralized organization is that individuals are admitted into the decision making structure, either in an advisory or discretionary capacity, on the basis of popular election. These individuals serve alongside career civil servants. Their status is "political" in the sense that they usually perform the role of advocates of a particular citizen or client group, thereby shunning the cloak of neutrality. This manner of selection is defended on the grounds that it makes government agencies more representative.

Conditions of Tenure. Under the traditional bureaucratic system a civil servant is appointed for life, notwithstanding any extraordinary act of negligence or criminality he may commit while in office. Originally established to counteract abuses of the spoils system, life tenure was meant to render government administrators independent of the influence of political leaders and interest groups. Not reliant on any individual or group for their tenure in office, these career civil servants were expected to perform their public duties in a politically neutral manner according to the dictates of their own professional standards and established rules of procedure.

Those individuals brought into the administrative process under political decentralization enjoy only a limited term of office. They usually serve at the pleasure of a constituency which may replace them in periodic elections. Advocates of political decentralization defend this institutional arrangement as a safeguard for responsible government. They reject the idea that administrative matters should be left in the hands of officials who do not owe their position to the public being served.

THE NORMATIVE ISSUE: REPRESENTATIVENESS

At the heart of the current discussion outlining the basic points of distinction between the New Public Administration and what we have chosen to call the old is the underlying normative issue of representative-ness. The structure of authority, method of selection, and terms of office which encompass a political system are all fundamental ingredients of an institutional formula which determine the aptitude of a government to be representative of and responsive to the general welfare. Viewing our traditional institutions essentially as the product of an age when political neutrality was the order of the day, contemporary reformers have raised some significant questions about the quality of representation which exists in the public bureaucracy. These are the very questions which will be dealt with in the forthcoming study. However, before approaching the subject from an empirical perspective, some further conceptual clarification is in order. What do we mean by the term "representative government"? Are its principles applicable to the administrative branch of the political system? If so, how? In what way does the concept relate to the subject matter of the proposed study on New York City?

Borrowing from the analytical classification drawn by Hanna Pitkin, one can identify three distinct levels at which the concept of representation may be understood.[17] These are:

1. formal representation—relating to the manner in which public officials are chosen

2. descriptive representation—which concerns the degree to which officials within the government reflect the social characteristics of the population they serve, i.e., race, ethnicity, sex, age, socioeconomic status

3. interest representation—which is concerned with whether public officials act in accordance with the wants and needs (interests) of their constituents

Formal Representation. Formal representation is concerned with the procedural arrangements by which a government official is selected. Such arrangements usually dictate for whom an individual public official is acting. For example, a senator elected by a statewide constituency is said to be a representative of that state, whereas a congressman chosen by a local constituency is deemed to be the representative of a local district.

The concept of formal representation can be rather simply applied to local neighborhood delegates who are elected to a politically decentralized administrative institution by a popular constituency. These individuals are the formal representatives of those citizens who have placed them in office. However, the concept is not so easily applied to our more traditional institutions. Depending upon one's understanding of these organizations, it is questionable whether career civil servants can be regarded as the representatives of any given group or whether their role in the political system is to act as neutral facilitators of policies decided upon by the true delegates of the people. The fact of the matter is that career public officials are not placed in office at the behest of any particular constituency, but are chosen on the basis of a uniform standard of merit.

In the absence of any direct link to a specific client group, it becomes difficult to establish a representative relationship between the career civil servant and the public he or she serves. So the question still remains, "How does one determine whether the manner in which non-elected officials are chosen is consistent with the value of representative government?" Part of the answer can be found by examining the established terms of eligibility. Is the system open, or is access restricted to a select few? To put the question more succinctly, one might ask, "Does every citizen have an equal opportunity to serve in an official capacity as a career civil servant?"

The equal opportunity issue becomes an important consideration with regard to the career civil service for at least two reasons. The first can be seen from the standpoint of the representative norm. Taking into account those individuals who perceive the career civil servant as a potential advocate for a particular interest or constituency, the equal opportunity principle gives each group a fair chance of having its representative chosen to fill a position which is vacant. Thus, the formal requirements of representativeness are satisfied.

The second consideration is seemingly more practical in nature. It stems from the fact that the public service has historically served as a means of employment and social mobility for the disadvantaged in this country. Given this significant historic function, it has always been of great import to such groups concerned that the method of recruitment remains fair and open.

Advocates of the merit system have hailed its representative and egalitarian virtues on the grounds that it constitutes the "broadest possible basis for recruitment."[18] Complemented by a policy which calls for objective and politically neutral criteria in hiring, the mechanism they describe appears to have all the makings of a fair and open system. However, another major purpose for the design of the merit system was to insure that those individuals chosen for government service possessed a minimum level of skill and competence to carry out the duties of office. At times these technical standards of qualification have seemed to display a certain logical tension with the open employment principles of the system. In reality, the merit system was never meant to work as a completely open system of employment but rather as one based on the principle of equal opportunity for all those found qualified. This principle is commonly referred to in the literature as one of "career open to talent."[19]

As demands by the poor for public service jobs have grown more intense, it has become increasingly apparent that particular care must be taken to guarantee that merit standards established for recruitment are fair, non-discriminatory, and relevant to the functions of the jobs to be filled. In recent years the courts, while making some active attempts to protect the right of equal opportunity in public employment, have at the same time been rather vague in setting down specific guidelines as to how this right might be enforced. For example, in March of 1971 the Supreme Court in *Griggs v. Duke Power Company*[20] declared that an individual could not be denied a job on the basis of merit unless the criteria for selection were directly related to the responsibilities of the position being sought. Thus, the Duke Power Company was ordered to make a janitorial job available to a black woman who had been previously excluded from qualification because she lacked a high school diploma.

While the latter case may have represented a step in the right direction for preserving the equal opportunity principle in public employment, the truth remains that on the whole the courts have shied away from evaluating the content of merit examinations for the purpose of establishing their validity. Instead, the courts and civil service officials alike have resorted to investigating the degree of "descriptive representation" which exists in government agencies as a means to assess the fairness of current hiring practices.

Descriptive Representation. Descriptive representation can be said to exist in a public agency when the social composition of its workforce reflects that of the general population within its jurisdictional environment. While the Supreme Court has not gone so far as to maintain that the social character of any public organization must reflect its constituent environment, a number of recent lower court decisions have placed the burden of proof of non-discrimination upon government bureaus in cases where descriptive representation was found to be weak.[21] Taking an even more active position on the issue, the United States Civil Service Commission has gradually moved towards the support of employment goals as a guideline for recruitment in the public sector. Until 1970 the Civil Service Commission had still defended equal opportunity in terms of the career open to talent principle of the traditional merit system, rejecting the use of goals as a violation of that principle. Within one year, however, under militant pressure from minority groups, the commission reversed that position. The reversal came at the end of a slow, incremental process of change evidenced by a number of policy decisions made by various agencies within the federal government as early as 1964. At that time the Equal Employment Opportunity Commission adopted rules requiring each private sector employer with more than one hundred employees to maintain records of the racial composition of its workforce. Two years later this commission extended this provision, mandating the same employers to submit data annually on both the race and sex of their workers. The major turning point in the federal policy towards goals took place in 1967 with the implementation of the Philadelphia Plan. With that the Office of Federal Contract Compliance issued a requirement that all bidders for federal contracts in the Philadelphia area submit "affirmative action plans" which outlined specific goals for the employment of minority group members. Shortly thereafter the Office of Management and Budget, the Department of the Army, and several other federal agencies expressed an interest in adopting specific employment goals for minorities. Then, finally, on May 11, 1971, the Civil Service Commission distributed a memorandum to the heads of all federal departments and agencies stating:

Employment goals and timetables should be established in problem areas where progress is recognized as necessary and where such goals and timetables will contribute to progress, i.e., in those organizations and localities and in those occupations and grade levels where minority employment is not what should reasonably be expected in view of the potential supply of qualified members of minority groups in the work force and in the recruiting area and available opportunities within the organization.[22]

That point marked the beginning of an era in which the federal government sanctioned the practice of "compensatory selection" for racial minorities to be used thereafter as adjunct to the merit system of selection. In 1972 Title VII of the 1964 Civil Rights Act was amended to require all state and local governments in the nation to submit annual reports on the racial composition of their workforces to the federal government. Thus, within a short period of time the traditional equal opportunity principle of recruitment was supplemented by a policy designed to support specific goals of employment.

The Supreme Court has yet to hand down a definitive ruling with regard to the use of goals in public sector hiring. In July of 1978 it did begin to deal with the issue in terms of university admissions when Allan Bakke, a white male who had unsuccessfully applied to a California medical school, claimed that he had been denied admission on the basis of race. It had been the practice of the medical school to reserve a specified number of seats for minority students in order to compensate for past discrimination. While Bakke saw this as a double standard which discriminated against whites, the California courts upheld the university policy. Then in *Regents of the University of California v. Allan Bakke,*[23] the Supreme Court, in 1978, ruled in favor of Bakke, stating that while race may be used as one factor in the selection of prospective students, it could not be used as the sole criterion. While the Bakke case represents the most significant court ruling on the subject of compensatory selection practices, it has provoked a good deal of confusion among civil rights leaders, university admissions officers, and personnel directors as to what constitutes a legal affirmative action program. Most important of all for the purposes of this study, there still remains a great deal of doubt concerning the future use of goals in hiring for the career civil service.

Nevertheless, from a comparative perspective, the administrative service has been subjected to more stringent standards of descriptive representation than any other branch within government. No other branch has been the target of such rigorous testing by a public overseer, nor has any other applied goals as a guideline for official recruitment. Part of this intense concern over descriptive representation in our government bureaucracies can be explained in terms of the dual role which these institutions play in society. As explained earlier, in addition to the governmental functions which it performs the career civil service is a major source of employment in the United States. Therefore, various groups which have been victimized by job discrimination in the past, particularly minorities and women, have used descriptive representation as a means for assessing whether they have received a fair share of the current governmental positions which are available.

Viewed from a political perspective, the significance of descriptive representation becomes more uncertain. It remains an object of individual determination whether career civil servants will project themselves as active participants of the social groups to which they belong or merely as passive facilitators of the policy process. Moreover, there is no guarantee that descriptive representation in our administrative institutions will necessarily be transformed into public policy which responds to the needs and wants of all groups within society. While descriptive representation may be used as a means to evaluate the fairness and suitability of the formal arrangements by which public officials are chosen, it is a less useful barometer for assessing the degree of interest representation which may be found. Interest representation can more readily be measured by analyzing the policy outputs of the institutions with which we are concerned.

Interest Representation. Harold Lasswell has defined politics as the determination of "Who Gets What, When, How."[24] David Easton has referred to the political system in terms of the authoritative allocation of values or valued things.[25] In either sense, the policy process is appropriately portrayed as a contest between individuals or groups in competition for favorable decisions from governmental officials. Interest representation is concerned with determining which individuals or groups are the winners of this contest and which, in turn, are neglected in terms of their political wants and needs. Thus, Pitkin writes:

The substance of the activity of representing seems to consist in promoting the interest of the represented, in a context where the latter is conceived as capable of action and judgment, but in such a way that he does not object to what is done in his name. What the representative does must be in the principal's interests, but the way he does it must be responsive to the principal's wishes.[26]

The values which governmental authorities allocate may be of a tangible or intangible nature. Both types have a potential for being highly significant determinants of an individual's or group's life chances in a competitive social environment. For example, an intangible allocation may appear in the form of a favorable decision for a public utility by a regulatory commission or the enactment of a law to protect human rights by the legislature. Tangible allocations would deal with such matters as the distribution of public resources to the poor or the application of resources for the delivery of public services. The advantage of the latter type from the point of view of the policy analyst is that it provides an opportunity to examine not only "Who got what?" but also the chance to ask "How much?"

In the past several years the courts have taken an increased interest in the issue of resource and service allocations among citizen groups, and have viewed it in terms of its relationship to the equal protection clause of the Constitution. One of the first major decisions came in 1971, the same year as the *Griggs* decision. Then in *Hawkins v. Shaw*[27] a federal circuit court found the manifest under-servicing of black neighborhoods by a local government in Mississippi to be a violation of the equal protection clause of the Constitution. The court ordered Shaw to prepare a plan for the equitable delivery of services for all citizens. However, as was the case with the equal employment opportunity issue, the court failed to provide any legal guidelines for determining how service equity might precisely be defined.

More recent federal decisions have only added to the confusion already begun in the *Hawkins* case. For example, in *Beal v. Lindsay*,[28] occurring in 1972, a group of black residents charged the City of New York with discrimination, claiming that the conditions of their local park facilities were not up to par with those available in white neighborhoods. The circuit court did not find the allegations made with regard to the relative conditions of facilities in error. However, it ruled in favor of the City because evidence showed that expenditures in the minority areas had exceeded those in white neighborhoods, and that the poorer conditions in the former were the result of excessive vandalism rather than a lack of commitment on the part of the City with regard to minorities. The court appeared to be saying that while all citizens have a right to an equitable allocation of public resources, governments are not responsible for establishing equal living conditions among neighborhoods after non-discrimination has been demonstrated. The definition of fairness or equity, however, still remained unresolved.

The equity issue has also captured the attention of the state courts, particularly with regard to matters concerning school financing. The year 1971 was again significant when the Supreme Court of California in *Serrano v. Priest*[29] found that the state system of educational financing discriminated against the poor and therefore violated both the Fourteenth Amendment of the Constitution and state constitutional law. Subsequently the state courts of Minnesota, Texas, New Jersey, and Michigan handed down similar decisions.[30]

It was not until 1973 that the Supreme Court of the United States became involved in the school financing controversy. Then a one-vote majority, in *San Antonio School District v. Rodriguez*,[31] found that disparities in per capita expenditures for school children are not a violation of the equal protection clause of the Constitution. While the Burger Court deplored the conditions in the San Antonio schools, it, in characteristic fashion, exercised a philosophy of judicial restraint, and handed down a decision which leaned heavily on the side of the states' prerogative in the field of education. Two weeks later a unanimous New Jersey court, in *Robinson v. Cahill*,[32] upheld the right of the state judiciaries to challenge school financing schemes on the basis of state constitutional and legislative enactments.

Thereafter in June of 1978 New York joined the ranks of those states which had become involved in the equity debate. In the case of *Levittown v. Nyquist*[33] State Supreme Court Justice L. Kingsley Smith found that a school financing system which is based on local tax revenues is discriminatory against poorer districts and ordered a restructuring of the state financing scheme. The decision has generally been interpreted as a victory for local urban areas like New York City, which are forced to bear the burden of a wide range of essential municipal services that most suburban and rural districts are not required to support.

The San Antonio decision turned a large part of the legal responsibility for the school financing controversy over to the state courts, thereby leaving a wide range of latitude for the determination of who deserved what and how one's rights might be defined.[34] As was the case with the equal opportunity question, therefore, the courts have not brought us much closer to what might be considered an operational definition of social equity with regard to public service delivery.

A Theory of Justice. The questions still remain:

1. What general criteria should be used in order to determine what constitutes a fair share of public goods and services for each individual or group within society?

2. How can the individual right to equal employment opportunity be balanced against the need for standards of competence within the government service?

There are several criteria one might apply in order to determine how government resources should be distributed among the public. Each criterion has its own rationale and carries with it both advantages and disadvantages that may not be found in the others.[35] The most simple operates in terms of pure equality, granting to each individual a fair claim to the same measure of public goods and services as that to which all his fellow citizens are entitled. The obvious advantage to this method of allocation, at least on the surface, is that it does not seem to favor any one individual or group. All would be treated alike. Despite its egalitarian features, however, this type of distributive process does raise some practical and normative problems, none of which can be avoided in terms of the equity issue.

To begin with, equal allocations to all may eliminate considerations of individual preference or public choice. It is conceivable, for example, that one neighborhood in a city prefers spending public funds on park facilities, while another favors an emphasis on library services. A distributive process which directs appropriations in accordance with such wants is more justifiable in terms of the responsible government ideal than is one which gives the same things to everyone. Depending upon other aspects of the distributive system, the substantive mixture of goods and services which is allocated to each group under this arrangement may or may not be of equal value.

A distributive process which calls for allocations of public goods equal in terms of either substance or value may be criticized on the grounds that it operates in contradiction to the notion of human need. Given the fact that individuals and groups live under a variety of social conditions, it is understandable that the total amount of public benefits which each requires for daily survival also varies. An obvious example of this difference can be found by comparing the situation of the high salaried corporate executive with that of the individual who is dependent upon public assistance. On another, less apparent, scale, there is good reason to wonder if it makes for either a fair or efficient public policy to allocate such essential services as police or fire protection among communities without any consideration of the relative demands for service in terms of crime or fire rates. Thus, another method of distributing public resources would be on the basis of some indicator of actual need.

Of course, there are those who might object to the latter method, claiming that it leads to a disproportionate allocation of the public goods. They might argue that each citizen, as a contributor to the public fund, has an equal right to equal benefits, particularly in cases where essential services are concerned. Taking this argument to a more extreme point, one might even contend that public benefits should be distributed on the basis of one's contribution to the general revenues. In either case, these points of view would call for a distributive process which disregards the need factor. These approaches undermine the social welfare role of the state which would otherwise redistribute public resources in favor of the poor and the disadvantaged. From these latter examples, we can begin to see that one's approach to the equity issue is very much a function of his individual social philosophy.

Let us suppose, for a moment, that the equity issue were resolved, and a method of distributing government services agreed upon. The next matter to be dealt with would be to determine who might be responsible for the provision of these services. To deprive any individual of an equal opportunity to serve in an official capacity or to acquire gainful employment is unjustifiable. Yet some standard of qualification is in order, for it would also be unjustifiable to place an unqualified individual in the position of teacher or to give the responsibility of fire protection over to a person who is physically unfit. Assuming that some fair standard of selection is reached, we are still left to wonder about the fate of the individual who is found unfit for public employment. What is the responsibility of the state to him? Has it expired once he has been given the opportunity to qualify? Does this individual forgo the right to be represented in the administrative branch of government once he has failed to qualify for service in an official capacity?

As was the case with the issue of equity in services, one's responses to the proposed questions will to some extent be an outgrowth of individual social philosophy. In a political system where the principles of equal opportunity and representativeness are valued governmental ideals, the state would retain a responsibility to the individual who does not personally qualify for office. A portion of that responsibility can be met in terms of the distributive process which determines to what share of the public resources each individual is entitled. In this sense, the substantive issues of service equity and public employment are closely interrelated.

In an important book on the subject of social justice, John Rawls has proposed what he calls a "maximin" conception of the ideal as it is understood from the perspective of a liberal democratic state. It begins with a requirement for maximizing the minimum share of public goods distributed among all individuals in society. Thereby each individual would have an "equal right to the most extensive total system of equal basic liberties for all."[36] However, recognizing the inevitability of social and economic inequalities in a liberal democracy, Rawls sets down two principles of distribution concerning public offices and public goods which are most relevant to the issues with which we are concerned.

Rawls begins by stating that an unequal distribution of primary social goods, such as liberty and opportunity, income and wealth, and the bases of self-respect, is justifiable only when it works to the advantage of the least favored.[37] He then goes on to argue that social and economic inequalities are to be arranged so that (1) the greatest benefits are given to the least advantaged, and (2) they are attached to offices and positions open to all under fair equality of opportunity.[38]

On the latter point, Rawls concedes the fact that not all individuals will enjoy the benefit of public office and accepts an unequal distribution of such offices on the basis of merit. On the former point, benefits of which he lists in order of priority, Rawls also accepts the notion that the state must serve as a mechanism to redistribute economic and social goods so that the allocation of public resources will work to the benefit of the disadvantaged. From this arrangement Rawls imposes an obligation upon the officeholder not to exercise authority for the sake of private interest, but rather to use the position of office in a way which provides the socially disadvantaged with the necessary resources to improve their social condition.

When one considers the Rawlsian system of justice in terms of the representative norm, the implications are of a diverse nature, and several significant questions arise. From a practical standpoint, it is the socially disadvantaged who are in a least favorable competitive position to qualify for office according to most standards of merit. Thus, for these groups the Rawlsian system could be used to deny them descriptive representation within the government. Rawls provides a means for dealing with this dilemma by prescribing a distributive arrangement based upon social need. Under it those same individuals who are at a competitive disadvantage insofar as public offices are concerned would be favored in terms of public allocations. Distributions are discussed here in terms of those primary goods that "every rational man is presumed to want" and which "normally have a use whatever a person's rational life plan."[39]

While Rawls's formula for achieving social justice is normatively defensible from the liberal democratic position appearing in his book, there is still ample room for questioning whether its institutional safeguards are either adequate or feasible in the world of real politics. One might hope that a disproportionate allocation of public goods in favor of the disadvantaged would eventually raise their social position to the point that they would also be able to compete for positions within the government. However, until such an eventuality is realized, the poor may find themselves in a rather dependent, perhaps precarious, position. One is left to wonder just to what degree a system of merit would work to deny the disadvantaged descriptive representation in government. Given the fact that the consequent situation might be severe, these groups are then left reliant upon the willingness, indeed self-enforced obligation, of those in office to represent the interests of all people. Thus, John Chapman has commented:

Despite Rawls's insistence that his principles of justice match the right and the good, and meet the criteria of collective and individual rationality, political activity in the liberal democratic state remains an amalgam of the just and the unjust.

... A gap exists therefore between Rawlsian ethics and democratic politics. As he remarks in an uncharacteristic overstatement, "The democratic political process is at best regulated rivalry...." (p. 226)[40]

In all fairness to Rawls, it must be emphasized that his book is designed to provide us with a normative ethical theory. It is not meant as a descriptive analysis of politics. Therefore, such "practical" considerations as those raised above cannot fairly be accepted as a criticism of Rawls so much as they constitute a departure from his original purpose. It is in such a context that these considerations are suggested here.

Taking the liberty of such a departure, the question remains for one who would attempt to implement the Rawlsian system of justice in a particular social environment: given the idea that politics is by nature a contest motivated by a multiplicity of self-serving interests, is it feasible to expect that a formal system of government with a logical potential for denying descriptive representation to some groups has a real capability of representing the interests of all people?

THE POLITICAL ISSUE: FEASIBILITY

Over the past decade, as political science research has become more concerned with the content of public policy rather than with the mere process which brings it about, some students of the subject have urged their professional colleagues to retain a keen awareness of the political implications inherent in any given set of policy options.[41] They have come to recognize that what might at first seem to be an effective policy choice for dealing with a particular governmental or social problem may not be "doable" in the real world of politics. Thus, Charles Schultz writes, "What we can do best analytically we find hardest to achieve politically."[42]

If the policy analyst is going to serve as a useful resource to the governmental decision maker, he is admonished to identify the relevant political environment, specify the proponents and opponents of the policy being considered, and make a political judgment of the option which is being selected.[43] Such political prudence is also required of the long-range social planner who would go about the business of recommending more basic reforms within our governmental institutions in order to achieve a given social end. It is particularly relevant as contemporary scholars consider the relative merits of the old and the New public administrations.

At issue here is the capability of our administrative institutions to remain representative of and responsive to the public they serve. Particular concern is paid to the poor and the disadvantaged, of which racial minorities constitute a disproportionately high number. The broader options lie somewhere between two alternative types of institutional arrangement. On the one side are the proponents of decentralization. For the most part these individuals deny either the possibility or existence of political neutrality in our traditional administrative institutions. They denounce the bureaucracy for its failure to represent the general public either socially or politically and propose reforms designed to provide new channels of access to the poor. These reforms are political in the sense that selection would be made on the basis of popular election. Their purpose is to bring more representatives of the poor into our administrative institutions, which they believe will result in a more equitable distribution of public goods and services on their behalf.

While the electoral process does not subject aspirants to political office to the same technical standards of selection as does the merit system, many of the social conditions that work to the competitive disadvantage of the poor who would hope to serve in the traditional civil service have been known to have a similar effect with regard to the political process. There is an extensive literature in political science which shows that successful participation in politics tends to be a function of class and status.[44] On the whole, the poor, and particularly the non-white poor, have not participated in politics because they do not have the social resources that are necessary for political effectiveness.[45] As the analysis in the next two chapters will show, those minorities who have attempted to break into the political system have often been confronted by the opposition of more established and powerful interest groups.[46]

These are the unfortunate facts of political life which the architects of decentralization will need to overcome if their program for reform is going to serve as a means to improving the political and social status of the disadvantaged. In many respects the history of decentralized government in American cities has been too short to assess whether it will succeed. It is not the primary concern which the present study is about. However, a recognition of these facts is certainly useful in putting a consideration of our traditional administration institutions into a more meaningful comparative perspective.

Perhaps the distinguishing feature of the old public administration is that its proponents believe political neutrality to be both a worthy and an achievable goal. The current reformers not only challenge this assumption but have also raised some basic questions concerning the capacity of bureaucratic institutions to fulfill the normative ideal of representativeness. We have already seen from our consideration of Rawls that a formal system of selection based upon merit does not necessarily lead to descriptive representation in government. Thus, the first order of business in judging the representative character of our traditional institutions is to test the empirical compatibility between the merit system, as it exists today, and descriptive representation. While the logical tie between these two concepts may be rather thin, those groups who feel excluded from public employment and the opportunity to serve in the administrative branch certainly have the right to know what the empirical consequences of the present recruitment policy are.

Given the understanding that descriptive representation may not be attained under the merit system, the next important question concerns the ability of our public institutions to represent the interests of all people. Rawls would appropriately evaluate this capability by examining the distributive process of government. His formula for equity calls for a distributive arrangement which favors the disadvantaged regardless of the social composition of the authority structure. Its outcome is efficient in the sense that it concentrates public resources where they are most needed. It is "non-political" in the sense that it favors the least influential members of society.

When one attempts to apply the Rawlsian formula to the administrative branch of government, the normative ideals espoused within the old public administration become significantly relevant. Recognizing the fact that public bureaucracies have often been the focal point for the activities of powerful organized interests, it is appropriate to ask how real the politics-administration dichotomy truly is. In search for an institutional mechanism within government to respond to the needs of the disadvantaged, it is essential to investigate the degree to which the operation of efficient standards of performance has led to an equitable distribution of resources.

EMPIRICAL RESEARCH

The general purpose of the empirical research in this study is to evaluate whether traditional bureaucratic institutions in New York City are representative of and responsive to the black and Puerto Rican communities within the population. It will do so with the completion of two research tasks:

1. an analysis of the racial composition of the New York City workforce prior to 1972

2. an assessment of the allocation of service resources among racial communities within the city, with particular reference to the Police, Fire, and Sanitation departments during 1972 and 1973

The methodologies which will be used to carry out these tasks will be described in more detail in chapters 4 and 5 where the data are presented.

Employment. The first part of the research will examine the percentage of white, black, Puerto Rican, and other minorities who occupy civil service positions in the city government. The analysis will be done according to occupational level, salary level, and agency. For purposes of comparison, the research will also analyze employment data for the federal, state, and private sector workforces in New York.

There are two reasons why the year 1972 was chosen as the chronological cutoff point for our employment analysis:

1. There is a significant quantity of detailed data available for the period chosen for study.

2. This year marked the time that the traditional merit system began to be supplemented by other methods of recruitment for the New York civil service, e.g., the use of employment goals.

Deployment. The second part of our research will concentrate upon the allocation of manpower resources among administrative districts which are categorized according to the racial composition of their resident populations. These allocations will be analyzed in terms of relevant indicators of service need for each government function studied. The analysis will cover the administrative districts which encompass the entire geographical commands of the Police, Fire, and Sanitation departments of the city.

There are several reasons why the three uniformed services were selected as the focus of our manpower deployment study:

1. All three represent essential functions for almost every local government.

2. Each of these services accommodates essential needs of the entire public, and therefore none can be linked with a particular clientele.

3. These agencies all have an established practice of allocating services on the basis of identifiable geographical units.

During the period being studied (1972–73) the New York City government was in the midst of a major effort to improve both the efficiency and effectiveness of its service delivery system. Among the several managerial strategies employed within this "Productivity Program" was a systematic attempt to deploy agency resources according to objectively determined criteria of service need. Studying the deployment patterns of three traditional bureaucratic institutions for this period will allow us to assess whether there may exist a logical and empirical relationship between the operational performance goal of efficiency and the normative ideal of social equity.

The Race Issue. Perhaps some explanation is in order as to why we have chosen to focus this study on the black and Puerto Rican populations of the city. New York is the home of many ethnic and racial minorities. However, blacks and Puerto Ricans are among the most easily identifiable in terms of their geographic distribution throughout the city. It is for this reason that they have been chosen as the focal point of the study. Their selection is not meant to undermine the impact which discrimination or prejudice exerts on other racial minorities or women in the city.

It is also worthy to note that the United States Census Bureau does officially classify residents of Puerto Rican heritage as Caucasian. Therefore, they are technically not a racial minority. However, it is also true that many immigrants from Puerto Rico are from mixed racial backgrounds, and most suffer from the same discriminatory social practices that are imposed upon blacks. As the data in table 1.1 show, Puerto Ricans in New York generally find themselves in a more unfortunate socioeconomic condition than do black residents of the city. It is for these reasons that we will treat Puerto Ricans as a minority group in the forthcoming analysis.

TABLE 1.1

SOCIOECONOMIC CHARACTERISTICS OF
RACIAL GROUPS IN NYC, 1970[1]

	Total Population	Whites	Blacks	Puerto Ricans
Education % persons 25 yrs. or over with 4 yrs. high school	50.44	52.05	43.27	23.98
Median family income	$9,682	$10,424	$7,150	$5,575
% persons below federal poverty line	11.4	9.23	20.49	20.35

1. These data were taken from New York City Planning Commission, "Community Planning District Profiles, part 2: Socioeconomic Characteristics," NYC CPD 73-08 (September 1974), unpaginated.

Thesis. The thesis of this study is as follows. When operating under the traditional merit system of recruitment and hierarchically determined standards of efficiency, New York City agencies have provided racial minorities with descriptive representation within the local public bureaucracy and an equitable share of the services which they deliver.

Descriptive representation will be measured in terms of the degree to which the percentage of public service jobs held by blacks and Puerto Ricans at the various levels of responsibility proportionally reflects their percentage of the total population in the city.

An equitable share of service will be defined here as a geographic distribution of agency resources (particularly manpower) which corresponds to the specific service needs of administrative districts throughout the city in those services studied. An operational calculation of service needs will be defined and explained for each of the three agencies. By efficient standard of performance we mean the application of a managerial strategy designed to increase the quantity and/or quality of services provided per public dollar invested. In more general terms, efficiency may refer to the selection of a mode of action which enables a service organization to achieve its operational goals in the least costly way known possible.[47]

Significance. The idea that bureaucratic institutions serve a representative function within government is hardly an original one. J. Donald Kingsley coined the term "representative bureaucracy" in his 1944 study of the British civil service.[48] However, Kingsley used the term in a prescriptive rather than descriptive sense, in search for an institutional arrangement to counter-balance the upper class domination of British politics.

Eight years later the American political scientist Norton Long adapted the idea to this country. Long claimed that the government bureaucracy in the United States is the most representative governmental institution in terms of class composition, race, ethnicity, religion, and the variety of interests found among its members.[49] While Long did not go about the task of documenting his findings himself, there is now available a significant volume of research which investigates descriptive representation within our administrative institutions. We will see in a review of this literature in chapter 4 that some research supports the Long thesis while some does not. The outcome often depends upon which particular government agency at which level of government is the subject of analysis. These assorted findings document the need for social planners in specific governmental jurisdictions to evaluate carefully our present institutions before making assumptions about their representative features and recommending reforms. The empirical analysis of descriptive representation appearing in the present study is therefore presented as a first and essential step taken in a more general assessment of representation in the local government bureaucracy of New York City.

While the research on resource allocations by government agencies is not so voluminous as that existing on public service jobs, the recent thrust in the social sciences towards policy analysis has brought with it a growing interest in that kind of work. For example, in 1970 one student in New York City analyzed the distribution of budgetary expenditures for seven local agencies among community planning districts.[50] While that analysis showed expenditures to be uneven, it did not relate them to either the demographic characteristics of the areas studied or any indicators of service need.

Research conducted by a number of social scientists on the delivery of police services in the cities of Chicago, St. Louis, and Berkeley has revealed a pattern of disproportionate expenditures in favor of low income areas.[51] These findings seem to indicate that local governments do take into consideration the need factor when allocating this essential community service. A more wide ranging study completed by Benson and Lund on a variety of local services in Berkeley has shown that public expenditures among income groups vary according to the type of service function.[52] For example, while expenditures for police, health, and remedial education were greater in low income neighborhoods, middle class neighborhoods of the city tended to absorb more public funds for library, college preparatory, and recreational services. Thus, the evidence from the Berkeley study seems to suggest that public expenditures there tended to be a function of both community need and public choice or preference.

In 1974 Levy, Meltsner, and Wildavsky conducted a similar study on education, street construction, and library expenditures in the city of Oakland.[53] One of the most significant features of that study is that its authors made a comprehensive effort to identify those policy-related factors which affected the outcome of distributive decisions in each service. For example, while compensatory state education programs for the disadvantaged were found to result in more public dollars and more teachers per student in minority areas, library acquisition funds tended to favor white upper class neighborhoods where circulation rates were higher. In the area of street construction and repair expenditures, the policy determinants were found to be more complex. Professional engineering standards called for a concentration of construction funds in a select street system where the highest traffic flows occurred, with the remainder going either to newly built upper income areas where paved streets had not yet existed or to older lower income areas where federal urban renewal monies made construction possible. This system of allocation for new construction was found to work to the advantage of the upper and lower classes and to the neglect of the middle class. Street resurfacing expenditures, on the other hand, tended to work to the exclusive advantage of the upper class in response to high traffic flows, deterioration, and, most importantly, citizen complaints.

Another detailed analysis of factors influencing service distributions in an American city is that completed by Robert Lineberry in 1977. Lineberry investigated six local services in San Antonio, Texas, comprising fire protection, libraries, parks, water supply, sewage, and police protection. He found that neither ethnicity, political power, nor economic status was a reliable predictor of service allocations to neighborhoods. Instead, he identified ecological factors, such as population density and age of housing, as variables more significantly related to distribution.[54] Lineberry further concluded: ". . . urban public bureaucracies, through their discretion both to make delivery rules and to fit a particularistic claim to one of several rules, probably have more to do with the allocation of services than does the distribution of political power."[55]

The Oakland and San Antonio studies represent significant attempts to assess the differential impact of political and professionally neutral factors on the distribution of public resources. Like preceding studies, each allows the student of public policy to gain additional insight into the important question of "Who got what, when, and how?" However, to take the state of the art a step further, it is necessary to evaluate such allocations in terms of the specific service needs existing among those population groups being studied. Only then can a judgment be made concerning both the equity and efficiency of current government policies.

There still remains a relative void in the empirical research dealing with the relationship between operational efficiency within local agencies and social equity in the allocation of their service resources. At a time when a growing proportion of our urban population is composed of disadvantaged minorities, when cities are under increased pressure to conduct their business more efficiently, and when the demand for social equity is still being heard rather loudly, we can no longer neglect research of this type. It is hoped that by studying resource allocations in New York, during a period when the City was involved in a program designed to increase the productivity of its service delivery system, we can begin to eliminate that void.

CHAPTER OUTLINE

The remainder of this study will be organized into six chapters. Chapter 2 will serve as a review of the relevant literature in public administration. It will discuss in more explicit detail the cycles of administrative thought referred to in the introduction and relate this thinking to the development of administrative institutions and practices in the United States. Particular emphasis will be placed on a definition of and comparison between the New Public Administration and the old, stressing their similarities and differences, strengths and weaknesses, and treating more explicitly the aberrations of the two general models that were outlined in the present chapter. Viewing public administration as a professional field of study, this chapter will address such questions as: Where have we been? What have we learned? How can it help us to get where we want to go?

Chapter 3 will provide the general historical background of administrative reform in New York City. Its purpose will be to describe the political and social setting existing during the period about which the empirical research is concerned. Here we will see the administrative principles and thinking outlined in chapter 2 applied in a particular social environment. We will observe how the political realities of New York forced the Lindsay administration to temper an original strategy of reform based upon political decentralization to one which became more reliant upon moderate changes epitomizing traditional principles of administrative thought.

Chapters 4 and 5 will present respectively the research findings on the allocation of public jobs and of services to racial groups in New York City. Each will begin with a brief review of the relevant research literature. Each will also include a description of the respective research methodologies that were used and an explanation of the rationale for their selection. Chapter 5 will also provide a brief overview of the three service agencies upon which it will focus and a description of how decisions concerning resource allocations were made.

Chapters 6 and 7 will serve as a conclusion. The former will concentrate upon the research findings of the present study. The latter will move from the specific details of the present study to a more general proposition concerning the compatibility between the normative ideal of social justice and the principles and practices associated with traditional bureaucratic institutions.

2

AMERICAN PUBLIC ADMINISTRATION
Lessons of the Past

The concern for normative issues within the professional study of American public administration is by no means a novel one. The pursuit of equity, justice, and fairness in government is an integral part of our rich though brief intellectual heritage. While at times these ethical values have been coupled with more "practical" goals such as economy and efficiency, demands for better operational performance in government have rarely been advocated as an alternative to our more fundamental normative ideals.

If the history of American public administration has sometimes been a turbulent one, it is not because we have been troubled by an ambivalence or uncertainty regarding the ends to which government activity should be devoted. What has often been a source of debate within the profession is the methods advocated by various scholars for achieving these ends. For example, in elucidating the various techniques which have been employed throughout the development of this country to accommodate the representative ideal with regard to recruitment for the public service, Van Riper explains:

To refine the concept of representative bureaucracy, . . . it is possible to develop such a bureaucracy in at least three ways: through the spoils system, the closed system, and what we have termed the opportunity system of the Pendleton Act. In the United States we have tried all three of these avenues—the closed system under the Federalists, the spoils system under the Jacksonians and early Republicans, and the opportunity system from 1883 to the present.[1]

As Van Riper suggests, even the Jacksonian spoils system, which became the target of a vociferous nineteenth-century reform movement, was originally instituted as a means to a more representative and democratic government. Prior to the incumbency of Jackson, the federal administrative structure was dominated by what Mosher called a "government by gentlemen,"[2] where class and family lineage were set down as the proper criteria of selection for the public service. It was alleged by defenders of the system that individuals of "good family stock" possessed the proper moral capacity and adequate judgment to qualify for office.

Jackson had the good sense to recognize the discriminatory and inegalitarian features of the system he inherited. Thus, he instituted a practice of patronage not only designed to reward political loyalists with the advantages of office, but also meant to provide the "common man" with access to and representation in government. While the spoils system did not succeed in altering the social composition of the higher civil service to the extent that many of its originators might have hoped for,[3] this revolt against class prerogative did serve to dramatize the political and normative implications inherent in the method by which non-elected public officials are recruited for their positions.

The Jacksonian movement is merely one early manifestation of the important role politics plays in the administration of government. From that point onward the definition of that role has emerged as a central issue within American public administration. This issue has been formulated in terms of both empirical and normative questions. The former type of question focuses on the determination of the actual role which politics plays in the administrative process. The latter type is concerned with determining the role which politics should play in administration in order to fulfill the more normative ideals of the profession.

Throughout the development of our administrative history politics has been both blamed and praised by various students of the subject as either the cause of or the solution to corrupt and unjust government. At identifiable periods of time the well-formulated interpretations of our more renowned scholars have served as a catalyst to new directions in public policy. At less admirable intervals the ideas of insightful students have merely been used as a justification for the policy preferences of political zealots.[4]

It is not without good reason that Allen Schick has titled a recent essay on public administration in the sixties "The Trauma of Politics."[5] The movement for a new New Public Administration, which grew out of that decade, represents a return to politics as a method for alleviating both the operational and ethical problems its proponents found in government.

It brought with it conflict and turmoil in both the political and intellectual arena. However, its ideals and outcomes were not without precedent.

While the professional study of American public administration has developed in a somewhat uneven and controversial fashion, there is much to be learned from the experience and scholarship of the past. This chapter will focus on that history. It will be organized in four distinct parts, each of which corresponds to a particular approach to governmental administration. The first three include what we will call the classical, neo-classical, and technocratic approaches. Here we will trace the development of the old public administration from its original form to that in which it is usually found today in our bureaucratic institutions. The last section will focus on the New Public Administration, which will be seen as a response and reaction to the previous approaches and organizational structures. Thus, the analysis in this chapter will not only serve to further clarify the dichotomy between the old and the New public administrations, but it will also allow us to draw upon the lessons of the distant and the immediate past.

DISPARATE ORIGINS OF A CLASSICAL APPROACH

What is frequently referred to as the classical approach to public administration[6] was the product of two independent movements which occurred contemporaneously in the latter part of the nineteenth century. The first was the reformist crusade against corruption in government, which led to the institution of the merit system. The second, originating in the private sector, was the scientific management movement, sometimes referred to as Taylorism after its chief exponent, which espoused efficiency and economy as the operational goals of administrative conduct. While the two movements had distinct origins and purposes, the principles which grew out of them established a conceptual foundation for modern public administration as we know it today.

The Merit System. The spoils system which was introduced by Jackson as a device designed to make government more responsive to the will of "the people" soon depreciated into a decadent system of patronage that reached down into all levels of government. Jobs were freely exchanged for political favors and, as the public sector became an open marketplace for individual cronyism, ineptitude began to pervade the entire governmental structure. Bossism and graft were particularly rampant in large urban areas. This situation was carefully documented in a series of articles written by one of the nation's first investigative journalists, Lincoln Steffens. It is quite appropriate that his classic reporting was finally compiled into a single volume under the title *The Shame of the Cities.*[7]

The period gave rise to a significant number of reform-oriented organizations intent on eliminating corruption in government. Among the more notable of these were the New York Civil Service Reform League, the National Civil Service Reform League, and the National Municipal League. Their campaign to promote specific guidelines for the manner in which government should operate began to display some semblance of accomplishment in 1871 when President Grant, himself a symbol of much that was wrong in government, appointed the first Civil Service Commission. The designated purpose of the commission was to draw up rules and regulations for the selection of administrative officials. Unfortunately, it received only symbolic support from Congress, and within a short time its activity was allowed to dissipate.

It was not until 1883 that the Pendleton Act established the merit system of recruitment within the federal service. The key feature of the merit system was to utilize written competitive examinations as a criterion for determining one's qualification for appointment. Once an individual was granted a position in this manner, he would ordinarily be assured life tenure. It was believed by the architects of the 1883 law that competitive recruitment and job security would allow public officials to remain independent from political influence. These assumptions were consistent with the overall purpose of reform, the creation of a politically neutral public bureaucracy.

In order to insure that the merit system did not impose an unfair barrier to job accessibility for the disadvantaged, the Pendleton Act stipulated that examinations must be "practical in content" and directly related to the job position being filled. In this sense, the American civil service differed from the British, where the scholarly nature of examinations gave an unfair advantage to the better educated members of the upper class. Thus, it might be said that the merit system amounted to a more objective mechanism for achieving the Jacksonian goals of an egalitarian and open government than did the original spoils system.

One might expect that an advantageous by-product of the new system would be a tendency to recruit better qualified individuals into the government service. Whether or not this was factually the case, it must be stressed that reform movements which brought about the passage of the Pendleton Act were more concerned with eliminating corruption in government than they were with improving the operational performance of administrative institutions. As Paul Van Riper, one of the most authoritative historians of the period, has emphasized:

It is quite clear that only secondarily—and not a very close second at that—were the reformers interested in efficiency and economy, the dollars and cents value of the merit system. They mentioned these things, but they almost invariably referred to the "greater" moral issues . . . efficiency in administration was but a corollary to the major purpose: the achievement of a new morality in public affairs.[8]

It would be some time before the reform movement took a managerial thrust. Nevertheless, while the reformist campaign against corruption was being carried on in the public sector, Frederick W. Taylor was at work in the private sector developing the conceptual and methodological tools which would eventually serve as a basis for a more systematic approach to governmental operations.

Scientific Management. Frederick W. Taylor was a job foreman in the Pennsylvania Steel Company during the last decade of the nineteenth century. His whole approach to the production process was based on the idea that management is a true science resting upon clearly defined laws which could be discovered by methodical research and experimentation.[9] He firmly believed that, once discovered, these laws could be applied to derive a better quantity and quality of work from employees, thereby leading to more efficient operational performance.

Taylor's sophisticated experiments with steel cutting techniques led to the development of high speed cutting steel and the improved design of tools. He was an originator of time and motion studies, functional or divided foremanship, differential pay rates, and the modern cost system. His attempt to fit all personnel, tools, and capital equipment into a highly integrated and finely tuned organization was motivated by a commitment to finding and applying the "one best way" of getting a task accomplished. For Taylor, the "one best way" was the most efficient, that is, the one which produced the maximally productive output for the least costly input of resources.

The scientific management movement brought with it a strongly hierarchic approach to organizational structures. The one best way orientation left relatively little room for discretion at the middle and lower levels of a productive unit. In later years anti-Taylorists would criticize this approach as a threat to democratic values. They would also criticize the functionalist orientation of its author, which they alleged treated individuals as a mere appendage of an inorganic mechanism without any consideration for the human side of management.

The Taylorism being applied in the industrial world of the nineteenth century did have some common ground with the merit system that was induced by political reformers. There was a logical link between Taylor's determination to find the "right man for the right job" and the practice of selecting individual government employees on the basis of merit. Moreover, the idea of a scientific approach to management was consistent with the reformer's commitment to utilize objective procedures in administration of government.

The principles underlying scientific management and the merit system were not practically integrated into a singular approach to public administration until the turn of the century. However, by 1887 Woodrow Wilson had already written a now famous essay which set down essentially what we understand today as the classical model.[10]

Wilson's Synthesis. Wilson's model was normative. It was concerned with what should be rather than with what actually was at the time. It was constructed by a man who was disturbed by what he saw as legislative domination of the American government. Wilson was an ardent admirer of the British system. He did not believe in the division of power between two or more branches of government. For Wilson, the only way to keep government responsible to the people was to focus responsibility at one source, the executive.

While Wilson would have placed ultimate responsibility for governing in the hands of the president, the model he constructed called for a distinction between purely administrative functions within the executive branch and those functions which were concerned with actual policy making. It recognized the importance of having men who were politically loyal to an elected chief executive in the latter positions, but for the former type it prescribed recruitment on the basis of merit. "The strictest rules of business discipline, of merit tenure and earned promotion must rule with every office whose incumbent has not to do with choosing between policies."[11]

Wilson perceived the merit system not merely as a judicious way of awarding individuals public jobs but also as a means for promoting competence in government along the same lines that Taylor was advocating in the private sector. Likewise his emphasis on the idea of "one rule of good administration for all governments alike"[12] bears a striking resemblance to the one best way postulated by scientific managers. Thus, it might be said that in the formulation of a classical model of public administration Wilson added an operational dimension to the concept of the merit system which complemented the ethical ideals of political reformers.

Wilson's organizational model brought with it all the hierarchical features that were present in the Taylorist one. Authority would be concentrated at the top. Moreover, even though it was concerned with the public sector Wilson's structure allowed little room for interference from outside the executive branch. While Wilson was dedicated to the principle of democratic government, he did not assume that this necessarily included democratic administration. He saw the public's role in the administrative process as one of a distant critic whose final judgment could be imposed through the electoral process when it chose a chief executive. Thus, he wrote: "Self-government does not consist of having a hand in everything, anymore than housekeeping consists necessarily in cooking dinner with one's own hands. The cook must be trusted with a large discretion as to the management of the fires and the ovens."[13]

Henceforth it should be clear that when we refer to the classic model of public administration, we are dealing with a system which is open only in the sense that it allows equal opportunity of access to all who meet the qualifications to participate as authorized officials within the bureaucracy. It does not include any active role for clients in ordinary administrative decisions. The classic approach is more concerned with the introduction of business techniques within government in order to maximize efficiency and economy.

THE CLASSICAL MODEL: FROM THEORY TO PRACTICE

The Wilsonian ideal would not become a viable guide for action within government until its underlying principles captured the enthusiasm and support of the American people. At the turn of the century a large proportion of the positions within the federal service remained outside the jurisdiction of the merit system, and the use of more sophisticated techniques in administrative management was still generally restricted to the private sector.

One of the most significant contributions of the early twentieth-century reform movements was that it added operational objectives to the agenda for change. As Dwight Waldo had explained in 1948,[14] the new reformers recognized the political acceptability which the demand for efficiency in government had with the American public. It was a much more tangible ideal than those that had previously been espoused and one which a people with a conservative leaning could accept gladly. This became especially true as the national economy began to firm up for the eventuality of a world war. Thus, the reformers paired appeals for efficiency with the moralistic crusade which was already in progress, and inaugurated a campaign which possessed the valuable ingredient of political feasibility. The evidence of this junction is apparent in a large quantity of literature which grew out of the period, some of which was cited by Waldo in his subsequent study.

For example, in 1907 W. H. Allen proclaimed in his book *Efficient Democracy:* "To be efficient is more difficult than to be good.... The goodness that has lasting value to one's fellow-man will be greatly increased and more widely distributed if efficiency tests are applied to all persons and all agencies that are trying to make tomorrow better than today."[15] Shortly thereafter M. L. Cook wrote an article appearing in the *Journal of Political Economy* under the title "The Spirit and Social Significance of Scientific Management." There he stated: "In my opinion, we shall never realize fully either the visions of Christianity or the dreams of democracy until the principles of scientific management have permeated every nook and cranny of the working world."[16] Then, in 1939, T. V. Smith, in a cooperative work with Leonard White, once again reminded us:

Don't misunderstand what we administrators mean when we use the shorthand of efficiency and economy.... When we say efficiency we think of lives saved from disease, of boys and girls in school prepared for life, of ships and mines protected against disaster.... We do not think in terms of gadgets and paper clips alone. And when we talk of economy, we fight waste of human resources, still much too scanty to meet human needs.[17]

The literature of the period also had to its credit the publication of a number of important textbooks. Among these were the classic works of Goodnow and Willoughby,[18] each of which advocated a necessary distinction between political and administrative functions within government in a fashion somewhat similar to the way Wilson had done years earlier. Thus, as the twentieth century began to unfold, it became apparent that Wilson's 1887 essay would prove to be prophetic.

In 1909 the Civil Service Reform League began to emphasize efficiency as one of its major programmatic goals. The first decade of the new century also witnessed the evolution of the "bureau movement," characterized by the formation of independent study groups dedicated to improving the operational performance of government administration. The most notable of these at the local level was the New York Bureau of Municipal Research. Its closest counterpart on the federal scene appeared in 1910 with President Taft's appointment of the Commission on Economy and Efficiency in Government.

The first major piece of reform legislation was not enacted, however, until 1921 when Congress passed the Budget and Accounting Act. The stated purpose of that legislation was to "establish business organization in government." Its most important feature was the creation of an executive budget which would be the responsibility of a newly appointed Bureau of the Budget. At that point fiscal planning was instituted at the federal level under the leadership of a chief executive who, in fulfillment of Wilson's fondest hopes, stood at the threshold of a new era of presidential power.

It has been a recurrent lesson of our institutional history that a necessary by-product of a national crisis is the increase in presidential authority. One of the glaring examples of this phenomenon is Franklin Roosevelt's response to the economic depression of the thirties. Faced with the dilemma of widespread unemployment, Roosevelt took the prerogative to resort to the creation of sixty new federal agencies in 1934. While the so-called alphabet agencies functioned to provide jobs for many desperate Americans, Roosevelt's executive action also represented a major blow to the merit system. According to Paul Van Riper, only five of the sixty new agencies recruited personnel on a competitive basis.[19] Thereby, for the first time in its short history the merit system was put aside by a national program to create employment for the disadvantaged.

In 1937 Roosevelt appointed the Presidential Committee on Administrative Management composed of Louis Brownlow, its chairman, Luther Gulick, and Charles Merriam. The designated purpose of the Brownlow committee was to make recommendations which would lead to a more economic, efficient, and effective operation of the federal government. While the committee was criticized by some as a device designed to justify a further absorption of power by the incumbent President, the report of the committee symbolized a governmental endorsement of the classical model of administration which already had been appearing in the professional literature for some time.

In accordance with the fears of its most vehement critics, the underlying message of the committee's report was the need to centralize administrative authority and responsibility in the hands of the chief executive.[20] In terms by now familiar to the reader, the committee called for a delineation between policymaking positions within the executive branch and those career positions which are concerned with the ordinary details of administration. It prescribed that only a few positions at the upper levels of administration be filled by means of presidential appointment; for all others it recommended recruitment on the basis of the merit system. The latter positions, it was believed, would provide the government with those skilled, objective, and politically neutral ingredients required for competent administration; the former would insure the existence of a centralized, hierarchic structure which would enable the president to exercise administrative and political leadership.

It still remains a question whether or not Roosevelt used the good graces of the expert committee merely to add legitimacy to a feat he had all intentions of accomplishing from the outset. However, there is little reason to doubt that the committee's recommendations were based on the deep-seated convictions of its members that hierarchy and centralization were the answer to government inefficiency. Gulick, perhaps the major literary spokesman of the committee, had come out strongly for centralization four years prior to its convening. He listed as its advantages: facilitated planning, economies of scale, specialization, expertise, and a single focus for public attention and control.[21] The final point listed among these is of particular importance. It is evidence of the fact that Gulick, in the Wilsonian tradition, perceived centralized organization not only as a key to efficient administration but also as an institutional means to responsible government.

Four years later Gulick could be quoted in a widely read article contending, "In administration the highest goal is efficiency."[22] This declaration was not meant to undermine the normative ideals and democratic principles which appeared in his earlier writings, but rather, in the classical vein, to reemphasize the limited and distinct role assigned to administrative matters. The old public administration does not allow for a mixture between the normative goals of politics and the operational objectives of administration. Thus, in 1937, Gulick would once again admonish his readers, ". . . politics and administration cannot be combined without sacrificing efficiency."[23]

The labors of the Presidential Committee on Administrative Management did not go unheeded. In 1939 the White House Executive Office was established in order to grant the President tighter administrative control over the executive branch. That same year the Hatch Act was enacted, which set down legal restraints on the political activity of federal employees. A year later the Ranspeck Act was passed prohibiting discrimination in federal employment on the basis of race, creed, or color.

It is not an exaggeration to claim that the convening of the Brownlow committee represents a watershed in our administrative history. By 1939 W. F. Willoughby had written one of many articles which alleged, along Taylorist lines, that there do exist principles of administration comparable to scientific laws which could be discerned by the application of a rigorous methodology to public management.[24] In the meantime Leonard White had completed the first textbook which attempted to combine the study of politics with the science of administration.[25] Within two decades the nation experienced the appointment of two Hoover Commissions[26] which were set up to study administrative organization and public management in the federal government. Both, particularly the latter, again dwelled upon the functional distinction between political and career executives.

Despite the general influence which the recommendations of the Brownlow committee enjoyed, or perhaps because of it, the committee report also encountered considerable criticism among professionals. Ideological opponents of the New Deal like Lilienthal, Tead, and Wallace offered arguments in favor of government decentralization from both a normative and an operational perspective.[27] The political scientist Marshal Dimock challenged some of the more basic assumptions of the committee, alleging that the politics-administration dichotomy was essentially false and impractical.[28]

In some ways the classical model of public administration gave rise to more questions than it answered. Is there really an identifiable area of government activity which can be removed from the realm of politics? To what extent can objective criteria for decision making be expected to prevail? Can the techniques of science be applied to a human organization in the same way that they are used in a natural environment? These questions and others like them became the source of considerable commentary as the nation entered the postwar era. Much of the resulting literature was critical in nature. However, as individuals who were in agreement with the fundamental principles of the classical model were forced to subject it to more penetrating analysis, a modified version of that model evolved which today seems more consistent with the realities of political and organizational life.

NEO-CLASSICALISM AND ITS CRITICS

Amitai Etzioni has written that one of the distinguishing features of latter day organization theory is a recognition of the inevitable conflict between individual and organizational goals.[29] It was believed by many students of the latter persuasion that the rationalist model of the Taylorists relied too heavily on the hierarchic and disciplined structure of an organization to impose order and direction upon its activities. So far as they were concerned, the mechanistic approach of Taylorism failed to recognize the human element inherent in collective social action. Throughout the thirties a group of psychologically oriented scholars from Harvard Business School worked diligently at developing techniques which would integrate individual employee needs with the goals of an organization. It was at that time that the term "human relations engineering" became prominent.[30]

There were also those theorists, however, who believed that the inevitable conflict between man and bureaucracy is irreconcilable. Among the most important was Robert Merton. In 1936 Merton wrote the first of a pair of articles which struck a caustic blow at the idea of rational organizational action.[31] Merton argued that bureaucratic action involves secondary consequences which are contrary to its overall purposes. These dysfunctions, he alleged, are a symptom of human resistance to the structure of an ordered environment. His central thesis was that bureaucracy and human nature are incompatible, and therefore individuals can be expected to function in a way which will displace the original goals of an organization. In a companion article, Merton attacked the specialized and routine nature of bureaucratic operations. There he argued that the devotion to the procedures of an organization inevitably becomes an end in itself. Therefore, he would have us believe, the worker becomes inflexible and is socialized into a system of trained incapacity.[32]

One of the best-formulated responses to the anti-organizational literature that abounded, and Merton's is merely a sample, came from a practitioner in the private sector. Chester Barnard, a former president of the New Jersey Telephone Company, put forward an "equilibrium theory" of organization.[33] In it he described the function of the executive as the regulation of an economy of incentives for individual employees who for no inherent reasons of their own could be expected to displace personal objectives which might run contrary to the purposes of their organizations. He categorized the inducements which an executive might offer to his employees into four types:

1. material—in the form of salary or wages
2. personal—in the form of prestige, distinction, or authority
3. environmental—relating to conditions of work
4. ideal—such as pride in workmanship, altruism, or loyalty

Barnard also recognized the important functions of informal organization and personal relations among workers as a means to facilitate communication, cohesiveness, and personal integrity. His writing was no doubt a revision of the mechanistic approach espoused by the classical school. Yet Barnard put the effort to rationalize collective social action back on its right course. He once again made the idea of efficient organizational performance into a defendable and practicable goal.

Barnard's book laid important groundwork for a much more comprehensive study to be completed by Herbert Simon in 1945. Simon's classic, *Administrative Behavior*,[34] is the seminal work on what we have chosen to call the neo-classical approach. In it the author modified two concepts within the classical model: rationality and hierarchy. At the same time he remained faithful to the basic tenets of the classical approach.

Above all else, Simon was interested in defining the limits of rationality within administrative decision making. He did so by first drawing a distinction between two types of administrative issues: those concerned with questions of fact, and those concerned with questions of value. According to his analysis, the first type involves propositions whose truth or validity can be tested empirically, while the latter refers to preferential choices that are concerned with values. It is the factual questions which are most susceptible to scientific solution by the administrators. For Simon, issues relating to the pursuit of particular values are of a policy-making nature and in a governmental organization remain the prerogative of political leaders.

Simon returned to the politics-administration dichotomy, designating to political leaders the responsibility of setting the objectives of a public organization while leaving for administrators the more operational task of determining the most efficient and effective method for attaining these objectives. In accord with the principles of the classic tradition, Simon emphasizes, ". . . efficiency is a basic criterion of administrative choice."[35] He goes on to explain: "The criterion of efficiency demands that, of two alternatives having the same cost, that one be chosen which will lead to the greater attainment of the organization objectives; and that, of two alternatives leading to the same degree of attainment, that one be chosen which entails the lesser cost."[36]

Simon believed that through the use of empirical analysis rational choices could be made to enable an administrator to adopt the most efficient operational means to a given organizational end. However, he also recognized the limits to rationality in administrative decision making. According to Simon, total rationality is impossible because the administrative decision maker does not possess the necessary information which is required for determining all the possible choices which are open to him and their respective consequences. Therefore, in an organizational setting the individual tends to "satisfice" rather than optimize rationality in the selection of a particular course of action. More often than not, Simon tells us, administrative decisions are incremental in nature, relying heavily on past practices to minimize the risks inherent in drastic change.

Of course, choice is only the first phase of the decision making process. Once a course of action is selected, the task of the organizational executive is to implement it. Simon was in agreement with the idea that organizational structures are by nature hierarchic. However, benefiting from the lessons of Barnard, he recognized the limits of structural authority, and further developed an equilibrium theory designed to enable executives to work within these limits.

Simon identified three major restraints on hierarchic discipline:

1. the individualistic needs and objectives of subordinate workers previously defined by the "human relations school"

2. the particularistic orientations of specialists and professionals who possess lateral authority in an organization

3. the wants and demands of an organization's clientele [37]

With regard to the first factor, Simon realized that employees could not be dealt with as mere cogs in the wheel of administrative machinery. Contrary to the assumptions of the classical school, he knew that management was not simply a matter of the issuance and following of orders. Therefore, like Barnard, he advocated a system of planned incentives where subordinates would be compensated by their superiors for the demands being made upon them.

Dealing with restraints of the second order, concerning specialization and expertise, would be much more difficult. Very often the decisions of specialists or experts at the middle levels of an organization are incontrovertible to superiors who do not possess adequate expertise to question the judgment of these professionals. Students of bureaucracy, from Weber onward, have characteristically identified specialization and division of labor as intrinsic features of complex organizations. Simon was one of the first to emphasize in an elaborate way how these features tend to decentralize power and authority in an organization. In line with his rationalist approach to administrative decision making, Simon urged executives to consider the factually relevant admonishments of experts in the formation of policy choices.

Simon's third reference group in his theory of equilibrium was perhaps the most original. Barnard had concentrated on the problem of internal resistance to change. Simon recognized that in order for an organization to maintain its viability, it is necessary for it to meet the needs and demands of its clients. Therefore, his theory turns our attention outward to a dynamic process which takes place between an organization and its social environment. [38]

It should be pointed out, however, that while Simon stressed that an organization must adapt to the ever-changing preferences of its clientele, unlike advocates of the New Public Administration his model does not allow for any direct participation of clientele in the organization's decision making. He leaves little doubt on the matter of who should be in charge. Like Barnard, he sees the organization executive as the regulator of a system of incentives designed to maximize control in a pseudo-hierarchic structure of administration.

Taken together with his emphasis on the politics-administration dichotomy and his orientation towards maximized (or "satisficed") efficiency, Simon's client-exclusive model of decision making fits well into the classification we have called the old public administration. For the purposes of the following study, the major contribution of Simon's work is that it provides us with a sufficiently realistic version of the classical model to enable us to compare the merits of the old public administration with the anticipated consequences of the New.

This is not to say that Simon's analysis provides us with any final solutions to the perennial issue concerning the role of politics in the administrative process. While it functioned to sustain some of the underlying principles of the classical approach, Simon's concessions to its critics opened the door to further attacks. Four years after the publication of *Administrative Behavior*, Philip Selznick completed his provocative study of the Tennessee Valley Authority, which pointed up some of the severe consequences which may result from an organizational strategy designed to moderate external resistance by capturing the political support of client groups.[39] In that particular case federal officials sought to defuse local resistance to the establishment of the TVA through political cooptation— that is, by inviting local officials to participate in the planning and implementation of the federally supported program. The net result, according to Selznick, was a drastic reorientation of the program in line with the priorities of local power groups, and an undermining of the original purposes for which it was created.

Selznick's book was followed by a large number of political studies which began to analyze the degree of influence which interest groups enjoy over public agencies. In 1955 J. Leiper Freeman wrote about subsystem politics involving the mutually beneficial coalitions of congressional committees, federal bureaucracies, and powerful client groups which cooperatively supported the same policy options in particular spheres of influence.[40] Four years later Charles Lindblom took up Simon's "satisficing" notion and offered a defense of incrementalism as a rational approach to administrative decision making.[41] That well-received article provided other political scientists with a theoretical foundation for arguing that bureaucratic decision making is really a function of political bargaining rather than of systemic analysis.[42] By the early sixties it was not unusual for students of government to portray public bureaucracies as just another form of interest group within the system, which plot and deal for political favors[43] like other political organizations.

As the professional literature began to focus on the political rather than the managerial side of public administration, the image of the rational and objective government bureaucrat declined in credibility. The new analytical thrust also coincided with the emergence of the civil rights movement. It is not surprising, therefore, that articulate minority group leaders started to demand equal representation within government agencies, as they had done regarding every other form of political institution.

The typical government response to these demands throughout the early sixties was a moderate one. The United States Civil Service Commission initiated an affirmative action program designed to pursue more actively the equal opportunity principles of the merit system.[44] In addition to its traditional programs to prevent employment discrimination in the federal government, the new Civil Service Commission policy called for:

1. an active attempt to publicize the availability of federal jobs among minority groups

2. the delivery of job-related training to the disadvantaged which would enable them to qualify for merit entry

3. a concentrated effort to assure that qualifying examinations do not unfairly discriminate against people from minority cultures

The initial CSC program runs in striking contrast to the affirmative action program implemented in 1971, which was described in the last chapter. The latter supported the principle of compensatory or benevolent discrimination in the form of employment goals and timetables; the original one prohibited such action as a violation of the equal opportunity principle of the merit system.[45] The more moderate position supported by the CSC prior to 1971 was spelled out in detail in a letter written by CSC Chairman Hampton to the U.S. Civil Rights Commission, rejecting a report which demanded a policy which would bring about proportional descriptive representation in the federal service:

The report presumes that the only manifestation of a successful equal employment program is immediate proportional representation of minorities at all grade levels, in every occupation, in all regions of the country. This is tantamount to a quota system and is inconsistent with the Executive Orders on equal employment . . . as well as with the concept of the merit system itself.

. . . The establishment of numerical minority quotas is not the answer, as implied in your report. This concept would result in employment on the basis of race or national origin, rather than merit or fitness.[46]

Throughout the sixties the United States Civil Service Commission initiated a number of programs designed to sensitize the merit system to the special needs and circumstances of the disadvantaged, particularly those groups belonging to racial minorities. As we shall see in the next chapter, the impact of many of these federally sanctioned programs would be felt at the local government level, not only in terms of revised recruitment policies but also in the form of new employment and job training opportunities. Suffice it to say at this point that, like the conceptual innovations made by Herbert Simon, affirmative action in its original form served the classical model of administration as an adaptive response to the realities of the times. In this way the merit system was sustained, at least temporarily, as the primary criterion for recruitment in the public service.

TECHNOCRACY AND THE NEW SCIENCE OF MANAGEMENT

While the movement for human equality was forcing civil service officials to reevaluate personnel practices that had been in existence for many years, the sixties were also a time when the executive branch came under increasing pressure to upgrade the quality of management in its large and cumbersome bureaucracies. President Johnson's determination to eradicate poverty on the domestic scene while at the same time pursuing an unreasonably costly war in Southeast Asia made it necessary for federal policy makers to search for new managerial techniques that would help to economize in the operations of government without any detriment to the effectiveness of ongoing programs. Thus, executive leadership at the federal level once again turned to the private sector in order to recruit specialists who could introduce the latest methods of planning, analysis, and performance evaluation within government. The new tool which these managerial technicians adapted to the public sector was systems analysis. Its financial counterpart was program budgeting, commonly referred to as "PPBS" (Program-Planning-Budgeting System).

According to the Rand analyst E. S. Quade, systems analysis may be broadly described as: "... an inquiry to aid decision-makers choose a course of action by systematically investigating their proper objectives, comparing quantitatively, where possible, the costs, effectiveness and risks associated with alternative policies or strategies for achieving them, and formulating additional alternatives if those examined are found wanting."[47] As Quade's definition suggests, the purpose of systems analysis was to force policy makers to identify and justify their objectives and to designate alternative courses of action for their achievement. While its operational component was concerned with the efficient management of existing systems, its financial component (PPBS) was oriented towards assessing the cost and resource requirements among alternative strategies for achieving the same goal.[48] The hope of its proponents was to rationalize decision making in government agencies and streamline its operations.

The emergence of systems analysis within public management can be said to represent a throwback to Taylorism in the sense that its practitioners were more concerned with the technical aspects of administration than with the human aspect emphasized by organization theorists like Barnard, Simon, and the Harvard School of the thirties. The ranks of its profession were conspicuously filled by individuals from the fields of engineering and the natural sciences, and, except for economists, not very well populated by social or behavioral scientists. As was the case with Taylorism, the methods of systems analysis once again brought to the forefront an interest in research, quantification, and the structured organization of men, material, and ideals.

The origin of systems analysis is usually traced to the field of operations research which itself rose to prominence in the military during the Second World War. At that time the talents of physicists, biologists, mathematicians, and other professionals in the hard sciences were drawn upon by the Allied field commands to devise strategies for the application of new defense-oriented technologies; e.g., radar and unconventional weapons systems. In later years Charles Hitch of the Rand Corporation combined the work of operations researchers and economists to develop a systems approach to operational and financial decision making in the military.[49]

Systems analysis and program budgeting were finally introduced into the federal government in 1961 when President Kennedy appointed Robert S. McNamara secretary of defense. McNamara, who had already utilized the systems approach successfully as a corporate executive in the auto industry, was summoned to incorporate the device in the Department of Defense. It was at that juncture that McNamara and a group of specialists from the private sector—sometimes called the whiz kids—descended upon the defense establishment and for the first time implemented the systems technique as a decision making tool in a federal agency.

There were several reasons why the Defense Department had seemed to be a logical place to initiate the utilization of the systems approach in government. To begin with, operations research had had its start in the military. Moreover, by 1961 the Rand Corporation had been experimenting with the application of the systems technique to defense-related problems for more than five years. Thereby, when McNamara came to office he found at Rand a ready-made package of technology and a group of experts who were familiar with the operations of the Defense Department and the particular issues that needed to be addressed.

From a political perspective, the Defense Department also seemed to be a highly susceptible place to implement a new management system, for, as the one-time Rand analyst James R. Schlesinger had explained, that agency had enjoyed a relatively advantageous degree of autonomy and freedom to operate without interference from outside parties like Congress, other agencies, or the general public.[50] Thus, managerial decisions could be made without the need to bargain with groups who were outside the administrative hierarchy of the department. In this sense, the decision making structure in Defense was relatively closed, attuned to tight managerial control, and thereby more closely resembling a corporate environment than any other federal agency.

The arrival at the Pentagon of a new group of technically trained professionals was accompanied by a certain transfer of power from career military personnel to civilian specialists who functioned under the wing of McNamara. These changes signaled a significant redesign of bureaucratic organization and practices which would take place in the public sector as the systems approach began to infiltrate the entire federal structure.[51] By 1967 President Johnson would hail the accomplishments witnessed in the Defense Department and prescribe an application of the systems technique in civilian agencies.

While this was not the first time an incumbent president had called upon individuals from outside the career structure of government to implement managerial reform, the magnitude of the "technocratic revolution" was such that it did represent an alteration of the ordinary organizational arrangement of the public bureaucracy. These managerial specialists who had been neither popularly elected nor qualified according to the traditional civil service system of merit entered the government laterally in either a staff or a consultant capacity. Yet, they accumulated a portion of power that was large enough to rival that possessed by career officials. As the systems approach gained more recognition and credibility at the federal level, a similar phenomenon began to occur within the organizational structures of several state and local governments, of which we shall see New York City become a prime example.

Notwithstanding these organizational changes, however, the new technocracy retained enough of the traditional managerial ethos to fit rather comfortably into the category we have called the old public administration. Commenting on its retention of this orientation, Ida Hoos writes:

The ethos of efficiency was translated into operational terms and became the prescription for all government agencies through the introduction of techniques already well known in military planning. Cost-benefit analysis, cost effectiveness ratios, and program budgeting became the accepted way to run the government's business. Comparable labels and terms of the past forgotten, the new, advanced concepts, purported to bring rational and systematic methods into the bureaucratic image, were the order of the day.[52]

While the bearers of the appropriate talents entered government through an appointee or contractual arrangement, they could usually be expected, in traditional fashion, to portray themselves as neutral instruments of the policy makers by whom they were employed. To those individuals who would question the validity of the politics-administration (or management) dichotomy, the claims of these new technicians appeared no more convincing. In some ways these specialists were less accountable to the public they served than were career officials, for they brought with them their own technology which defied evaluation by a non-professional citizenry.

Less concerned with the more esoteric issues related to the policy process than were neo-classicalists like Simon, the technocrats were also less inclined to preoccupy themselves with defining the limits of their own rationality or the broader normative issues of the day. Yet, the disastrous manifestation of military planning exhibited by the Vietnam War, not to mention its amorality, led many to wonder about the degree of efficiency, let alone wisdom, inherent in the systems approach. Whether or not the same deficiencies existed in the application of these techniques to domestic problems remains to be examined in the subsequent pages. Nevertheless, we should henceforth understand that the demand for public representation and accountability which emerged as part of the New Public Administration was as much a reaction to the professional technocracy as it was to the career component of the government bureaucracy. Thus, Frank Marini has characteristically concluded a compendium of papers on the "Minnowbrook perspective" with the charge:

... management science ironically enough is limited in the same way that scientific management was. Its utility increases as the programmed nature of its problems and the predictability of its environment increases. Its utility increases as efficiency increasingly becomes its dominant goal. Its utility is increased as the problem is moved toward the "attainment of consensual goals" and away from "deciding between conflictual goals" or the "inventing-of-goals" end of the continuum.... But if the view presented in this volume of our society and the demands upon Public Administration in these times is anywhere near accurate, these limitations are critical.[53]

THE NEW PUBLIC ADMINISTRATION

The old public administration in its various forms thrived on the idea that politics and administration are distinct functions of government which should remain separate in terms of both organizational activity and responsibility. While the managerial technicians of the sixties purported to be preoccupied with the operational aspects of government and their efficient attainment, the theorists of the classical and neo-classical schools defended the politics-administration dichotomy as a means to achieving both the operational and normative ideas of government. Early critics of the traditional approaches thought the separation of these two functions to be impossible. Proponents of the New Public Administration assumed the same, and then took the matter a step further.

The New Public Administration represents a reincarnation of politics as a vehicle for the attainment of social equity and justice in government. Its advocates propose that administrative institutions should establish new political channels whereby clients can directly participate in the decision making of public agencies. In the meantime they are ready to concede that their model of administration may function to undermine the efficient operation of government. This attitude is most apparent in an article written by H. George Frederickson, a key participant at the Minnowbrook Conference. He claims: "A preferred form of deprived-minority involvement would be routinized patterns of communication with decentralized organizations capable of making distributive decisions that support the interests of deprived minorities, even if these decisions are difficult to justify in terms of efficiency or economy."[54]

The advocates of the New Public Administration take their political admonitions even further. Rather than being merely neutral objective participants in the governmental process, public administrators are urged to become agents of change who would alter the present institutional arrangement of government in pursuit of social equity. One member of the Minnowbrook group goes so far as to recommend a new form of "confrontational administration."[55] Thus, the Minnowbrook perspective involves the incorporation of politics into the administrative process at two levels. On the one hand, it calls for the direct involvement of clients in that process, whom classicalists (and neo-classicalists) would have excluded. On the other hand, it encourages administrators to pursue their value preferences, a responsibility which early theories had reserved solely for policy makers.

Not all the members of the Minnowbrook group supported the position with the same degree of militance. While faithful to the new theoretical thrust which came out of the conference, many individuals recognized the dangers of an increasingly politicized bureaucracy and the still important managerial role of public executives. Note, for example, the moderating tone of W. Henry Lambright, who suggests:

Politicizing administration through the device of client participation or confrontation techniques might make public organizations more responsive to change. It might also destroy them if carried too far. Somehow the basic work of the organization still has to get done. The service . . . has to be performed. Administration in a democracy need not be "efficient," but it should be effective. Needed is a balance between the managerial and political roles of the public administrator at all levels of government.[56]

The New Public Administration must be understood, at least in part, as a reaction to the behavioral movement which swept through the political science discipline during the fifties and sixties. That phenomenon, which was an attempt to impose scientific standards upon social research, led to a de-emphasis of normative issues by many scholars who supported it. The New Public Administration sought to undo the temporary moratorium placed on the introduction of values into political inquiry. Thus, one participant of the Minnowbrook Conference laments: "It is an odd commentary on Public Administration that normative issues have been shunned on the grounds that they are in some sense less ascertainable than are facts about the organizations, administrative processes, and other such matters."[57]

Frederickson is quite correct in depicting the Minnowbrook group as a brand of "second-generation behaviorists."[58] Their emergence occurred at a time when the political science profession was undergoing an evaluation of the course it had followed with the rise of behavioralism. In addition to a rekindling of an interest in normative concerns by traditional political theorists,[59] this self-examination resulted in a reorientation of empirical political research from the study of the processes of government to an examination of the policy outputs of our political institutions.[60] The New Public Administration incorporates both these recent trends into a singular approach. As Frederickson explains: "A new form of distributive analysis is emerging. This approach focuses on equity in the distribution of government services within a jurisdiction."[61]

In terms of scholarship the Minnowbrook Conference is a good indicator of what was going on in the political science profession during the late sixties and early seventies. However, the New Public Administration is more than an act of intellectual housecleaning or statement of professional goals. Its precepts actually define a "revolution" which had already begun to take place in our administrative institutions before the Minnowbrook Conference was even in the planning stage. In practice, a New Public Administration resulted from the transformation of the American civil rights movement to a demand for black power and self-determination by minority group leaders who were not satisfied with the goods and services they were receiving from government.[62] It emanated from the White House. Its driving force was the presidential leadership of Lyndon Johnson. Its program for action was the Great Society's War on Poverty. Its outcome was a political assault on centralized administrative institutions in several large cities in America. Part of its legacy is the direct participation of client groups in newly decentralized administrative structures located in many, though not all, of those same American cities.

According to Piven and Cloward, the "hallmark of the Great Society" was "the direct relationship between the national government and the ghettos, a relationship in which both state and local governments were undercut."[63] From its moment of origin it was apparent that President Johnson's War on Poverty would serve as a mechanism through which federal funding would be channeled directly to the poor. This strategy permitted Washington officials to avoid any direct involvement with big-city mayors who were well entrenched in political alliances with white ethnics. In another sense, it might also be said that this strategy removed city mayors from the politically embarrassing position of being the intermediaries in a large urban aid program which did not bear any benefits for their traditional political allies. However, the anti-poverty program turned out to be much more than simply a method for allocating federal monies. It also became the basis for a federally supported campaign to restructure administrative decision making in large metropolitan areas.

It was the Community Action Program of 1964 which called for "maximum feasible participation" of the poor in federally sponsored programs designed to eradicate poverty. In its original form CAP legislation entailed the representation of the poor, local businesses, and organized interest groups on citywide policy boards. Then in 1966 the Quie Amendment was added, which specifically required that one-third the membership of Community Action boards be representatives of the poor. Thereby the federal legislation established a legitimate role for clients in the administration and decision making of the program.

The Community Action Program was a major milestone in the direction of decentralized client-responsive administrative institutions. It enjoyed significant support from university and foundation-based social scientists, many of whom contributed to the design and implementation of the new program.[64] It was these individuals who set down the theoretical and political foundations for a New Public Administration. Within several years three federal advisory commissions would recommend the further institution of administrative decentralization and client participation not only for federally sponsored programs but for local government units as well.[65] In the meantime a plethora of literature came forth from urban scholars supporting the same.

The Community Action Program received its most formidable opposition from the mayors of the nation's larger cities. Not only were they being ignored in this major federal effort which was being undertaken to eliminate urban blight; CAP was laying the foundation for the development of a political substructure in minority neighborhoods which would rival the traditional Democratic organizations that brought local chief executives to power. As one analyst describes it, CAP was an anti-establishment program which utilized federal funds to exert pressure against local bureaucracies.[66]

The nation's local government executives finally grouped their forces at the United States Conference of Mayors' meeting held in 1965. There Mayors John Shelly of San Francisco and Sam Yorty of Los Angeles sponsored a resolution accusing Sargent Shriver of fostering class struggle in urban areas. Mayors Robert Wagner of New York and William Walsh of Syracuse were among the others who came out against the new federal program. Finally the conference formed a new anti-poverty committee under the chairmanship of Chicago Mayor Richard Daley and adopted a resolution urging the Office of Economic Opportunity to recognize City Hall–endorsed local agencies as the proper channel for community action.

The mayors eventually took their cause to Congress, and their efforts were not without consequence. In 1967 Congress passed the Green Amendment to the Economic Opportunity Act. This removed the maximum feasible participation clause from the CAP and stipulated that local governments could either set up a central Community Action Agency themselves or designate an organization to fill that role. The Green Amendment was also similar in tone to the Model Cities legislation which had emerged from Congress the year before. That program, while intended to provide area residents with a means to introduce their viewpoints on policy issues, left ultimate authority for decision making in the hands of City Hall.[67]

There is much reason to doubt how successful the Community Action Program was in mobilizing the poor for political action. Despite the hopes of "democratizing" the local decision making process, the fact remains that no more than 5 percent of the electorate turned out to vote in the poverty program elections in areas that were affected.[68] A number of studies have also documented the fact that those individuals who did become involved with CAP at the community level, who purported to be representatives of the poor, were generally drawn from the upper socioeconomic strata of their localities.[69] In most cases they were local notables and experienced activists who had dominated the politics of their communities prior to the implementation of CAP.

Many students of the Great Society program, several of whom supported the social welfare thrust of its agenda, did not hesitate to launch vehement criticisms against CAP. Daniel P. Moynihan attacked the new brand of participatory democracy advocated by his university colleagues as a substitution of political ideology for social science.[70] Theodore Lowi condemned what he perceived to be the parceling out of public authority to private parties as a violation of the conflict of interest principle and an undermining of the law.[71] Other scholars were quick to point out what the successful campaign of big-city mayors against CAP had already proved: the poor did not have adequate political resources, nor did CAP provide them, to launch an effective challenge to established local interests.[72]

Despite the significant setbacks for CAP at the federal level, the Great Society program did function to establish a sound ideological footing for decentralized administration in the local sector. As client-based institutions were becoming the order of the day in several experimental urban government programs, the public administration literature began to reflect a continuing debate over a new hierarchy of values within the profession.[73] Citizen participation emerged to displace efficiency as the higher order goal for decision making in many local governments.

As has been the case throughout most of the nation's administrative history, the reforms of the sixties continued to be advanced in the name of social justice. As time wore on, the latest wave of reform not only took issue with the traditional hierarchic structure of bureaucratic institutions but also began to question the degree of fairness which was manifest under the merit system of recruitment. While not ostensibly linked with the movement for a New Public Administration, recent criticisms of the merit system are definitely consistent with the demand for "social equity" which began to appear in the public administration literature after the convening of the Minnowbrook Conference. In some sense, the term social equity has been adopted as a password for all those who have found reason to challenge traditional institutions. For example, in an article which appeared in a symposium on "Social Equity in Public Administration," Eugene McGregor writes: "Social equity doctrines in public affairs are popularly regarded as the enemy of merit principles. The equity camp defends popular (i.e., reasonably equal) distribution of opportunity and reward, and the merit system connotes elitism and competitive excellence."[74]

By the time the seventies had arrived, the old public administration had weathered a number of storms which struck at the very core of its meaning. Public servants were being urged to become political activists rather than neutral instruments of policy, decentralization was being offered as an antidote to the hierarchic structure of traditional institutions, and participation had begun to rival efficiency as a higher order value for administration. In the meantime a reversal in 1971 of the United States Civil Service Commission's position on racial quotas, time-tables, and employment goals had challenged the merit principle as a method by which government employees were chosen.

AN INTELLECTUAL HERITAGE: WHAT CAN BE LEARNED?

A distinct pattern pervades our entire administrative history. While all the reforms of the past were proposed in the name of social justice, the final impact which each exerted on the administrative process was ultimately decided in the political arena. The spoils system, the merit system, affirmative action in its various forms, and administrative decentralization were all purported to be mechanisms by which the government could work to attain the highest ethical and moral standards. Even scientific management was defended as a device which would allow society to realize the ideals of Christianity and democracy.

Nevertheless, the realities of politics are indisputable. It was the election of Andrew Jackson which began to bring about an end to class discrimination in the public service. It was the organized activities of nineteenth-century reformers which led to passage of the Pendleton Act. It took the good political sense of early twentieth-century reformers to recognize and exploit the political viability of a campaign to promote economy and efficiency in government. It took the bold decisions of Franklin Roosevelt to assure that Woodrow Wilson's classical model was actually reflected in the operations of government. Without the political momentum of the civil rights movement, demands for equal opportunity and community power would have gone unanswered. Without the aggressive determination of Lyndon Johnson, the campaign to establish client-responsive administrative institutions would not have gone as far as it did.

Our normative concerns notwithstanding, it is politics which determines the ends to which administrative action is devoted. This is not to say, however, that there is no room for objective rational thinking within the administrative process. Herbert Simon did designate an identifiable sphere of administrative decision making which, at least in a relative sense, is susceptible to the use of systematic analysis. It is that concern with the selection of techniques which will allow an organization to accomplish its purpose in the most efficient way known. That particular sphere of activity became especially recognizable each time the federal government turned to the private sector to borrow from the recent technological and methodological developments in the field of management.

The most valuable attribute of Simon's administrative model is its element of realism. While consistent with the operational goals of scientific management, Simon's model takes into account the limits of rationality in human organizations. Henceforth, when we refer to the rational approach to decision making inherent in the old public administration, it must be understood in terms of Simon's "satisficing" notion. For Simon, the optimal level of rationality in a human organization is actually a "bounded rationality" which functions within the confines of the limited information possessed by individual decision makers.

The neo-classical model of the old public administration also leaves room for a consideration of the political restraints which are often faced by organizational executives in the implementation of decisions. Simon was aware of the fact that organizational employees at the middle and lower levels have the capacity to resist policies handed down from above. He also knew that in order for an organization to survive it must respond to the wants and needs of its clientele. However, Simon retained enough of the classical ethos to believe that it is the responsibility of the executive hierarchy to assure that neither the resistance of employees nor the demands of clients could work to undermine the efficient fulfillment of the organization's purpose.

It is with regard to the latter point that the old public administration can be distinguished from the New. The New Public Administration is anti-hierarchy. It encourages administrators to resist the patterns of the past. It calls for a redesign of our administrative institutions so that public clients enjoy a direct role in the decision making of agencies which serve them. The rallying call of the Minnowbrook Conference was social equity. Its participants sought to undermine the traditional operational goal of efficiency and replace it with the ideological goal of citizen participation. Although their efforts to reestablish the significance of normative issues within the social science disciplines is commendable, our brief overview of the literature in public administration should serve to substantiate the claim that ethical values also played an important part in formulating the ideals of the more traditional theorists.

Both the merit system of recruitment and scientific management were offered by their supporters as alternatives to corrupt, unjust, and incompetent government. Proponents of the New Public Administration have raised some serious questions concerning the ability of our bureaucratic institutions to fulfill the normative ideals of the governmental system. However, while history has proved both merit recruitment and efficient performance to be feasible political goals, there still remains some doubt as to whether politicizing the poor against established interests is a practically attainable agenda for reform.

The administration of President Lyndon Johnson is particularly interesting because it was one which pursued a dual program of reform embracing principles that were consistent with those underlying both the old and the New public administrations. Through the use of managerial technicians from the private sector, Johnson strategists, following the lead of the preceding Kennedy administration, incorporated new managerial systems which centralized decision making in several federal agencies, particularly defense, to upgrade the operational efficiency of government. With the inauguration of the War on Poverty, the Johnson team also sought to decentralize administrative decision making at the local level in order to provide clients, especially the poor, with an opportunity to participate in government. At the same time the Johnson administration provided an impetus for a reevaluation of the merit system so that more public jobs would become available for the chronically unemployed.

A similar pattern of reform was being carried out, almost simultaneously, in New York City under the administration of Mayor John Lindsay. Taking his cues from Washington, Lindsay introduced the idea of maximum feasible participation into the local government structure of New York; yet, in an effort to improve the delivery of local services, Lindsay relied heavily on the talents of managerial technicians brought in from the private sector, particularly the Rand Corporation. In the meantime Lindsay's agenda for reform also included an evaluation and revision of the local merit system. As was the case with the federal reforms, the initiation of the programs and the degree of success which each achieved were very much an outgrowth of the political environment in which they appeared.

3

ADMINISTRATIVE REFORM IN NEW YORK CITY

New York City has traditionally served as a hatching place for administrative reform movements in the United States. Its history in this regard dates back nearly a century when the city stood at the forefront of the national reform movement which took place during the latter part of the nineteen hundreds. The New York Civil Service Reform League and the National Civil Service Reform League, both products of the same town and the same era, enjoyed widespread national membership by the turn of the century. George William Curtis, the original chairman of the United States Civil Service Commission, and Dorman Eaton, who succeeded him after the passage of the Pendleton Act, both emerged from the momentum generated by the New York reform movement. The Bureau of Municipal Research, whose efforts to improve public service became a model for the entire nation, still maintains its headquarters in New York under the chairmanship of Luther Gulick.[1]

While many of the demands for government reform which grew out of New York had a national focus, a large part of the political fallout resulting from these efforts descended upon the city's own local government bureaucracy. As the national government stood under increased pressure to put its own administrative house in order, Washington also implemented a number of policies designed to encourage cities to do the same. This ripple effect was somewhat evident at the turn of the century when a national consensus on the wretched state of affairs in the cities focused much attention on the need for municipal reform. It was again evident in the sixties when the demand for racial equality by minorities forced the federal government to implement a number of programs that would promote change in the nation's urban centers.

New York City became a major target of the Washington-based initiatives which took form in the federal anti-poverty program. The manner in which its governmental structure responded to these initiatives can generally be understood as an outgrowth of two interrelated factors. On the one hand was the local political environment of the city itself, which was quite indicative of the racial discontent evident in other parts of the country. On the other hand were the personal leadership styles and individual priorities of the two mayors who presided over the city's large government bureaucracy during the turbulent sixties and early seventies.

This chapter will trace approximately one decade of administrative reform in New York. It will describe the events which led to and shaped several moderate changes in the traditional civil service system, a variety of experiments in decentralized government, and finally the Productivity Program of the early seventies. For the purpose of providing a meaningful historical perspective, this chapter will include a brief account of the developments which characterized the final years of the Wagner administration. However, its focus will be on the administrative reforms initiated under Mayor John Lindsay.

Lindsay presided over the city during the period with which our empirical research is concerned. His administration is particularly interesting because it serves to illustrate an important lesson we have already drawn from the previous chapter: no matter how worthy the ends to which it may lead, an essential ingredient for successful administrative reform is political feasibility. Lindsay's case is one exception which proves the rule. An unconventional mayor who sought to oppose the established power structure of the city in which he rose to office, Lindsay found it necessary to retreat from a more "radical" program for change to one which was more moderate in both purpose and tone. Entering office as a vocal supporter of decentralization and community control, Lindsay retired from a highly centralized government espousing the traditional administrative principle of maximum efficiency in the delivery of local services.

WAGNER AND LINDSAY: A CONTRAST IN STYLE

Sayre and Kaufman have described three different styles of leadership from which an incumbent chief executive might choose in going about the business of governing New York City. These are classified as:

1. an "initiator or innovator" who sponsors new solutions to city problems

2. an "arbitrator" who chooses among the solutions offered by others and works for their adoption

3. a "mediator" who seeks to moderate issues of conflict between competing forces and to cultivate a consensus for compromise[2]

On the basis of their analysis of the pluralistic nature of power in New York, Sayre and Kaufman conclude that most mayors are compelled to act as arbitrators rather than innovators, and when possible as mediators rather than arbitrators.

Of course, the true range of options which are open to any individual mayor are directly related to the political resources which he has brought to the office and the specific goals for which he plans to use them. To discuss administrative reforms in a city apart from the political forces and motivations which brought them about would be to tell only half the story, and perhaps, it would mean leaving out the most interesting parts.

While Robert F. Wagner came to the mayoralty as a result of a hotly contested primary battle between the regular county organizations of the Democratic party, he managed eventually to consolidate a power base in the city that enabled him to enjoy three terms in office. He represented the epitome of Sayre and Kaufman's mediator style of leadership. Thus, his approach to administrative reform was a rather moderate one, and he responded in kind to the many demands for change which came to the city by way of federal anti-poverty programs.

John V. Lindsay, to the contrary, was a self-styled mover, who described his own manner in office as that of an "advocate mayor."[3] He came to City Hall in an unorthodox fashion with no real power base of his own. Bent upon reorganizing the power structure of the city, Lindsay saw administrative reform as a means to do battle with the city's long-standing multiplicity of elites. He used the federal initiatives undertaken by the Johnson administration as a first attempt to cultivate a new base of support in the city.

Wagner: The Politics of Moderation. Robert Wagner was one of that rare breed who are capable of maintaining a cordial and usually cooperative relationship with both the reform elements and the established interests of the Democratic party in New York. A former borough president of Manhattan, he had originally been elected mayor with the support of the powerful Tammany Hall organization. However, after two terms in office Wagner, under pressure from Manhattan reform clubs, finally broke with the Tammany leader Carmine DeSapio.

The break with DeSapio could have been catastrophic for Wagner. Tammany enjoyed widespread loyalty from the city's old ethnic groups. It had provided a variety of services to a large number of immigrants in the form of facilitated citizenship, voter registration, and jobs for the unskilled laborer—not to mention the proverbial Christmas turkey. No New York Democrat could afford to lose the support of these groups.

Manhattan reformers came out of an altogether different mold. Their movement was essentially an attempt by outsiders to gain access to the mainstream of city politics. According to Wilson's vivid portrayal, the Manhattan reformer of the late fifties was usually drawn from the recently educated Jewish middle class or was a "better off" white Anglo-Saxon Protestant.[4] Many of those older and less educated Jews who broke with the Democratic party machine did so by joining the ranks of the Liberal party, which had its origins in the International Ladies Garment Workers Union.

Wagner managed to court the reform factions of the Democratic party without alienating the traditional ethnic stronghold which consistently delivered large majorities at the polls. He did this in part by developing and maintaining a close friendship with the city's large and powerful municipal labor unions. The son of a prominent United States senator, whose labor-oriented legislation bears the family name, Wagner sought to do for the New York laborer what his father had already done at the federal level.

New York has a long history as a labor town. As far back as 1909 clerical workers within the City workforce organized to form the Civil Service Forum. A year later policemen and firemen established similar organizations. Since at the time of their founding public employees were prohibited from collective bargaining with the City, these associations concentrated most of their efforts on political action and lobbying. Because a good deal of labor legislation came out of the state capitol, these associations learned to focus a large part of their attention on Albany instead of City Hall.

During his first campaign for the mayoralty in 1953, the then borough president of Manhattan promised labor leaders in the city that he would work for the passage of a local version of the Wagner Act. Soon after his election Wagner signed an executive order which recognized the right of City employees to be represented in collective bargaining by organizations of their own choosing. He also established a City Department of Labor which was authorized to recognize employee associations and establish grievance procedures.[5]

Wagner took pride in the personal role which he assumed in negotiating with local labor leaders. His efforts on their behalf not only enhanced his own individual stature in the local political process, but it served to reorient a major part of organized labor's efforts from Albany to City Hall. These accomplishments by Wagner would prove to be a significant liability to his immediate successor, John Lindsay.

Lindsay: The Politics of Confrontation. John Lindsay came to the mayoralty with a number of disadvantages. Perhaps the most detrimental was the
fact that he was a Republican chief executive in a town where the Democratic registration outnumbers that of any other party by a margin of
more than three to one. Moreover, Lindsay sought to use his New York
office as a place to establish a national reputation in the Kennedy image,
whereby he would project himself as an ally of the poor, a catalyst for
change, and a spokesman for the American city. His apparent willingness
to raise controversial issues which threatened the interests of established
groups did not fare well with representatives of organized labor who had
just enjoyed three terms with Robert Wagner.

Lindsay originally declared his candidacy in 1965 as a fusion candidate,
bolstered by a Democrat and a Liberal as his two running mates. Although
he did receive substantial financial support and some organizational back-
ing from his own party, it was common knowledge in New York City that
Republican clubs had rarely demonstrated a potential to deliver votes.
Therefore, Lindsay relied very heavily on his own personal organization
composed of approximately 120 neighborhood storefronts. According
to one estimate, these local organizations succeeded in recruiting some
ten thousand active volunteers, most of whom were veterans of the Democratic reform movement.[6]

Lindsay's partnership with middle class Jewish reformers would prove
to be a valuable asset. Not only do Jews constitute the strongest ethnic
voting bloc in New York City, but the Republican WASP Lindsay needed
all the help he could get to defeat his leading contender, Abraham Beame,
a Jewish candidate from the Brooklyn Democratic organization. His
final margin of victory in 1965 was merely 102,000 votes.

The conglomeration of neighborhood storefronts that successfully
elected a fusion candidate in 1965 would stay in existence after the
election in the form of local Civic Improvement Organizations. By the
time Lindsay was ready to seek a second term in office, these storefront
associations would be organized into five separate county organizations,
closely resembling a local party structure. Each storefront and county
group was headed by a ranking city official.

While Robert Wagner had illustrated the feasibility of maintaining a
cordial relationship with both Democratic reformers and organized labor,
Lindsay's political thinking did not allow for such a convenience. The
new Mayor wanted to make inroads into the racial ghettos of New York.
He hoped to foster a cadre of fresh leadership in these areas and join it in
challenging the existing power structure of the city. Lindsay seemed to
work on the assumption that in order to win the confidence of alienated
minorities he would have to show that he was at odds with the standing

government bureaucracy and the unions which inhabit it. Nat Hentoff described the Lindsay rationale rather well when he wrote: "The demographic shifts that are taking place in New York—the growing numbers of Negroes and Puerto Ricans—make it all the more important for him to maintain certain enemies."[7]

Whatever the shortcomings of his overall political strategy, it did not take long for Lindsay to demonstrate that he suffered from a hostility with labor. His first day in office was greeted by the most crippling public transit strike in the city's history. It was during this grueling episode that the new mayor made what was probably the keynote speech of his entire administration. There he condemned the "power brokers" of the city and pledged, "I shall not permit the public interest to be flouted."

Throughout Lindsay's eight years in office the people of the city would suffer through a number of public employee work actions which would compromise the health, safety, and convenience of the average citizen. These included a seven-day sanitationmen's strike, a firemen's walkout, two sickouts by the police, a bridge tenders' and sewer workers' strike, and three actions by teachers which closed the city schools. During the seven-day sanitation walkout seventy thousand tons of garbage were left on the streets, creating a citywide health emergency. The longest teachers' strike lasted for a period of eight weeks. In the meantime organized labor succeeded in acquiring some of the most significant wage gains in the city's history. In most cases these pay raises even exceeded those acquired under the Wagner administration.[8]

In 1967 Lindsay replaced the city Department of Labor with a new Office of Collective Bargaining. This new tripartite agency composed of City, union, and "public" members would assume full responsibility for negotiations between the City and labor leaders. Unlike his predecessor, Lindsay rarely played a personal role in the conduct of such business, a practice which made many union people feel slighted. It did not take long for Lindsay to develop a reputation as a Mayor who could not adequately deal with organized labor. As the City workforce grew younger and more militant, union leadership was forced to make more severe demands upon the City for services rendered by employees. Given this situation and his original political orientation, it is not surprising that Lindsay embraced administrative reform as a technique to declare war on the bureaucracy.

Lindsay's approach to administrative reform really proceeded in two directions simultaneously. On the one side he moved towards a centralization of the bureaucracy in order to extend his own span of control and consolidate executive discretion at City Hall. This strategy became most apparent with the creation of ten "superagencies" which incorporated more than fifty independent city departments into less than a dozen larger organizations. On the other side he moved towards decentralization. This strategy became apparent in a number of experiments which were implemented at the neighborhood level. As former Budget Director David Grossman explained it:

There was both a centralizing and decentralizing concept within the Lindsay administration which occurred at the same time. The centralizing concept was manifest in the creation of the superagencies. The decentralizing concept was manifest in several areas, but most significantly in the field of education. We did not see any inconsistency in the two approaches. We believed that there was a need for more responsiveness, both centrally and at the roots of government in the communities.[9]

THE MAYORS RESPOND TO THE POVERTY PROGRAM

The Economic Opportunity Act which was signed by President Johnson in 1964 represented a two-pronged national attack on the problem of poverty. Its first thrust was to decrease the unemployment rate among the poor through the infusion of federal funds into local governments. While not necessarily intended to circumscribe the traditional merit system, the poverty program was designed to emphasize the "equal opportunity" aspect of the merit concept. It would do so by an intensive program of job training that would enable the poor to qualify for public employment and by making more money available for the creation of new local government jobs.

The second thrust of the federal legislation, that which called for maximum feasible participation, was designed to increase the role that the disadvantaged would play in decisions concerning programs which were implemented to meet their needs. In a general sense, it would be expected that client groups would be provided with a mechanism through which they could articulate both their service demands and their level of satisfaction with locally administered programs.

As is the case with most legislative mandates, a good deal of doubt existed in the early stages of the poverty program concerning just how it would be administered. Many questions remained to be answered. The creation of an Equal Employment Opportunity Commission indicated that the federal government would be placing a greater emphasis on the enforcement of anti-discrimination laws with regard to job placement. Did this mean that local governments should be reevaluating or redesigning their own civil service procedures? The maximum feasible participation clause made it apparent that client groups were no longer to remain a passive entity at the output end of the political process. But just how much authority were they to be granted in local decision making?

The vague character of legislative enactments usually provides an administrator with a wide range of discretion in both interpreting the meaning of laws and determining how they will be implemented. Most local chief executives took advantage of that situation with regard to the poverty program by implementing it in a way which was consistent with their own priorities. The differing ways in which New York Mayors Robert Wagner and John Lindsay chose to respond to the same piece of legislation are a case in point. They serve to illustrate the fact that administrative reform, no matter how worthy its designated ends, cannot be understood apart from the political process.

Jobs and the Merit System. New York, the first American city to do so, has had a competitive system of job recruitment since 1883. In 1954 a recently elected Mayor Robert Wagner announced the abolition of a sixty-eight-year-old Municipal Civil Service Commission and its replacement by another three-person commission whose chairman would also serve as director of a newly created Department of Personnel. According to the state legislation which brought it into being, the primary purpose of the new bi-partisan Civil Service Commission was to act as "guardian of the merit system" in New York City.[10]

While the overall function of the new commission did not vary significantly from that of the one which it succeeded, the institution of a new city department to serve as its administrative arm was evidence of a growing awareness on the part of city officials that operating according to the merit system is both a serious and a complex civic responsibility. From the time of its inception until 1964 most activities of the commission and the department were concentrated in four general areas, namely, the formulation of civil service rules and regulations, the classification of job positions, the preparation of competitive examinations, and the hearing of employee grievances which originate in the various city agencies.

Throughout this period the Wagner administration emphasized the role of the merit system as a means of selecting the most qualified individuals for employment within the city government. This priority became most visible in 1963 when Wagner requested the Brookings Institution to conduct a study to recommend ways in which the City could successfully compete with the private sector in attracting skilled professional personnel. Despite the fact that the Brookings study was highly critical of the department's recruitment and qualifications practices,[11] the Wagner administration continued to defend the way in which it administered the merit system. In the same year that the Brookings study was published, the annual report of the Civil Service Commission and Department of Personnel emphasized, "The prime tool for selecting the best qualified candidates for City employment remains the competitive examination."[12]

In 1964 the City Department of Personnel began to take on new responsibilities. In response to the inauguration of the national War on Poverty, the Personnel Department became a clearing house which would coordinate the numerous training and employment programs which were made possible by the influx of new federal dollars. It was at that time that Project Join was initiated. Project Join involved the creation of new jobs for the hiring and career development of minorities who had been the chronic victims of unemployment in the city.

In the following year an anti-poverty program unit was set up in the department. Under its guidance a wide range of opportunities were made available to the disadvantaged in the city. Among these were:

1. College Work Study Program, which allowed students to work part time in a city agency and continue their education

2. Neighborhood Youth Corps, which brought high school dropouts back to school and allowed them to work a half-day and attend classes the other half

3. Municipal Cooperative Education and Work Program which permitted potential high school dropouts to alternate a week of school with a week of work

4. Preparation Retraining and Education Program which trained and rehabilitated male heads of households which were supported by welfare

By the end of 1965 the anti-poverty program unit, after nine months of operation, had succeeded in providing employment and/or training for nearly nine thousand individuals.[13]

Under Mayor Wagner's administration the Department of Personnel had also begun to inaugurate a Job Restructuring Program in eight city agencies. Through this program the department would review the job descriptions and functions of all professional and semi-professional positions in the agencies affected. Its purpose was to determine what aspects of the jobs examined might be performed by non-professional or less skilled individuals. It was hoped that through the results of these job analyses the City would make more positions available for unskilled workers and at the same time increase the attractiveness of higher level positions for the professional talent pool in the city.

The Job Restructuring Program was as much a response to the criticisms incorporated in the Brookings study of the previous year as it was an attempt to increase employment opportunities for the disadvantaged. The fact remains, however, that during its charge over the City's personnel system, the Wagner administration moved slowly towards the task of reforming the job qualification policies that had been in practice for many years. While Mayor Wagner welcomed the availability of federal funds from the anti-poverty program to provide jobs for the poor, he had refrained from being directly critical of the merit system as it existed in 1965. In this respect he differed quite considerably from his successor.

While Robert Wagner focused on the creation of new public service jobs as a method for dealing with minority unemployment, his successor, John Lindsay, was outwardly critical of the merit system in the form that he found it. Lindsay wanted to open the public bureaucracy to those groups which he felt were unfairly excluded from public service by outdated civil service rules and regulations. He sought to revamp the merit system so that it would not function as an obstacle to minority groups, but rather serve as an active mechanism capable of reaching out to the black and Hispanic communities. As a former member of the Civil Service Commission who served under both Wagner and Lindsay explained:

The Lindsay approach to civil service reform was far more direct and aggressive than that of Wagner's. While Wagner concentrated on the creation of new job titles, the Lindsay people wanted to change the civil service system itself. They wanted to bring about change quickly and their strategy was to break down the job and recruitment structure so that minorities could more easily qualify for employment.[14]

Most of the civil service reforms which were implemented as a result of the Lindsay administration's efforts took shape under one of three major types of programs:

1. an evaluation of merit qualifications in order to determine which requirements discriminated against individuals from minority cultures but did not have any direct relationship to the job to be performed

2. a campaign designed to make minority groups more aware of the employment opportunities which exist in the public sector

3. the inauguration of training programs which would help those who were educationally disadvantaged to prepare for civil service qualifying examinations

Students of government and civil rights activists alike have raised serious questions about the validity of the examination system which is used to qualify individuals for employment or promotion within the civil service.[15] They have criticized the exams for testing skills which are not commensurate with the responsibilities of the positions they are used to fill. Thus, some have alleged that the system is arbitrary and, at times, downright discriminatory.

Lindsay accepted many of these criticisms as fact and soon after his election took a number of steps to modify the traditional hiring practices of the City. His position on the issue was open and determined. He even demonstrated a willingness to take his cause outside city limits. In 1967 three members of the City Civil Service Commission appeared before a state Constitutional Convention and appealed for an amendment of a long-standing statute which governed the local merit system because, they claimed, "it is discriminatory against those who can perform the jobs to be done, but who cannot do equally well on competitive tests."[16] They advocated the adoption of a new law which would require that, "Appointments and promotions shall be based upon merit and fitness, to be ascertained by examination *or by other evidence of fitness*" (emphasis added).

That same year the City Commission revised its own local hiring standards along the same lines as the recommendations which it made to the state. Among the reforms implemented were:

1. reduction of height requirements for police trainees
2. removal of employment prohibitions for persons on parole or probation
3. allowance of individuals with conviction records to compete for most civil service positions
4. elimination from personal history questionnaires questions relating to the arrests, social status, and behavior of relatives
5. establishment of a general policy which called for "judging each applicant on the basis of current fitness and ability for a specific job" as opposed to "an absolute set of standards for all positions"[17]

In 1969 the Department of Personnel began to employ several language consultants whose responsibility it was to review civil service examinations for the identification and elimination of those features which were culturally biased. By 1971 the department began to experiment with the use of partially bilingual tests; and it soon became a regular policy to include bilingual sections on exams whenever 5 percent of the applicants requested it.

In addition to initiating a number of local programs designed to sensitize the city's civil service system to the social condition of minorities, the Lindsay administration undertook a concerted effort to encourage these groups to take advantage of the many opportunities that were becoming available as a result of the federal anti-poverty program. In 1966 the Personnel Department established a Community Relations Division in order to help individuals who were in need of employment. Through this new unit the department began to hold job fairs and career day programs at high schools and colleges throughout the city. The Community Relations Division was also responsible for sponsoring several training programs, many of which were held in conjunction with the City University and local high schools. By the end of 1966 more than twenty thousand individuals received job training and/or employment with the funds made available from the anti-poverty program alone.[18]

In October of 1967 the Department of Personnel took a further step in order to expand employment opportunities for the poor. With the cooperation of the federal and state governments, a pilot program was set up in the Brownsville section of Brooklyn which directly involved local organizations in the campaign to employ the poor. Community groups not only were used as a vehicle to publicize job opportunities in their neighborhoods but also assisted in helping to prepare local residents for civil service examinations. The Brownsville pilot project eventually became a model for the Three Faces of Government Program, a more comprehensive effort sponsored by federal, state, and city funds. Three Faces of Government utilized Community Action corporations in the same manner in which the Brownsville organizations had functioned. Thereby the campaign against unemployment was further disseminated to the neighborhood level.

The political implications of the latter program, particularly the way it was administered, are quite apparent. Lindsay had already made it clear that he wanted to establish his own political base in the black and Puerto Rican sections of the city. By using Community Action corporations as an instrument for channeling employment opportunities, Lindsay was enabling these recently created organizations to fulfill some of the same functions that traditional political clubs had performed. However, while the older clubs provided a source of jobs for European immigrants, Lindsay had hoped that the Community Action corporations would bring more racial minorities into the City bureaucracy.

Lindsay concentrated a major part of his recruitment drive on the uniformed services, where minority employment was known to be low. The Department of Personnel launched several cooperative campaigns with the black and Hispanic societies of these forces in order to attract more minority employment. In 1971 the department created the positions of police aide, fire aide, housing police aide, and sanitation trainee aide for residents of Model Cities areas. These positions were created to provide minorities with new entry-level jobs in the uniformed services where they were not well represented, with the hope that the relevant job experience would eventually help them to qualify for regular positions as police, fire, and sanitationmen. Because these opportunities were limited to Model Cities residents, the new positions were vehemently criticized by public employee unions, who claimed that the policy was discriminatory and unfair.

By 1970 it appeared that Lindsay was prepared to move towards a more extreme policy of affirmative action in the city; that is, one not only designed to insure equal employment opportunity for the disadvantaged but also one involving preferential treatment in hiring practices. Whether or not this was the case to any significant extent, it should be emphasized that the City never relied upon the use of racial quotas or employment goals under Lindsay's administration. As one Lindsay appointee to the Civil Service Commission, Frank Arricale, explained to this author: "Racial quotas were never really considered as a serious option during the Lindsay years. It was never really discussed to any great extent. We did target recruitment drives in urban renewal areas and worked with black and Hispanic groups to encourage minorities to apply for jobs, but there were never any employment goals or timetables set."[19]

In 1970 the Department of Personnel was given an added responsibility to reduce the overall size of the City workforce because of imminent budget restraints which had to be faced. Thus, there was not much to be gained from an extremely controversial hiring policy at that point. Moreover, John Lindsay reserved his most radical policy of administrative reform for those local programs which were related to the maximum feasible participation clause of the Economic Opportunity Act. Lindsay espoused the concept of "client participation" as a means to provide minorities with administrative representation from outside the traditional boundaries of the bureaucracy. His enthusiastic support for establishing a mechanism whereby citizens could become directly involved in administrative policy making and the manner in which he went about it served to further distinguish Lindsay from his predecessor Robert Wagner.

Maximum Feasible Participation. In his provocative study on the subject Daniel P. Moynihan has gone to great lengths to emphasize that while the poverty program of the Great Society was Washington-based, the "ideology of participation" which is associated with it is really a product of New York. He writes:

Community action in both its conservative and radical formulations was a product of New York. The war on poverty was a product of Washington. The one deeply concerned with society, the other preoccupied with government; the one emotionally no less than ideologically committed to social change, the other profoundly attached to the artifacts of stability and continuity; the one fascinated by racial, ethnic and religious diversity,

the other still fiercely loyal to the Republic and still trying to fashion a
nation out of a continent. It is a contrast between ideas and information,
between brilliance and endurance, between innovation and preservation.[20]

It was a year prior to the Economic Opportunity Act when a group
of New York-based social scientists, with the endorsement of President
Kennedy's Committee on Juvenile Delinquency and support from the
Ford Foundation and other private organizations, gave birth to an experiment designed to overcome the alienation of youth in urban society
by encouraging them to become active participants in their environment.
Based on the "opportunity theory" of Richard Cloward and Lloyd Ohlin,[21]
the Mobilization for Youth Program which was instituted on the Lower
East Side of Manhattan, served as a precursor to the more ambitious
Community Action Program which would emerge from Washington a
year later.

The incumbent Mayor Wagner responded to the Mobilization for Youth
Program with cooperation. To a large extent, few had recognized the social
implications of the new project during the first year of its existence.
Moreover, the Wagner and Kennedy administrations enjoyed a relationship
of mutual support. Mobilization for Youth remained very much in the
hands of the local welfare establishment, with whom Wagner had also
worked rather cordially. In addition to the Ford Foundation, it was
sponsored by such local organizations as the Henry Street Settlement,
the New York School of Social Work at Columbia University, the Kaplan
Foundation, and the Taconic Foundation. The original board of directors
included among its membership a priest, a rabbi, a minister, a black man,
a Puerto Rican, a trade unionist, a woman, representatives of the major
local settlement houses, and the dean and associate dean of the New York
School of Social Work.[22]

Wagner's own political orientation was not entirely alien to the idea
of citizen participation, so long as it was channeled through the established
sources of power in the city. As borough president of Manhattan, Wagner
had created twelve Community Planning Councils with advisory powers
concerning land use, budgeting, and zoning in their particular districts.
Therefore, he deserves personal credit for establishing the first formal
structure for direct community participation in the decision making
process of the City. It is important to emphasize, however, that Wagner
retained for himself the sole authority of appointing the membership
of these local advisory bodies in Manhattan. In this sense, the new
neighborhood institutions served to help consolidate his power in the
borough.

The inauguration of the Community Action Program in 1964 changed the stakes of community politics rather considerably. At a minimum, maximum feasible participation called for an institutional arrangement which would enable representatives of the poor to make decisions, and not merely in an advisory capacity, concerning what kinds of local policy were most responsive to their perceived needs. Of course, just who might be considered representatives of the poor, and how far they might be able to carry their authority, remained to be decided.

As chief executive of New York, Mayor Wagner implemented Community Action in a way which permitted him to keep a good handle on the monies and programs that were implemented under its auspices. According to Stephen David, the federal Office of Economic Opportunity twice refused funding proposals submitted by the City because the local decision making structure administering the program did not include sufficient representation of the poor.[23] Wagner did eventually create a citywide policymaking board called the Council against Poverty in which one-third of the membership were direct emissaries of the poor. However, decision making on this board continued to be controlled by city officials and the private welfare establishment.

The new federal legislation also called for the establishment of a local community committee in each of the original sixteen poverty areas which participated in the program. In three of these areas Mayor Wagner designated established juvenile delinquency agencies as the organizational representatives of the poor. In the remaining thirteen representatives were chosen by neighborhood conventions which, for the most part, were dominated by the traditional religious, business, and social welfare institutions of those communities.[24]

Under Mayor Wagner the Community Action Program was administered in a way which protected the interests of the established power structure of the city. While some participation of the poor was allowed, the program itself concentrated on the improvement of service delivery rather than on the promotion of political action. This policy not only was consistent with the priorities of white political leaders but it also pleased those members of the black clergy who were able to maintain their domination over politics in the ghetto.

Although Wagner did a rather effective job of keeping the Community Action Program within the usual parameters of city politics, there was growing evidence by the time he was ready to leave office that the federal effort to eliminate urban poverty would give birth to a new current of reform. In late 1963 the Mobilization of Youth Program had become responsible for organizing low income groups for a variety of political actions. These included voter registration drives, rent strikes, school boycotts, and a number of violent demonstrations against city agencies. The War on Poverty was quickly beginning to be identified with black militance, urban malaise, and an attack on the traditional power structure in cities.

While the incumbent Mayor Wagner was one of several big-city mayors to appear before a House Committee in 1965 to urge that Community Action Program funds be channeled through elected city officials rather than be appropriated directly to neighborhood groups, mayoral candidate Lindsay denounced his predecessor for not providing the "unaffiliated poor" with adequate representation in local policy making. It was obvious even before he assumed office that Lindsay approached the ideal of citizen participation with an entirely new set of expectations.

There were a number of notable changes made in the content and the structure of the Community Action Program after Lindsay's election. To begin with, he expanded the size of the program from the original sixteen to twenty-six district poverty areas. These areas included a total population of 3.16 million people. Lindsay also reorganized the citywide Council against Poverty so that half its members would be representatives of the poor. These individuals were appointed by local community corporations which themselves were selected by direct popular elections. By 1969 the program content had changed from one which was service, employment, and training-oriented to one which focused upon political advocacy.

It is important to emphasize, however, that while Lindsay provided many new neighborhood organizations with a significant voice on the citywide Council against Poverty, he was still able to maintain virtual control over the Community Action Program. This was accomplished through the creation of a Community Development Agency whose staff, which was appointed by and loyal to the Mayor, retained ultimate responsibility for evaluating funding proposals.

Lindsay was willing to give more authority to community groups because his political goals were similar to theirs. Both sought to challenge the established power structure of the city. Nevertheless, Lindsay was careful to insure that these emerging community groups did not develop a self-sufficient capacity that would enable them to pursue a policy which was inconsistent with his own priorities. In this latter sense, Lindsay's operation of the Community Action Program closely resembled that of Wagner.

While Mayor Lindsay instituted the use of direct popular elections for the selection of Community Action Corporation members, the fact remains that, as was the case in most other American cities, participation in the local poverty program elections seldom exceeded 5 percent of the eligible voters. From this experience, one might raise some legitimate questions concerning how representative these corporations were of the communities they served. There is also serious reason to doubt the degree of equity which was present in the Community Action Program at the time. A study prepared by the State Charter Revision Commission for New York City has shown that during the early years of the Community Action experience fourteen of the twenty-six local corporations managed to acquire only 80 percent of their fair share of available funds as defined by federal formulas, while five corporations received 150 percent of their share.[25]

When the Demonstration Cities and Metropolitan Development Act (Model Cities) was passed by Congress in 1966, Lindsay issued an order declaring that those neighborhood corporations which came into existence as a result of the Community Action Program were not eligible to serve as representatives of the three local areas affected by the new legislation.[26] He prohibited dual membership by any individual on both a local Community Action corporation and a Model Cities committee. These restrictions not only gave rise to additional new power groups in those areas of the city participating in the Model Cities program, but they also set the stage for the development of bitter, sometimes violent, rivalries between Community Action and Model Cities organizations which shared the same neighborhoods. Some of this competition exhibited racial overtones, with the newer Hispanic groups in Central Harlem and the South Bronx making a bid for their share of community power which had been previously concentrated in the hands of more "established" black organizations.

As was the case with the Community Action Program, the Model Cities legislation of 1966 called for "widespread citizen participation." However, under the latter program local chief executives were given much more discretion concerning what form that participation would take. Lindsay exercised his mayoral prerogative by deciding that all Model Cities programs in New York would be operated by city agencies and departments.

When Model Cities funds first came to New York, authority to determine what types of programs would be implemented was fairly evenly divided between a central Model Cities Committee composed of city officials and Local Policy Committees elected by the residents of each of the participating neighborhoods. Under this arrangement the Local Policy Committees were granted the responsibility to determine the particular program priorities for each of their own areas. Therefore, the communities enjoyed a major role in the planning phase of the program.

In April of 1970 this institutional arrangement was altered. At that time the Mayor appointed a central Model Cities administrator, who assumed ultimate control over the citywide program. The Model Cities administrator would in turn appoint an assistant administrator for each of the demonstration areas, who would coordinate local programs. While the Local Policy Committees were retained, they began to function in merely an advisory capacity. Therefore, community participation in the decision making process was reduced to a minimum.

According to a study completed by the staff of the State Charter Revision Commission for New York City in 1973, the restructuring of the Model Cities program in 1970 represented a changeover from a "shared responsibility model" of decentralization to one of "administrative decentralization."[27] While some decision making was being carried out at the neighborhood level after 1970, it was being done by city officials directly responsible to the Mayor in cooperation with line personnel from operating agencies. The role which the local citizenry played at that point was inconsequential.

By 1970 the Nixon administration had begun to dismantle the federal poverty program to such an extent that one might reasonably argue that it would not matter how Model Cities was administered locally. However, Lindsay's reorganization of the Model Cities program remains significant for other reasons. It is indicative of a general reversal which was taking place in his overall strategy for administrative reform. During his four years as mayor Lindsay had begun to recognize the limits of a strategy designed to use the poor, particularly the nonwhite poor, as a battering ram against the city's established power structure. His plans for political decentralization of the City bureaucracy had proved to be politically unfeasible. Moreover, Lindsay's association with black militance and racial turmoil had developed into a personal liability which affected his own political fortune.

LINDSAY'S RETREAT: FROM RADICAL TO CONTROLLED REFORM

Elected without strong organizational support in 1965, the Republican John Lindsay found it imperative to set up an institutional network which could rival the political clubs that provided a grassroots mechanism for the majority Democratic party. In 1966 Lindsay created an Urban Action Task Force which was designed to operate as a means of communication between City Hall and several local neighborhoods which had been known to be brewing with racial tension. Through the task force Lindsay could interact with community leaders and at least begin to rectify grievances which were directly related to particular City services. At its peak the task force opened twenty-two neighborhood offices. However, most were run by city officials who had other responsibilities, and there was little funding available for their operation. Thus, there was a limit to how much they could be expected to accomplish.

During that same year Lindsay requested City money for the establishment of thirty-five neighborhood city halls so that his activities in local areas could be expanded. A Democratically controlled City Council denounced the proposal as an attempt to set up political clubhouses and decided it was not worthy of public support. This episode was typical of the type of relationship the Republican Lindsay would share with Democratic city officials during his tenure in office. By the end of his first year at City Hall, the new Mayor had also fallen victim to a devastating transit strike and had become embroiled in a hotly contested controversy with the Patrolman's Benevolent Association over his creation of a Civilian Complaint Review Board in the Police Department.

Given the fact that Lindsay could expect a general spirit of antagonism from other city officials and organized labor, it is not surprising that he approached decentralization of the City bureaucracy with great favor. The Mayor had hoped that decentralization would provide access and power in government for the same groups with which he wanted to forge a political alliance. The basic problem with Lindsay's plan for decentralization is that he underestimated the capacity of traditional forces in the city to resist an attempt to compromise their power base. By the time he was prepared to serve a second term of office, the Mayor was forced to rethink his original political strategy. Thus, the chronicle of Lindsay's attempt to reform the City bureaucracy is one which begins with an attempt at radical reform but which ends with a relatively moderate policy. He began with a program designed to reorder the administrative power structure; he ended with a program which was more ostensibly designed to improve the performance of the traditional City bureaucracy. This is not to say that Lindsay's stated emphasis on administrative efficiency developed overnight or that it was ever perceived as an alternative to decentralization. What changed in the latter years of his administration was the point of emphasis.

School Decentralization. One of the first and most drastic steps which New York took in the direction of decentralized government occurred in the field of education. By the mid-sixties observers of the city school system had come to severely criticize the central Board of Education for being a closed bureaucracy which was neither accessible nor responsive to its quickly changing clientele.[28] Between 1957 and 1969 the proportion of black and Puerto Rican children attending city schools would increase from 31.7 percent of the total to 55.8 percent.[29] This significant change in the racial composition of the student population was accompanied by growing demands on the part of black and Puerto Rican parents that the educational policy of the city be made more adaptable to the particular needs of minority children. In the summer of 1966 vocal parent groups in the I.S. 201 school of Harlem began to give up their demands for school integration and adopted support of a program which called for community control. This reversal signified both an admission of defeat for the former goal of integration and a new reaffirmation of racial pride which grew out of the black power movement. Soon thereafter older civil rights groups in the city like the NAACP, CORE, and EQUAL underwent similar changes in their political programs.

John Lindsay had supported the idea of school decentralization as a mayoral candidate in 1965. One of his first actions as chief executive of the city was to appoint a blue ribbon panel to study and make recommendations for both political and administrative decentralization of the school system. The panel was headed by McGeorge Bundy of the Ford Foundation. In the fall of 1967 Bundy released a report which recommended the creation of from thirty to sixty autonomous school districts, each of which would have a popularly elected board with powers over personnel, budgeting, and curriculum.[30]

Bundy's recommendations were in keeping with the position which the Ford Foundation had previously taken on the issue of citizen participation. In the spring of 1967 the Ford Foundation added additional impetus to its commitment by making funds available to the City for the creation of three demonstration school districts, each of which would function with a community board. The three districts affected included Intermediate School 201 in Harlem, Ocean Hill–Brownsville in Brooklyn, and the Two Bridges District in lower Manhattan.

The Ford experiment proved to be a mixed blessing for Lindsay's program of government decentralization. While the state legislature would eventually approve legislation decentralizing the city school system in accord with the Mayor's priorities, the demonstration districts became the scene of a harrowing conflict which would turn into a major liability for the cause of community government.

From the outset teachers and school supervisors had objected to the idea of granting communities discretion concerning educational matters over which they had previously enjoyed a virtual monopoly. Thus, the demonstration districts became the arena of controversy between educational unions claiming professional prerogatives over school policy and angry communities demanding representation in government. The most devastating conflict occurred in the Ocean Hill–Brownsville district over the transfer of several white teachers whom the community board found undesirable. It was this event which led to the thirty-six-day teachers' strike in September of 1968.[31]

The most damaging fallout of the Ocean Hill–Brownsville episode was the serious degree of racial polarization it brought about in the city. A poll taken by Louis Harris Associates at the time revealed that while blacks sympathized with the community at a rate of 8 to 1, whites sided with the union by 6 to 1.[32] Opponents of decentralization, particularly the unions, took advantage of the situation by identifying decentralization with black militance, racial prejudice, and general disorder. Thus, the debate over decentralization evolved into a racial issue. In a city where 70 percent of the population is classified as white, and a much higher proportion of registered voters, these developments represented overwhelming odds against the prospects for decentralized government.

The events in Ocean Hill–Brownsville also led to a significant loss of popular support for Mayor John Lindsay, who endorsed the position of the militant community. This was particularly true among Jewish communities, from which Lindsay had received a large number of votes in 1965. While Jews in the city traditionally had taken a liberal position on civil rights issues, many reacted to the charges of anti-Semitism which teachers made against the community board in Brooklyn.

Although Lindsay succeeded in decentralizing the school system by 1969, it had also become apparent by then that he would have to go about the business of administrative reform in a more moderate manner. Community control of the schools, and particularly the events which ushered it in, left a bitter taste that made the Mayor's broader plans for government decentralization politically unfeasible. As one high ranking Lindsay administration official explained in a conversation with the author: "The school strikes had a shattering effect on just how fast it was possible to move in the area of decentralization. The school strike made us realize how thin the social fabric of the city was when it came to racial issues. It was a watershed in the movement towards decentralized government."[33]

Soon after school decentralization was implemented in the city, it became readily apparent that the process of electing individuals to local school boards would be highly partisan, with a large proportion of the candidates running on organizationally supported tickets. Among the most viable competitors in this process was the teachers' union itself. For example, in 1973 54 percent of those who won positions on local school boards were candidates supported by the United Federation of Teachers,[34] which spent an estimated $127,000 on campaign-related activity.[35] As was the case with the poverty program corporations, it was also questionable how representative local school boards were of their communities. Only rarely had more than 10 percent of the eligible voters participated in the elections, and in most instances the turnout was, and continues to be, significantly lower.

There is also reason to doubt whether the new institutional arrangement has resulted in a more equitable allocation of educational resources for the poor and the disadvantaged. According to the Charter Revision Commission Study, the New York Board of Education has tended to "equalize allotments of funds among districts and schools regardless of need" under decentralization.[36] It concludes that since the time when decentralization was established the City has "abandoned the principle of compensatory education under which the most needy districts would receive large numbers of additional personnel."[37] It goes on to explain that this general tendency towards equal allotments "in part results from the high visibility of allocations."[38] Thus, the authors of the study write: "Each district knows what the other districts receive; schools know what other schools receive. Faced with the hazardous task of awarding funds in full view of competitors, administrators often look upon 'almost equal' allotments as the most workable solution."[39] The conclusions set down in the Charter Revision Commission Study are also supported in a report conducted by the Fleishman Commission for the state.[40] Both reports serve to illustrate the difficulty of implementing a compensatory policy of resource distribution in a highly visible, politically sensitive environment.

Neighborhood Government: Evolution of a Plan. In 1969 the New York City Council passed legislation resulting in the creation of sixty-two Community Boards which were empowered to develop plans "for district welfare and orderly development" and "to advise any officer, agency, or legislative body with respect to any matter relating to the welfare of the district."[41] The legislation was the outcome of years of lobbying by the Citizens' Union, the Citizens' Housing and Welfare Council of New York City, and several other private organizations which sought to establish a citywide mechanism modeled on the Community Council concept that originated with Manhattan Borough President Robert Wagner in 1953. The new boards represented a moderate move in the direction of neighborhood government in the sense that their members were appointed rather than elected and their powers were merely advisory.

While Mayor Lindsay signed the 1969 legislation, there is good reason to believe that he had not endorsed it very enthusiastically. The Democratically controlled City Council had written a bill which reserved all power of appointment to the boards for the five borough presidents, thus minimizing the role which the Mayor would have in determining their composition.

In the following year the Mayor prepared his own "Plan for Neighborhood Government."[42] The plan called for a merging of the Community Board structure with the local Urban Action Task Force offices. Members of the new boards would be selected jointly by the mayor, City Council members, and the borough presidents. Each district would also have a salaried community director, assisted by a staff, who would be responsible for chairing a cabinet of local service officers representing a variety of operating agencies. The community director would be selected by the mayor from a list of five submitted by the board membership.

While Lindsay's proposal declared that Community Board members should eventually be chosen by means of neighborhood elections, no definite date was set for when this might occur. It appears that the manner of selection suggested was meant to appease the City Council members and borough presidents who would have to approve the proposal. Nevertheless, the Mayor's plan still represented a significant step backwards from the direct election system he had formerly supported. This turnabout was consistent with the restructuring of the poverty program which the Mayor was engineering at about the same time. Perhaps the Mayor had finally come to grips with the realities of the political situation in New York. Yet, despite this hard-earned awareness, his Plan for Neighborhood Government, which would have enhanced the powers of the mayor in the Community Board system, was destined to defeat.

In January 1972 Mayor Lindsay finally put into effect his own program of decentralization for the City. This was called the Office of Neighborhood Government (ONG). Coordinated by a cabinet-level official from City Hall, ONG initially established a network of offices at eighteen locations throughout the city. These offices were run by a district manager appointed by the Mayor, who would also chair a cabinet of local officials from operating agencies in the neighborhoods.

Unlike Lindsay's previous proposals for decentralization, the Office of Neighborhood Government did not include a strong community component. Therefore, it represented an experiment in administrative rather than political decentralization. Unlike many of the Mayor's previous experiments in decentralization, ONG offices were set up in both the poorer areas of the city and middle class neighborhoods. In this sense, ONG also represented an attempt by Lindsay to win the favor of the white electorate, many of whom he had alienated with his previous policies of political confrontation.

Most important of all, ONG was publicly portrayed as an effort to improve the efficiency and effectiveness of city services through better coordination at the neighborhood level. Such a program would not only help the Mayor to cast off an image he had developed as a poor administrator, it also was necessitated by the strained fiscal situation which had developed in the city. It was within the context of these overriding purposes that the citywide Productivity Program was inaugurated later that year.

THE PRODUCTIVITY PROGRAM

The Productivity Program which the Lindsay administration officially launched in August of 1972 was not an idea which was conceived overnight. The groundwork was set as far back as 1966 when a project management staff was established in the executive office of the Mayor which was designed to function as an instrument for program analysis and implementation for a variety of city agencies. Subsequent to this a Program-Planning-Budgeting System was set up in the Bureau of the Budget under its director, Frederick O. R. Hayes. Hayes commanded a newly organized staff of forty professionals in his own bureau and deployed an additional hundred analysts among operating agencies in the city, whose work was meant to complement that of his own group and the previous efforts conducted by the project management staff.[43]

During the early years of the Lindsay administration, the City also turned to the extensive use of outside consultants, whose analytical and technical expertise was applied to augment the newly developing managerial thrust. Among the several private firms to which the City became a client were McKinsey and Company, MDC Systems, and Meridian Engineering, not to mention several public and private universities. Among the notable efforts undertaken by an outside group, however, were those undertaken by the Rand Corporation, which by the mid-sixties had already gained a wide reputation for its work done in the Defense Department.

In 1968 the City signed a $2-million contract with Rand which agreed to set up a New York office maintained by sixty professionals. With an additional $900,000 of funding from the U.S. Department of Housing and Urban Development and the Ford Foundation,[44] the "New York City-Rand Institute" began to assume the role of an in-house analytical tool which could provide quantitative information for the upgrading of managerial decision making in the City. While the stated purpose of the various management programs implemented by the Lindsay administration was to improve the delivery of city services, these developments might also be observed as a more subtle feature of the Mayor's campaign against the standing bureaucracy. Lindsay utilized the newly appointed corps of Budget Bureau analysts and outside consultants as a means to infiltrate the bureaucracy. In this sense, the Lindsay strategy was similar to that utilized by President Kennedy in the Defense Department. Through the lateral introduction of personnel into operating agencies, he was able to remove a certain degree of decision making autonomy from career civil servants. As Greenberger, Crenson, and Crissey have written with particular reference to the Rand-related activities:

Rand's design was closely tied to Lindsay's goals. The mayor began his administration in 1966 by declaring war on "bureaucracy," special interests, "power brokers" and the obstructive alliance between them. Lindsay promised a program of reform that would liberate municipal agencies from the control of special interests (chiefly the municipal employee unions) and make it possible to streamline and rationalize the operations of city government. Most of the reform measures advanced by the Lindsay administration proposed to curb the influence of special interests by enlarging the power of the mayor—in particular his ability to direct the activities of the city bureaucracy.[45]

Lindsay's intentions aside, it was to the credit of several groups of consultants, particularly Rand, that they usually did not assume the role of protagonist in the agencies where they served. Of course, there were exceptions. Greenberger, Crenson, and Crissey have observed a certain antagonism which existed between Rand analysts and Health Department professionals attempting to perform the same functions in a single agency.[46] Hayes has noted similar problems which emerged in the initial stages of a Police Department project.[47] However, these cases were the exception rather than the rule, at least so far as the Rand group was concerned. The Rand analysts attempted to walk a rather narrow line by pursuing the managerial goals of the incumbent administration but at the same time taking advantage of a certain willingness they found at the operational levels of departments to improve the way in which things got accomplished. As one Rand analyst working in the Fire Department explained to the author:

We tried not to get involved in any conflicts between the Mayor and the bureaucracy. Instead, we tried to concentrate our efforts on improving the efficiency and effectiveness of the operations of the line agencies with the cooperation and support of the agencies. For example, the fire project was truly a joint effort between Rand and the Fire Department. Throughout the course of the project, chief officers and other department personnel were part of the research team. Institute staff bounced ideas off members of the department staff, got operational questions answered, and got the department's help in gathering data needed for the mathematical models. The Institute provided them with tools that could be used to evaluate their policy ideas.[48]

Perhaps the Rand group had benefited from the unfortunate experiences of many other outsiders who had entered the city bureaucracy as "shakers," proceeded to alienate line managers, and finally left frustrated. We will return to that subject in a later chapter. Suffice it to say at this point that between 1968 and 1972 several consultant groups developed a rather cooperative relationship with the career civil servants who ran the agencies where they were assigned. This was particularly true in the uniformed services, where both the greatest efforts and most notable accomplishments were made. Thus, it should be stressed that a good part of the managerial achievements which were publicized under the auspices of the Productivity Program in 1972 were the product of a joint effort between outside consultants and line managers who had come up through the ranks of the traditional civil service.

Given the variety of activities that went on in the city between 1968 and 1972, the formal announcement of the City Productivity Program in the latter year was somewhat anti-climactic. In essence, the most successful aspects of the program that were announced were the outcome of what had happened before. The major element of change which emerged in 1972 was a new determination on the part of the Lindsay administration to make public its interest and achievements in matters pertaining to public management.

By the end of 1971 the project management staff of the Mayor's Office was transferred to the Bureau of the Budget. Its two coordinators, Andrew Kerr and John Thomas, assumed the respective positions of deputy director and assistant director of the bureau and set up what eventually became known as the Management Service Division. Kerr and Thomas were the major architects of the Productivity Program that emerged a year later. However, while the Productivity Program was for the most part administered from the Budget Bureau, its major driving force was First Deputy Mayor Edward Hamilton, a former budget director who had succeeded Fred Hayes before going to City Hall. It was Hamilton who, with the support of the Mayor, went public with the program and used it as a mechanism for making known the managerial achievements of the incumbent administration. As Hayes explained it:

Hamilton approved the program and obtained Lindsay's concurrence because it was a good thing to do, because it had become feasible with the passage of the high tide of union militancy and with the rising citizen opinion critical of employee performance, and because it would give Lindsay some recognition for substantial managerial achievements that had gone almost unnoticed in the city.

The program was supported by a considerable public relations effort.[49]

In an article appearing in the *Public Administration Review,* Hamilton described the goal of the program as an attempt to "improve the quantity and quality of public services provided per dollar invested."[50] His description was consistent with the standard definition of productivity or efficiency used by economists, which is usually expressed in terms of the relationship between units of service outputs and units of resource inputs.[51]

He then went on to outline four major strategies which were followed in the implementation of the program. These were:

1. reduction in unit costs in those services which are easily measurable

2. improved deployment of resources so as to maximize the probability that they will be available at the times and places they are needed most

3. improvement in the organization and processing procedures in government, especially through the imaginative use of computers

4. development of new technological devices so as to make the best use of every employee

The first technique Hamilton listed, that concerned with the reduction of service costs, was a direct outgrowth of the situation which made the program necessary. The City was experiencing a depletion of its financial resources, so each public dollar had to be spent with greater care. In order to provide a mechanism for estimating the unit cost of services, the Budget Bureau in cooperation with the line agencies identified and/or developed 288 quantifiable performance indicators and 34 measures of service demands for the various departments throughout the city.[52] These indicators were used to set performance standards which were monitored on a quarterly basis in meetings between the deputy mayor and each city commissioner.

The second technique, that which is concerned with a better deployment of resources, actually emerged as a mechanism to compensate for the inherent limits of the first. Here the city's planners were attempting to come to grips with a perennial problem that has troubled municipal economists, the difficulty in quantifying municipal service functions.[53] Unlike manufacturing firms in the private sector, cities do not produce a tangible product. Therefore, the actual output of public employees, such as that of a fireman who stands ready to respond to an emergency, often does not lend itself to easy measurement. In order to accommodate this problem, the City followed a deployment strategy designed to assure that services were made available at the time and place that demands were known to be the greatest. Thus, more police were to be deployed to high-crime areas, more fire companies were to be placed in neighborhoods with high incidence rates, etc.

One of the significant by-products of this latter type of managerial strategy is that it exhibits an actual potential for allocating resources in what might be considered in Rawlsian terms an equitable manner. According to its logic, policy decisions concerning "who gets what" would be determined on the basis of need rather than of other considerations such as power or influence. To use Merton's terminology, one of the "unanticipated consequences" of utilizing a deployment strategy in local government management may be a greater allocation of services to the disadvantaged, who do not have the capability of winning such rewards in the political arena. To return to the basic theme explained in the introductory chapter, there may indeed exist an empirical linkage between the traditional bureaucratic goal of efficiency and the current demand for social equity in the public services.

Hamilton cites the "imaginative use of computers" as a third technique designed to improve the organization and processing procedures of the City. As we will see in subsequent pages, the application of computer-processed information was a key ingredient in the methodology which analysts used for determining the service needs of the many neighborhoods throughout this heterogeneous city. It was an essential tool for the utilization of the systems approach in the public sector. In a broader sense, it might be said that the computer represented one of several modern technological devices which served to further rationalize the decision making process in the city.

Among the other technological innovations which the City began to use in order to improve the delivery of services were:

1. fire alarm boxes with voice mechanisms so that the number of false alarms could be reduced

2. polymerized ("slippery") water which enabled fire companies to operate with thinner and lighter hoses, thereby reducing response times

3. containerized solid waste collection which reduced the unit cost per ton of sanitation collection services

4. improved communications systems in all the emergency services

5. the establishment of a computerized Parking Violations Bureau for the effective tracking of chronic traffic offenders

Within the context of the Productivity Program announced in 1972, the City also began to incorporate a practice of "productivity bargaining" in labor relations.[54] Under this practice increased employee benefits and salaries were exchanged for concessions on the part of union representatives which would bring about improved worker productivity. The practice became a regular part of labor negotiations in the city, particularly with respect to the uniformed forces where Mayor Lindsay had always maintained a running battle.

It is one of the greater ironies of the Lindsay years that while the Mayor and organized labor had an ongoing hostility, some of the most notable accomplishments of his entire administration were those related to improved service delivery. For example, in the area of street and highway repairs, resurfacing doubled despite a 250-man reduction in the workforce. The vehicle maintenance operation of the Sanitation Department improved to the extent that vehicle downtime decreased 350 percent. In the crucial area of rodent control the number of premises inspected increased from 6.1 to 20.1 per man day, and the number of exterminations performed was raised from 2.5 to 11.1 per man day.[55]

Some critics of the Lindsay administration would observe an additional dimension to this irony by noting that despite the rancorous relationship which existed between the Mayor and organized labor, during this time the unions gained some of the most generous collective bargaining agreements in the city's history. Raymond Horton has argued that the wage settlements agreed to during these years tended to undermine the purposes for which productivity bargaining had originally been implemented.[56] While this assertion may be true, however, the fact does remain that it was under Lindsay's administrative reforms that the City took its initial steps towards performance-oriented management. The citywide quantitative system that emerged as a result of the Productivity Program has provided the foundation for a more refined monitoring system being instituted in the city today.[57]

THE POLITICS OF REFORM:
A SUMMARY OF THE NEW YORK EXPERIENCE

This brief analysis of the Wagner and Lindsay administrations once again serves to illustrate the important role which politics plays in determining both the direction and the feasibility of administrative reform. In each case the program which the mayor chose to adopt was a product of a political environment shaped by Washington-based initiatives, vigorous activity on the part of local interest groups, and his individual priorities for the city. Wagner, who was very much tied to the traditional power structure of the city, sought to emphasize the job-related aspect of the poverty program and to steer away from any sort of political action which threatened the status quo. His programs were carried out with a relatively minimum amount of resistance from local political forces. Lindsay, who came to city politics as a virtual outsider, tried to use the poverty program as the first step in a more general effort to challenge the powers that were, especially those housed within the civil service bureaucracy. This strategy resulted in conflict.

While Lindsay enjoyed some success in the way of school decentralization, he was finally forced to retreat from his original program of reform. This reversal was manifest by his tightening of the reins over the local poverty program and his later increased emphasis on improved service delivery. Lindsay complemented his reform efforts with rather effective though moderate changes in the local merit system. Both his service-oriented and merit-related programs succeeded with a minimal amount of resistance from the bureaucracy, thus demonstrating the political feasibility of such types of reforms in the city.

The question still remains to be answered, however, whether reforms designed to provide equal employment opportunity and more efficient services are responsive to the specific needs of the disadvantaged, particularly racial minorities. Do these groups receive a fair share of public jobs in the city under the merit system? Are they adequately represented within the bureaucracy? Are they allocated an equitable portion of city services? We will turn to these questions in the next two chapters.

4

MINORITY EMPLOYMENT IN NEW YORK CITY

As was explained in previous chapters, the availability of public service jobs has both a social and political significance for the individual who is a product of a disadvantaged background. It not only provides him with a source of employment and a means of social mobility but also with an opportunity to participate in public affairs. Those who sit in positions of authority at the top of our government bureaucracies exercise a direct impact on public policy, and sometimes assume the role of advocates of those racial, economic, social, and occupational groups to which they belong.

The purpose of this chapter is to assess the level of employment opportunity which has been afforded black and Puerto Rican minorities in New York City under a recruitment policy governed by the traditional merit system. It will do so by empirically investigating the degree of descriptive representation which is found within the operating agencies of the local government bureaucracy. In accordance with the definition of the concept appearing in the introduction, descriptive representation will be examined in terms of whether the racial composition of the local government workforce reflects that of the city population as a whole.

The empirical analysis in this chapter will be conducted on several levels. In order to provide a simple criterion for judging how well racial minorities are represented in the City government and whether they receive a fair share of City jobs, it will begin by comparing the proportionate numbers of blacks and Puerto Ricans in the City workforce with their proportion of the general population in New York. Then a similar analysis will be made of data which are available on the federal, the state, and the total civilian labor forces in New York City. This will allow us to assess the level of opportunity which the local government has provided to racial minorities in relation to that which is apparent among the three other sources of employment within the city.

The major part of this chapter will be devoted to an in-depth analysis of the distribution of minorities within the City workforce. Particular attention will be given to examining the distribution of blacks and Puerto Ricans according to service agency, job level, and pay grade. Because these minorities are unevenly distributed among city agencies, merely investigating composite data on the entire City workforce could leave one with an inaccurate impression of the representation these groups share within specific units of government. Since public employment may be viewed as a means to both political influence and social mobility, it is imperative that our analysis consider minority representation by both job level and pay grade. While the former consideration will allow for a better understanding of the level of authority and degree of responsibility these groups enjoy in city government, the latter will indicate how much financial compensation they receive for the work they perform.

Fortunately for the student of the Lindsay administration, there is a significant data base on minority employment among local agencies. It is the result of two censuses carried out by the City Commission on Human Rights. The first, conducted by order of Mayor Robert Wagner in 1964, was "A Report on the Number and Distribution of Negroes, Puerto Ricans and Others Employed by the City of New York" in 1963.[1] The second, completed at the request of Mayor John Lindsay in 1971, was a more comprehensive study on "The Employment of Minorities, Women and the Handicapped in City Government in 1971."[2]

While the chapter will focus on data from the more recent survey, a comparative analysis of the information contained in the earlier report will make it possible to measure the change in the employment condition of minorities which occurred during the intervening years. This comparison will be particularly interesting in light of the fact that a variety of programs was implemented in the city between 1964 and 1971 which were designed to create new job opportunities for minorities and sensitize the local merit system to their particular circumstances.

An explanation of the methodology and data sources used in the two aforementioned studies will be presented in a forthcoming section. Before discussing these surveys, however, we will briefly turn our attention to some of the relevant work performed by other students of public employment. Most empirical research of this sort has been done with regard to the federal sector. Nevertheless, a brief review of the literature will place the forthcoming data on New York in a more informative perspective. It will not only provide us with another basis for evaluating how New York City has fared in the hiring of its minority population, but will better advise us on the state of the art of the type of research in which we have chosen to engage.

RELEVANT RESEARCH

In accordance with Kingsley's original notion of a representative bureaucracy, most of the earlier empirical research on the concept focused on the class variable, as opposed to ethnicity or race. Special attention was paid to identifying the social origins of America's "higher civil servants." Among the more significant earlier efforts were those of Bendix, Warner, Van Riper, Martin, and Collens.[3] More recent studies of the same kind were done by Kilpatrick, Cummings, Jennings, and Subramaniam.[4] Although somewhat different in nature and scope, all have served to document the fact that American federal executives are drawn primarily from the middle class.

While those scholars who had hoped to refute the idea of an elitist federal bureaucracy rejoiced at the evidence of a middle class–dominated government, the color-blind research of this period failed to recognize the racial implications of the carefully documented findings which emerged. Racial minorities in America, particularly blacks and Hispanics, are disproportionately found among the lower socioeconomic classes. Thus, the inevitable question must arise concerning whether these minority groups are underrepresented in the administrative branch of the government.

It was not until 1961, when the U.S. Civil Service Commission regularized the practice of keeping data on the racial composition of the federal workforce, that the criteria of ethnicity and color became prominent factors in empirical research concerning the concept of representative bureaucracy. The new abundance of federal data established a foundation for a whole new direction of race-oriented research.

In 1967 Cummings, Jennings, and Kilpatrick, using data collected for their previous survey, compared data on minority employment in the federal government with similar data on the generally employed public. They discovered that whereas only 11 percent of the American workforce was nonwhite, 21 percent of all federal employees were drawn from racial minorities.[5] Four years later Hellriegel and Short, utilizing U.S. Civil Service Commission data, designed an index for comparing black representation in federal employment with black representation in the population as a whole.[6] They found that by 1970 the percentage of blacks on the federal payroll exceeded their ratio in the general population by a margin of 15 percent to 11.2 percent.

Shortly thereafter Nachmias and Rosenbloom completed a more comprehensive study of minority integration in the federal government by agency and grade.[7] While their research supported the conclusion previously drawn by Hellriegel and Short that minorities are proportionately well represented in the public sector, they found great variances among specific agencies and lower minority representation at the higher grades. With few exceptions, they found integration to be highest in those agencies responsible for broad social programs such as the Equal Employment Opportunity Commission and the departments of Labor, HEW, and HUD.[8] Insofar as grade was concerned, integration was reported to be highest in grades one through six. The research also documented the fact that among minorities Hispanics, American Indians, and Orientals were more poorly represented throughout the federal bureaucracy than were blacks.

In 1975 Kenneth Meier completed a wide ranging review of existing published research which was designed to test Norton Long's more broadly defined concept of representative bureaucracy.[9] Drawing from material presented in some of the aforementioned works, U.S. Civil Service Commission data and information made available by the University of Michigan Survey Research Center, Meier concluded that, as Long contends, the federal bureaucracy on the whole is broadly representative of the American people in terms of social background, race, income, education, political attitudes, and age. However, in accordance with the findings of Nachmias and Rosenbloom, he added that the degree of representation does become weaker at the higher levels of administration where personnel tend to be white, better educated, more highly paid, older, and more politically conservative. With particular regard to the issue of race, the author did not suggest any belief in active discrimination against nonwhites at the upper levels of government, but instead noted that this "maldistribution" at the top may, in fact, be a function of education, qualification, or other factors.

It was not until 1976 that Harry Kranz completed what is to date and what will very probably remain for some time the most comprehensive study of public employment in the United States.[10] Kranz not only concerned himself with the employment situation in the federal sector, but, using information made available by the Equal Employment Opportunity Commission in 1974, also examined data on state and local government jurisdictions.[11] Therefore, his overall research effort covered material relating to 44 states, 1,791 counties, 2,249 cities, and 413 townships.

In general, Kranz's wide ranging investigation supported the findings that had emerged from previous federal studies, and these patterns tended to hold at all levels of government. While on the whole minorities tended to be well represented in public employment, blacks tended to fare better than did other minorities (Hispanics, Asians, American Indians). Minorities in general tended to be underrepresented in positions carrying more authority (e.g., official/administrative categories) and receiving higher pay. They were also concentrated in certain types of service agencies. Thus, minorities were most likely to be found in hospital, health, welfare, employment security, sanitation, and sewage work. They were least likely to be found in police and fire protection, natural resource preservation, and financial administration.[12]

These general patterns notwithstanding, Kranz's work did show differences in minority representation to exist among the various levels of government. While the representation of these groups was found to be better at the federal level than it was among state and township jurisdictions, minorities tended to be best represented within county and city governments, particularly the latter. The Kranz study also demonstrated that significant differences in representation existed within the same levels of government, depending upon geographical location. Thus, for example, while the percentage of minority group members within the general populations of California and Alaska is approximately the same (22.9 percent and 22.7 percent, respectively), the representation of minorities in federal employment in California is more than double that which is found in Alaska (26.5 percent versus 11.5 percent).[13]

The assortment of information which has been made available as a result of the Kranz book is significant for at least two reasons. On the one hand, the broad scope of the study provides one with the composite data which are needed for an authoritative overview of the public employment situation in the United States. On the other hand, however, its more in-depth analysis of public employment at different levels of government and in different geographical jurisdictions within the country serves to underline some of the basic limits inherent in the composite or macro approach to the subject. It shows that while composite data are useful for painting an overall picture of representation within our public bureaucracy, it can also be misleading so far as specific governmental units are concerned, for it does not consider local variations which may exist throughout different regions of the country.

The lessons of the Kranz book are particularly relevant for those social scientists who would use macro data on public employment as a basis for recommending broadly based reforms of our present governmental institutions. They would be better advised to rely more heavily on a micro approach which investigates the characteristics of specific units of government within particular jurisdictions. Only then would they be able to identify more precisely what problems need to be addressed and what types of reforms are appropriate under a given set of circumstances.

Once one goes below the federal level of government, one finds that each state and subdivision thereof is governed by a different version of the merit system. Thus, each has afforded minorities a varying set of opportunities for pursuing a career in the public service, and thereby each has provided these groups with a different quality of representation within the administrative branch of government. The student of New York City is particularly fortunate in having data available on the public employment situation in that local government for a period as early as 1963 and to have a comparable set of data for the period subsequent to the enactment of several types of reforms in the local merit system. An analysis of this data will once again show that not all government jurisdictions fall into the particular pattern that has previously been observed on a national scale. It will also serve to demonstrate what types of local reforms can be effective for bringing about change and what kinds of problems facing minorities fall outside the purview of the traditional merit system.

THE NEW YORK CITY EMPLOYMENT CENSUS

The 1971 census of the New York City workforce was conducted by means of a head count completed by first line supervisors for employees on the City payroll as of October 1, 1971.[14] All mayoral agencies were requested to participate in the project, and a number of non-mayoral agencies also cooperated.[15] Each of these departments or bureaus assumed responsibility for submitting an agency-wide report to the City Commission on Human Rights, based on the information compiled by its unit supervisors. City personnel were divided up into six ethnic categories: "whites," "blacks," "Puerto Rican," "other Spanish surnamed," "Chinese," and "others." The final category included such groups as American Indians, Japanese Americans, Filipino Americans, Indians (Asian), and Pakistanis.

While the same general method was used for data gathering in the 1963 survey, two significant differences should be noted as a prelude to any comparison between the two surveys. To begin with, not all the same agencies participated in the two studies.[16] The most significant difference in their participant populations resulted from the non-inclusion of Police Department data in 1963. By 1971 this department was maintaining a 35,310-man workforce, 87 percent of which was white. Therefore, it is reasonable to assume that the absence of police data from the 1963 survey tended to underestimate the total percentage of whites in the citywide workforce. In order to control for this factor, we will exclude 1971 Police Department data from any comparisons between the two studies. Police data will, however, be reported in all other analyses pertaining to 1971.

The second major difference between the 1963 and 1971 surveys concerns the number and types of categories into which the various ethnic groups were classified. Only three categories were designated in the 1963 survey: "Negro," "Puerto Rican," and "others." Because no distinction was made in 1963 between Puerto Rican and other Hispanics, both were listed under the classification "Puerto Rican." While this exaggerated the Puerto Rican count to some extent, it is worthy to point out that the number of non–Puerto Rican Hispanics living in New York in 1963 is believed to have been small.[17] The category "others" included all whites and the remainder of the workforce population which was not included among the "Negro" and "Puerto Rican" categories.

Minorities in City Government. According to the United States Census Bureau, the total New York City population in 1970 was 68 percent white, 20 percent black, 10 percent Puerto Rican, and 2 percent others. When one reviews the data on the overall composition of the City workforce in 1971, it appears that in relation to the general population of the city the local government is proportionately representative. The 1971 census conducted by the City Commission on Human Rights revealed that personnel within the city government are 67 percent white, 25 percent black, 6 percent Puerto Rican, and 2 percent others. The only minority group underrepresented among these is Puerto Ricans, whose proportion of City jobs is 4 percent lower than that of their population as a whole. Blacks were actually overrepresented by 5 percent, with "other minorities" breaking even. Thus, from a general standpoint, it can be said that racial minorities in New York are slightly overrepresented within the city government by a margin of 1 percent.

The results of this general survey of the workforce are particularly significant when one considers the fact that the racial distribution of the New York City population by age group is such that a higher percentage of the working age population is composed of whites than that which is reflected in the overall breakdown of the city population. Thus, as the data appearing in table 4.1 indicate, the racial composition of New Yorkers between the working ages of 18 and 64 is 71 percent white, 20 percent black, and 9 percent Puerto Rican. As one observes the data in the higher age brackets, the percentage of whites compared to minorities grows even more significantly. This outcome stems from the basic fact that minorities as a group are on the average younger than the white population in the city. Thus, while the average age for white men and women is 35 years, that of blacks and Puerto Ricans is 25 and 21 years, respectively.

TABLE 4.1
RACIAL DISTRIBUTION OF NYC POPULATION BY AGE GROUP (1970)[1]

	White	Black	Puerto Rican
18–24 yrs.	67%	21%	12%
25–34 yrs.	64%	23%	13%
35–44 yrs.	66%	23%	11%
45–54 yrs.	76%	18%	6%
55–64 yrs.	84%	12%	4%
45–65 yrs.	80%	15%	5%
18–65 yrs.	71%	20%	9%
Median age	35	25	21

1. These figures are based on data provided by the New York City Planning Commission in "The 1970 Census, Second and Fourth Count, Population and Housing Tables by Borough," vol. 18.

When one compares the employment data from the 1971 survey with that from 1963, the figures seem to document a rather significant improvement in minority representation over the eight-year period which elapsed. This is evident in table 4.2, which compares data drawn from the surveys taken during both years and relates it to information on the general city population at the time each survey was taken. In order to allow for comparability, 1971 statistics on white and other minorities are grouped together, and Police Department data are excluded.

During the eight-year interval which passed, black representation in the City workforce grew from 23 percent to 28 percent, while that of Puerto Ricans expanded from 3 percent to 6 percent. There is no doubt that this increased minority representation can be partially explained by the fact that these groups accounted for a larger portion of the city population by 1971. The percentage of blacks increased from 14 percent to 20 percent and that of Puerto Ricans from 8 percent to 10 percent. Nevertheless, the growing numbers of these groups within the government was still quite significant. The 5 percent increase in black employment reflected an addition of 26,000 individuals from that group to the City payroll. While Puerto Ricans were still somewhat underrepresented, 10,000 Puerto Rican workers were recruited to the City bureaucracy between 1963 and 1971. Although it is difficult to ascertain exactly what factors brought about the increased minority representation in the City workforce, it is reasonable to conclude that the various programs that were implemented by the City between 1964 and 1971 to make more jobs available and modify the merit system did have a positive influence.

TABLE 4.2
MINORITIES IN CITY GOVERNMENT

Group	1971		1963	
	% of city workforce	% of city population	% of city workforce	% of city population
White & others	66	70	74	78
Black	28	20	23	14
Puerto Rican	6	10	3	8

Minorities in the Citywide Workforce. Although the local government is the single largest employer of labor in New York, there do exist three other major sources of employment in the city. These include the federal, state, and private sectors. It should be emphasized that any valid comparison between minority representation in the local government workforce and that which is found in the other sectors must be limited, so far as the available information allows, to those total numbers of positions that exist in the New York City area. Since the composition of the local workforce in any geographical location is affected by the characteristics of its area population and job market, the data on the local government workforce in New York and the composite data on the total federal, state, and private sector workforces (whether it be on a national or statewide basis) are not directly comparable. Therefore, direct comparisons in this section will be restricted as nearly as possible to data concerning the New York City area. The one exception will be the federal data,

TABLE 4.3

CITYWIDE MINORITY EMPLOYMENT
BY SECTOR (1971)

	NYC govt.	N.Y. State govt.[1] (within NYC)	Fed. govt.[2] NY SMSA*	Total civilian[3] labor force
Total number	274,758	30,714	118,576 (1970)	3,330,803
Percent white	67	57	68	75
Percent black	25	36	26	19
Percent Puerto Rican	6	5	6†	7
Percent other	2	2	.5	N.A.

*The racial breakdown of the population in the New York SMSA is 75% white, 16% black, 7% Puerto Rican, and 2% other.

†This percentage includes other Spanish surnamed as well.

1. These data as presented in the City Human Rights Commission Report (1973) are based on New York State Department of Civil Service, *1971 Fifth Annual Report on the Occupations, Job Status and Ethnic Characteristics of Employees in New York State Agencies,* Albany, 1972.

2. These data as presented in the City Human Rights Commission Report (1973) are based on U.S. Civil Service Commission, *Minority Group Employment in the Federal Government,* November 1970.

3. These data as presented in the City Human Rights Commission Report (1973) are based on U.S. Department of Commerce, Bureau of the Census, *Population and Housing Characteristics for the United States, by State:* 1970 P.C. (sl.)–29, December 1972, tables P3, P6, P7.

which are not available on a citywide basis but are reported according to Standard Metropolitan Statistical Area (SMSA). Population data for the New York SMSA will, however, be provided during the course of the analysis.

Table 4.3 displays the racial breakdown of the population in the three public sectors and a similar summary for the entire local civilian labor force. The latter category includes both the public and the private sectors. Since federal data are computed on the basis of a Standard Metropolitan Statistical Area, it should be pointed out that the information in that column of the chart includes data on the five New York City counties plus the suburbs of Nassau, Rockland, Suffolk, and Westchester.

In relation to other employers in the metropolitan area, the New York City government ranks high as a source of jobs for black, Puerto Rican, and other minorities. Proportionately it ranks second only to the state government in the percentage of local personnel who are drawn from the nonwhite community. Let us consider each of these individual sectors in order, beginning with the state.

While only 20 percent of the city population is black, 36 percent of the state employees who work within the five boroughs are from that minority group. Puerto Ricans have fared less well, holding only 5 percent of the state employment positions within the city. This amounts to only one-half the percentage of Puerto Ricans within the entire city population and slightly less than the percentage of that group's jobs within the city government (6 percent).

In a general sense, it can be claimed that minorities receive a disproportionately high share of the state job positions available within the city. However, one must be cautious in estimating the role which the state government has played as a source of minority employment within New York. In actuality there were only 30,714 state positions within the five boroughs in 1971, while according to the Human Rights Commission Census City jobs numbered 274,758.

When one reviews the state employment situation from a statewide perspective, he receives a rather different impression from the one presented in table 4.3. According to the State Civil Service Commission Report[18] on which these data are based, the state positions in New York City and its four suburbs (Nassau, Suffolk, Westchester, Rockland), account for 74 percent of the black and 91 percent of the Puerto Rican employees in the entire state workforce. On the whole, the New York State workforce is 94 percent white. More than 83 percent of the minorities in the state government are concentrated in four agencies. These include the Department of Mental Hygiene, the Department of Labor, the Narcotics Addiction Control Commission, and the State University. Therefore, while minority representation in the state workforce is high in New York City, this is not the case within the state government as a whole.

When we turn our attention to the employment situation in the federal sector, we find that minority representation at that level of government is highly favorable. From the information presented in table 4.3 it appears that the composition of the federal workforce in the New York SMSA is similar to that found in the city government. While the percentage of whites within this federal grouping exceeds the percentage of whites in the city workforce by 1 percent, so does the percentage of blacks (26) by the same margin. The representation of Puerto Ricans appears to be the same (6 percent) for the city and federal governments, although the latter count does include non-Puerto Rican Hispanics. The representation of other minorities in the local federal workforce (.5 percent) is somewhat smaller than their representation in the city government (2 percent).

However, when one examines the general composition of the population in the New York SMSA, it is quite clear that minorities enjoy a disproportionate amount of representation in comparison to their percentage of the population as a whole. According to the data provided in table 4.3, the general population of the New York SMSA is 75 percent white, 16 percent black, 7 percent Puerto Rican, and 2 percent other minorities. In this sense, the proportionate representation which minorities have attained in the federal workforce exceeds by far that which is found within the workforce of the City, where the general population is only 67 percent white.

The disparity between the employment-population ratio of the city and SMSA areas can be largely explained by the fact that an overwhelming portion of both the minority population and the federal positions available in the SMSA are located within New York City. Since 89 percent of the black and Puerto Rican populations and 92 percent of the federal positions in the SMSA are found in the five urban counties of the city, it is understandable that the racial composition of the total federal workforce in the SMSA is more closely related to the racial composition of the city than it is of the population of the SMSA.

An examination of the information in the final column of table 4.3 bears evidence to the fact that the private sector is the largest source of employment in New York City. According to this data, the total size of the city labor force in 1970 was 3,330,803. While this figure includes both public and private employees, it far surpasses the total numbers presented in the other three columns (424,048), even with the fact that the federal data include public employees from the local suburbs. However, within this citywide workforce minorities hold a significantly smaller portion of the available jobs than they do in either of the three public sectors. Blacks account for only 19 percent of the labor force, while Puerto Ricans amount to 7 percent. Given the fact that these percentages are skewed upward by the inclusion of federal, state, and city government data in the totals, it is apparent that minority group representation in the non-public workforce in New York is considerably lower than their total portion of the population calls for. Thus, the figures in table 4.3 tend to substantiate a common claim made by defenders of the merit system that, on a proportionate basis, racial minorities rely more heavily upon the public sector for employment than they do upon the private labor market.

TABLE 4.4
NYC MINORITY REPRESENTATION BY AGENCY (1971)

Agency	Total number employees	% all minorities	% white	% black	% Puerto Rican	% others
Health & Hospital	40,646	70	30	55	10	5
Housing Authority	11,312	57	43	38	19	*
Social Services	23,237	52	48	44	6	2
Corrections Dept.	3,681	47	53	43	3	1
Health Dept.	5,962	46	54	36	7	3
Municipal Services	3,917	39	61	32	3	4
Rent & Housing Maintenance	2,349	38	62	25	13	*
Traffic Dept.	1,143	32	68	28	4	*
Triborough Bridge & Tunnel Auth.	1,052	25	75	23	2	*
Board of Education	88,641	25	75	18	6	1
Finance Admin.	2,043	22	78	18	3	1
Parks, Recreation & Control Affairs	4,895	21	79	19	2	*
Office of Comptroller	1,176	17	83	15	2	*
Sanitation Dept. & Admin. Serv.	15,304	15	85	13	2	*
Police Department	35,310	13	87	10	3	*
Highways Dept.	2,954	11	89	8	2	1
Water Resources	3,858	9	91	8	1	*
Fire Department	14,873	5	95	4	1	*

*Less than 1%.

THE DISTRIBUTION OF MINORITIES IN CITY GOVERNMENT

While the information covered thus far is useful for presenting an overall picture on the level of minority representation in the city government, and on how it compares with that of the other sectors, general information of this sort does not tell the entire story. Given what we already know about the public employment situation in the rest of the nation, such general data merely beg the questions which call for more detailed information about the distribution of minorities in city government according to service agency, job function or rank, and pay grade.[19]

Distribution by Agency. Table 4.4 contains a breakdown of minority representation in all those city agencies which had more than one thousand employees as of 1971. Agencies are listed in rank order according to the percentage of minority group members which each employs. In order to give the reader a better understanding of the actual number of jobs which each group holds within an agency, the table also includes figures on the total number of employees contained within each of the agencies as of 1971. All other figures are expressed in terms of percentages.

According to the data presented in table 4.4, the city government is similar to the federal and state sectors in the sense that minorities tend to cluster in certain types of services. Among those in which they are most highly concentrated and in fact overrepresented are agencies concerned with the delivery of health, housing, and public welfare services. With regard to housing services even Puerto Ricans, who tend to be underrepresented in the city government as a whole, hold a favorably disproportionate amount of positions with 19 percent of the jobs in the housing authority and 13 percent of the jobs in the Department of Rent and Housing Maintenance.

Generally, those agencies in which minority group members have pursued careers are ones which are particularly concerned with catering to the needs of nonwhite and poorer communities. In New York it is the black and Puerto Rican communities who are most reliant on the city government for preventive health and hospital care, low income housing, building code enforcement, and anti-poverty–related programs. Thus, it is not unreasonable to conclude that minority group members join the City workforce with some intention of serving their own people.

Minority representation tends to be poorest among those agencies which traditionally have been the strongholds of specific white ethnic groups. For example, the Irish have historically been attracted to the police and fire departments; Italians have always dominated the sanitation, water resources, and highway construction services; and the Jews have tended to pursue careers in education.

These patterns generally continued to exist in 1971, particularly in the uniformed services (police, fire, and sanitation). Since recruitment for these services is done by means of an open and competitive examination, one might assume that the persistence of these patterns is not the product of a systematic policy of discrimination, although some critics have claimed that the examinations themselves are culturally biased against

minorities. However, students of the city have observed a natural pro-
clivity on the part of its racial and ethnic groups to seek careers in particular types of services. As Moynihan and Glaser have long since taught us,
these tendencies are usually the outgrowth of long-standing social values
and cultural traits.[20]

Taking into consideration the employment situation in the city
government as a whole, the optimist might be led to conclude that
despite the inclination of ethnic and racial minorities to cluster in particular agencies, in the end most minorities have successfully carved out the
portion of City jobs which is rightfully theirs. The skeptic, on the other

TABLE 4.5

REPRESENTATION IN NYC GOVERNMENT
BY JOB CLASSIFICATION (1971)

Occupational classification	Total no. employees	% all minorities	% white	% black	% Puerto Rican	% other
Officials & administrators	11,060	23	76	20	3	1
Professionals	86,547	22	78	16	2	4
Tech. workers	2,489	37	63	29	6	2
Inspectors & investigators	3,557	15	85	13	1	1
Protective service workers	52,581	15	85	12	2	1
Paraprofessionals	16,072	77	23	49	25	3
Clerical workers	35,771	45	55	39	6	*
Craftsmen	6,491	8	92	5	2	1
Operatives	5,811	35	65	24	10	1
Service workers	33,060	72	28	58	12	2
Laborers	21,319	26	74	27	8	1

*Less than 1%.

hand, might be inclined to allege that, while minorities are proportionately
well represented in the bureaucracy as a whole, it is the white majority
which has managed to corral the more desirable positions. It is with
reference to the latter's interests, and they are quite legitimate, that we
turn to the next issue.

Distribution by Job Classification. Table 4.5 contains an analysis of the
proportion of jobs which each minority held at the various occupational
levels in the city government in 1971. The categories used are similar to

those adopted by the U.S. Bureau of the Census for reporting information on the general characteristics of the national workforce. The table also includes data on the actual number of positions contained within each classification.

An examination of the data appearing in the table reveals a similar pattern of minority representation as that which we have already seen with regard to the general city government workforce. Blacks and other minorities fare rather well within the top levels of the City bureaucracy, while Puerto Ricans are again underrepresented. Blacks, who represent 20 percent of the entire population in the city, have managed to obtain 20 percent of the official and administrative positions, 16 percent of the professional positions, and 29 percent of those jobs which are classified as technical. These figures represent a significant reversal of the pattern observed in relation to the public workforce in the nation as a whole. The ability of blacks to receive their due share of official and administrative positions is also significant in the sense that these positions carry with them a great amount of authority in city government and therefore a capability to affect policy decisions. Therefore, the placement of these minorities in such positions greatly enhances their ability to function as advocates of those racial groups which they represent.

Blacks do hold a smaller share of the professional positions in city government than that to which they are entitled, accounting for only 16 percent of those posts. Most of those professional positions that they do hold are found in agencies where blacks tend to dominate. For example, 31 percent of the social workers, 41 percent of the nurses, and 31 percent of the housing assistants in the city government are black. The slight underrepresentation of blacks in the professional fields is probably a function of their lower educational achievement as compared to whites. Blacks, however, have managed to gain entry into 29 percent of the technical level jobs in the city government.

Puerto Rican residents tend to suffer from several disadvantages when competing for the better occupational positions in the city government. With respect to educational attainment they fare even more poorly than the black population. While 4.5 percent of all blacks over the age of twenty-five have completed four years of college, only 1 percent of the Puerto Ricans in that age group have done so. The figure for the entire post-twenty-five population of the city is 11.5 percent. In addition to the impediment of education, Puerto Ricans also incur problems in competing for jobs because of the problem which many of them have with the English language. Thus, Puerto Ricans are found in only 3 percent of the official and administrative job slots, 2 percent of the professional positions, and 6 percent of the jobs classified as technical.

The impact of the educational disadvantage on Puerto Ricans is most clearly illustrated when one compares their employment situation with that of the other foreign born minorities who may experience some language related obstacles but usually enjoy better educational backgrounds. Other minorities hold 4 percent of the professional positions in the city government, a percentage twice the size of their representation in the population. A closer analysis of the groups within the other minorities category reveals that 42 percent of all non–Puerto Rican Spanish surnamed, 76 percent of all Chinese, and 73 percent of all other minorities within the city government are professionals. Only 37 percent of all

TABLE 4.6
REPRESENTATION IN NYC GOVERNMENT
BY SALARY RANGE (1971)

Salary range	Total no. employees	% all minorities	% white	% black	% Puerto Rican	% other
$25,000 +	2,140	17	83	15	1	*
$18,000–24,999	6,169	11	89	9	1	*
$13,000–17,999	23,690	16	84	10	1	4
$10,500–12,999	100,551	18	82	14	4	1
$ 7,300–10,499	68,841	26	74	22	4	*
$ 5,200– 7,299	61,955	70	30	53	15	1
Under $5,000	4,998	53	47	34	18	1
Unknown	6,303	55	45	38	14	1

*Less than .5%.

whites fit into the professional category. Thus, while professional positions within the city government are closed to all but those with higher educational achievements, the merit system of recruitment for these careers does not appear to discriminate against individuals because of national origin or race.

Distribution by Salary Range. When one considers the racial distribution of New York City employees on the basis of the level of compensation they receive for their work, the results of the 1971 survey are not so encouraging for minorities. Despite the fact that minorities, particularly blacks and non–Puerto Ricans, have managed to obtain a fair share of jobs within the higher and more prestigious classifications of the city government, minorities on the whole do not appear to be paid as well as whites.

Table 4.6 includes data on the distribution of minorities and whites in city government according to seven basic salary scales. The figures in it show that minorities in general, and especially Puerto Ricans, tend to be disproportionately concentrated at the lower salary ranges of the city pay system. While minorities constitute 32 percent of the city population, they only hold 17 percent of the positions in the highest pay grade ($25,000 and over), 11 percent of the positions in the second highest ($18,000-$24,999), and 16 percent of the positions in the third highest ($13,000-$17,999). Overrepresentation of Puerto Ricans is found only in the three lowest pay scales. The only nonwhite racial groups holding a disproportionate share of the higher paying jobs are those classified in the other minorities category. They constitute 4 percent of the third highest salary range ($13,000-$17,999). The latter outcome is consistent with the high degree of professionalism that was observed among this group in the previous section.

Why, one might ask, are minorities, particularly blacks, so poorly represented at the better paying levels of city government when they have done so well in qualifying for the higher and more prestigious job classifications? There are two types of explanations one might offer for this apparent disparity. The first is directly related to the personnel system of the City. While there are a number of factors which come into play which determine how much compensation a civil servant receives for his work, to some extent salary is a function of seniority. While employees may enter the City workforce at any one of the several job classifications, the amount of compensation they derive within that classification is to some extent determined by their longevity. Since minorities in New York tend to be younger than whites, then it may be expected that those within the local civil service system are also younger and therefore have less seniority than do their white counterparts. As the data in table 4.1 at the beginning of this chapter show, while 68 percent of the city population is white, 80 percent of those individuals within the senior age groups (45-65 years) are white. Therefore, to some extent the low representation of minorities at the higher pay scales of the city government may be a function of age.

The second explanation which might be offered for the disparity is more indirect. However, it may also be more significant. Salary determinations for those individuals who work for New York are to a large extent the outcome of a collective bargaining process which takes place between city officials and the leadership of municipal employee unions. Historically, those unions which have been most successful in attaining high levels of compensation for their members are the ones which are found in predominantly white city agencies. For example, according to a study completed by Raymond Horton, the most successful participants in this collective bargaining process, in terms of both salary and fringe benefits, have been the unions which represent the uniformed forces.[21] The data in table 4.4 of this chapter indicate that these agencies are 90 percent white. According to Horton's study, the second most successful major collective bargaining unit in the city, in terms of both salary and fringe benefits, is the United Federation of Teachers.[22] The data in the survey conducted by the City Human Rights Commission in 1971 indicate that schoolteachers in New York were 89 percent white.[23] According to Horton's study, one of the less successful major labor unions in the city so far as salaries and fringe benefits are concerned was District Council 37.[24] While the members of this union are distributed throughout a number of city agencies, a large portion of them are found in either clerical positions or the health field, which the Human Rights Commission study indicates are more disproportionately black and Puerto Rican.[25]

In a major way, the reason for the varying levels of success which each of the city employees' unions has had in the collective bargaining process is political in nature. While District Council 37 is the largest public employee union in the city, it has only recently been as effective politically as have those unions which represent policemen, firemen, sanitationmen, and teachers. To begin with, in 1971 the black and Puerto Rican members of D.C. 37 were less likely to vote than their white counterparts in the other unions. Second, at that time the members of D.C. 37 were not organized to participate in campaign or election-related activity on the same scale that people in the other unions were. Hence, the heavily populated minority unions enjoy less leverage in the local political process than the others. This is why it is not unusual in New York City to find a professionally trained registered nurse drawing a lower salary than a less skilled sanitation worker. Thereby it can be said that in the one area of the City personnel system where minorities are under-represented, that concerning pay scale, the explanation appears to be more closely related to the political process of the city than it is to the merit system.

SUMMARY AND ANALYSIS

In the introductory discussion of the merit system which appeared in the first chapter, we observed a certain logical tension between the equal opportunity principle of the system and its imposition of standard qualifications for selection. There it was noted that while the civil service is open to all who qualify for a particular office, the socially deprived are at a relative disadvantage when competing for employment with those who enjoy more supportive educational and social backgrounds. Thus, it was found that the merit system displays a logical capability to deny socially deprived racial minorities descriptive representation within our traditional administrative institutions.

The competitive disadvantage of these groups becomes especially apparent when one reviews the relevant research literature on public employment in the United States. It shows that while racial minorities are well represented in our government bureaucracies on the whole, they have not done so well in competing for the higher ranking, more prestigious, and better paying jobs within the civil service. However, the research literature also reveals some notable variations and distinctions from these general patterns which are worthy of comment. The fact that local government bureaucracies, particularly those in cities, were found to be the most representative of all levels of government, is especially significant considering that these local administrative institutions have been the major target of reforms proposed by advocates of the New Public Administration. Our own research on New York is a relevant case in point; for while the City was in the process of attempting several experiments in decentralized government in 1971, our data show that the traditional bureaucratic arrangement was significantly more representative than some of its critics would have believed.

From the material appearing in the City Human Rights Commission surveys, it is evident that minorities in New York enjoyed a degree of representation in the local bureaucracy which was slightly higher than their proportionate part of the city population. While 32 percent of the city population was composed of racial minorities in 1971, 33 percent of the City workforce was made up of members from those groups. This general pattern was found to exist even at the higher levels of the civil service, a factor which greatly distinguishes New York City from the national trend.

A comparison between the 1971 and 1963 surveys has demonstrated that significant strides were made in recruiting minorities for the City workforce during those years when attempts were made to sensitize the merit system to the particular condition of blacks and Puerto Ricans. However, the data also show that among minorities Puerto Ricans continued to be underrepresented in the City workforce, particularly at the higher levels of the bureaucracy. The condition of the latter group appears to be a function of the educational and language barriers which continue to put Puerto Ricans at a competitive disadvantage when seeking employment with the City. It stands in bold contrast to the condition of other, better educated minority groups in New York, especially Asians and other Hispanics, who were overrepresented at the professional levels of the workforce.

Despite the general success which minorities have had in competing at the higher occupational levels of the City bureaucracy, the data from the present study show that they did not do so well in attaining comparable levels of compensation for their work. Thus, while the merit system of recruitment functioned as a means to equal employment opportunity for minorities, those aspects of the personnel system concerned with determining wage scales did not serve minorities so well. While merit selection is a relatively objective process governed by fixed standards, salary determinations are part of a political process which is affected by local influence. Thus, the underrepresentation of minorities at the higher salary levels of the City personnel system tends to support one of the basic lessons to be drawn from the present case study of New York City. While those aspects of the administrative process which are controlled by regularized standards of operation are capable of being responsive to the needs of minorities, those features of the system which are more susceptible to political influence tend to work against the interests of disadvantaged groups.

The latter point raises some serious questions so far as the representative nature of our administrative institutions is concerned. The data on the distribution of minorities in the City workforce indicate that these groups tend to be disproportionately concentrated in a small number of services such as health care, housing, and social welfare agencies, all of which are particularly concerned with serving minority clients in the city. It seems to suggest that minorities pursue careers in agencies which allow them to focus upon the problems of their own communities. This pattern of preference may be the first stage of a process by which proportional representation in particular agencies is transformed into active representation at the community or street level. There is no better way for a bureaucracy to represent the interests of a community than by the recruitment of individuals who join with that intention in mind.

Nevertheless, one may view the distribution of minorities in the City workforce from another perspective, for there are a number of agencies, such as the uniformed forces, which are predominantly white. Should one assume that the members of these organizations will become active representatives of the racial groups to which they belong? Will they thus favor their own communities when delivering services and ignore the needs of minority groups? To rephrase a question proposed in a previous chapter, "Is an administrative institution which lacks descriptive representation capable of representing the interests of all groups?" Is there a politically neutral aspect of bureaucratic decision making which enables these institutions to allocate resources and services in an equitable fashion? These are the questions which will be addressed in the next chapter.

5

THE ALLOCATION OF LOCAL SERVICES AMONG RACIAL GROUPS IN NEW YORK CITY

This chapter is composed of three case studies which will analyze the allocation of police, fire, and sanitation services among racial groups in New York City during 1972 and 1973. Its purpose is to provide an empirical basis for evaluating whether the city agencies studied allocate an equitable share of services to black and Puerto Rican minorities. In accordance with the Rawlsian concept of justice already defined, an equitable distribution of services will be considered one in which service-related public resources are allocated among communities on the basis of some appropriate indicator(s) of social need. Thereby, so far as most city services are concerned, police and fire in particular, the standard of equity which has been adopted would call for a disproportionate allocation of services among disadvantaged minorities, who are severely victimized by social maladies such as crime or fire hazards.

The analysis of allocations within the three services which have been selected is significant from three different but related perspectives, all of which contribute to the overall theme of the present study. These comprise:

1. The dichotomy between the old and the New public administrations: Because the three agencies which have been selected are all traditionally organized bureaucratic structures, the research in this chapter will allow one to determine whether the traditional institutions are capable of fulfilling the normative ideals that have been recently associated with the New Public Administration.

2. The relationship between descriptive representation and interest representation: As the data in the previous chapter have shown, each of the three agencies selected is one in which the descriptive representation

of minorities is low. The analysis in this chapter will allow us to evaluate whether a traditionally organized bureaucratic structure with poor descriptive representation is capable of responding to the social wants and needs of all groups, regardless of which group controls decision making within it.

3. The linkage between operational efficiency and equity in the distribution of services: All three agencies selected were, at the time with which the research is concerned, involved in a major effort to improve the efficiency of their service delivery systems. Since a major part of the program strategy implemented was concerned with the "optimum" utilization and deployment of resources, the research in this chapter will allow us to determine whether there exists both a logical and an empirical relationship between the operational goal of efficiency and the normative ideal of social equity.

The concept of efficiency has already been described generally, with reference to the New York City Productivity Program, as the application of an organizational strategy designed to improve either the quantity or the quality of services rendered per unit of resources invested. Yet, for the sake of clarity it will also be necessary to define the term operationally in terms of each of the services with which we are concerned. Therefore, this chapter will also include a description of the managerial goals defined and the techniques employed by those who were responsible for allocating resources in each of the respective agencies. All such techniques can be subjected to criticism, since they are designed and implemented in an organizational environment where decision makers, in Simon's terminology, must be content with "satisficing" rather than optimizing rationality in pursuit of their chosen ends. Therefore, our final analysis will also include an account of the shortcomings inherent in the techniques which were adopted.

RESEARCH METHOD

The general approach to be followed in this chapter will be to compare the racial composition of the population with the allocation of agency manpower within geographically defined districts in each agency studied. The same procedure for analysis will be used in all the services with which we are concerned. Here we will explain the rationale for that approach and consider each step of the research procedure in its appropriate turn.

The first order of business was to select an organizational level of analysis in each agency which would be small enough to allow for the identification of significant population groupings yet large enough for the comparison of manpower allocations at a meaningful level. We chose police precincts, fire battalions, and sanitation districts. In 1972 there were seventy-one police precincts, fifty-eight fire battalions, and fifty-eight sanitation districts in New York. Except for fire services, these administrative districts are the same organizational levels at which the city government will be subdivided in 1981 under its new plan for decentralization. The Fire Department will not participate in that plan on a district level.

The next order of business in our analysis was to determine the racial composition of these districts. This was done by superimposing departmental district maps over U.S. Census Bureau maps for each of the city's five boroughs and thereby identifying which of the more than two thousand census tracts were located in each district. After this was done, it was possible to ascertain with the use of Census Bureau data the number of non–Puerto Rican whites, non–Puerto Rican blacks, and Puerto Ricans of both races (hereafter referred to as whites, blacks, and Puerto Ricans) living in each of the service districts throughout the city.

With this information in hand it was possible to rank the districts in each department according to the percentage of blacks and Puerto Ricans which each of them contained. Orientals and "other" population groupings were included with whites. The ranked districts of each department were then categorized into five intervals of 20 percent, as follows:

Group 1, which we will classify as a "highly segregated white" category, comprises all those districts that contain 80 percent or more white populations (excluding Puerto Ricans).

Group 2, which we will classify as "moderately segregated white," comprises all those districts that contain between 60 percent and 80 percent white populations.

Group 3, which we will classify as "integrated," comprises all those districts that contain between 40 percent and 60 percent white populations. These, of course, also contain between 40 percent and 60 percent black or Puerto Rican populations.

Group 4, which we will classify as "moderately segregated minority," comprises all those districts which contain 60 percent to 80 percent black or Puerto Rican populations.

Group 5, which we shall classify as "highly segregated minority," comprises all those districts that contain between 80 percent or 100 percent black and Puerto Rican populations.

With the population characteristics of each district clearly defined and categorized, the next order of business was to go about the task of measuring levels of service which each district and group received from the three agencies being studied. Once again there was the need to select a methodology, and the state of the art of local government service measurement is such that there was a variety to choose from. For example, as early as 1938 Clarence Ridley and Herbert Simon conducted one of the first systematic investigations into ways of measuring local government services.[1] It resulted in the development of various types of indicators, such as expenditures, standards of effort, and the distribution of equipment. However, the passage of time since then has brought with it the development of more refined measuring and monitoring techniques. In 1960 Henry Schmandt and G. Ross Stevens made another significant contribution to the field by developing service-level indices for a variety of local government functions in Milwaukee County.[2] Their method permitted them to measure the "direct output" of many local agencies. Then in 1969 Bradford, Malt, and Oates established a technique which drew an analytical distinction between the direct output (D-output) of local government agencies and the consequences (C-output) of those outputs.[3] Their work provided the foundation for a landmark study carried out by the Urban Institute in 1972 which resulted in the development of a large number of indicators which could be used to measure both the output and effectiveness of urban services, particularly police and sanitation.[4]

Despite the great conceptual and methodological strides made over recent years for measuring local government services, each new technique has brought with it the excess baggage of its own deficiencies.[5] In selecting a methodology for analysis one must recognize these pitfalls and review the assortment with one basic question in mind, "Which technique will most completely tell me what I want to know?" In this instance, the particular question to be addressed may be stated, "Have three local agencies allocated their services among racial minorities in an equitable way?" Our major concern is to ascertain the level of commitment which these agencies display with regard to the needs of black and Puerto Rican populations.

One might begin to go about this business by measuring the direct output of the agencies. However, while this method is useful with certain "hard" services such as sanitation collection, which can be measured in terms of tons of refuse collected or the frequency of collections, it cannot be reliably or validly applied in such "softer" services as police or fire. For example, the number of fires a fire department extinguishes is more directly related to the number of fires that occur in an area rather than to the level of commitment displayed at the agency level. All fires reported are extinguished. Therefore, measuring the output of a fire department tells us little of what we want to know.

The same type of problem arises when one tries to use effectiveness criteria as a basis for measuring the level of commitment in softer services. There is no necessary or direct relationship established between the level of commitment displayed by local police departments and such commonly used effectiveness measures as crime rates. Crime is related to a variety of environmental and social factors such as employment, income, and education, over which the police do not exercise any direct control.

Since the publication of the Urban Institute study in 1972, there has been a greater emphasis placed upon the use of citizen surveys as a means for evaluating the effectiveness of local government services.[6] This technique has provided us with a valuable tool for measuring citizens' perceptions on both the level of services they receive and the quality of life they enjoy. However, as is the case with other measures of effectiveness, it does not serve as a direct indicator of the level of commitment made by local governments and their agencies in servicing the public.

It is because of such methodological difficulties in measuring government outputs and their effects that students of public affairs have relied heavily upon the use of resource allocations as a means for evaluating the degree of equity to be found within the distributive process. Here again the state of the art is such that the analyst has several techniques from which to choose. The one most commonly applied is the analysis of budget expenditures.[7] The chief advantage of this technique is that it permits one to determine the distribution of both capital and human resources among population groups or geographical areas. The basic problem with it, however, is that agency budgets are not easily broken down among geographical subdivisions. Therefore, it is difficult to ascertain which resources are devoted to support or maintenance functions as opposed to the delivery of services directly to the public. Wage differentials among employees at various levels of seniority may also present an inaccurate picture of the levels of service enjoyed among various communities.

The concentration on manpower resources as a method of analysis, which is the one we have chosen to use, appears to have several benefits which are not found in the other techniques that were mentioned. To begin with, manpower resources are both easily observable and highly measurable. Thus, their use facilitates the process of comparing service levels among districts. Moreover, manpower allocations provide us with a significant indicator for assessing the degree of commitment which an agency has for responding to the service needs of various population groups.

The analysis in this chapter will specifically focus on the deployment of agency manpower below the supervisory level. These include police-men below the rank of sergeant, firemen below the rank of lieutenant, and sanitationmen below the rank of assistant foreman. They are the individuals who remove the rubbish, extinguish the fires, and apprehend criminals on the city streets. It is they who deliver services directly to the public. Their numbers are also somewhat representative of the allocation of large capital equipment among communities because there are standard assignments of two patrolmen to a police car (excluding foot patrol), five or six firemen to an engine or ladder company, and three men to a sanitation collection truck.

With the use of departmental statistics it is possible to determine how many servicemen are allocated to each of the geographical districts within the agencies studied. These figures have been used to calculate the average allocation per district within each of the five racially defined groupings described above. Such information will allow us to compare allocations across racial lines. Since the populations within these districts vary widely in each service, allocation data will also be computed on a per capita basis expressed in terms of servicemen per one thousand population. Thus, it can ordinarily be expected that districts with excessively large populations will exhibit relatively low per capita allocations and districts with excessively small populations will exhibit relatively high per capita allocations. Since we are primarily concerned with the relative allocation of manpower among population groups, we will exclude from our analysis those non-residential districts which would misleadingly skew the averages within each group. The method for exclusion within each service will be more clearly defined in later sections.

Studies of service delivery which focus on resource allocations are occasionally criticized by practitioners of some of the aforementioned approaches for not considering such factors as performance or effectiveness. It should be kept in mind, however, that these criteria are built into the allocation methodologies which we will be describing. Therefore, performance measures such as tons collected per truck shift in the harder sanitation service and such "proxy" measures as response time in the softer emergency services will be dealt with at considerable length.

Finally, it must once again be emphasized that this study is concerned not only with the equal distribution of services among racial groups, but with the equitable allocation of service in terms of relative community needs. Therefore, our analysis will relate manpower allocations which exist prior to and following the implementation of new managerial techniques to such need determinants as crime rates, incidence of fire, and street miles. It should be noted, however, that it is not our intention here to establish value relationships between social indicators of service need and demands for manpower at specific levels. That would involve a highly complex, and one might add, arbitrary process, which lies outside the purview of the present study. We simply do not know, for example, how many additional police patrolmen are called for in an area which suffers from a 20 percent rise in reported crime rates. As the analysis in the forthcoming sections will show, the problem of identifying optimum manning levels or deployment distributions becomes significantly more complicated when other need factors are considered. The outside analyst does not have access to the detailed information which is needed to make such calculations.

Our purpose here is to compare general patterns of service need that are evident through the use of appropriate indicators with the manpower allocations that are found in the agencies being studied. We do know, for example, that a high-crime precinct in the city deserves more police manpower than a relatively safe one, even if we do not know exactly how much. An examination of the deployment strategies followed by decision makers in the agencies studied will provide us with a basis for determining whether they have made a rational attempt to respond to the particular needs of the communities they serve. An analysis of data on manpower deployment will allow us to evaluate whether the patterns of distribution established have been fair and equitable.

Each of the three agencies which we will consider in this chapter— police, fire, and sanitation—will be treated in a separate section. These three parts will each include a brief introduction to the nature and activity of the agency, a description of the deployment methodologies that were utilized, and an analysis of the results achieved with these techniques.

POLICE

According to a statutory prescription found in the City Charter, the mission of the New York Police Department is to preserve public peace, prevent crime, detect and arrest offenders, and protect the rights of persons and property.[8] These functions are supplemented by additional duties such as traffic control and response to individual and public emergencies of a non-criminal nature.

The Police Department is one of the many agencies which felt the crunch of austerity measures imposed by Mayor Lindsay between 1971 and 1973. As a result of the citywide hiring freeze in effect during this period, the manpower level of the department was allowed to drop by three thousand officers to a roster strength of approximately 28,600 men.

These personnel reductions took place at a time when crime was rapidly on the rise in New York. The total number of reported felonies had grown to over one million in 1973, representing a 38 percent increase over the actual amount in 1966 when John Lindsay first took office. Within the category of felonies, murder and non-negligent manslaughter had leaped 130 percent, rape by 71 percent, and robbery had exceeded the 1966 figure by 209 percent.

New York was evidently becoming a more violent place to live. As the size of the police force patrolling the city streets began to shrink, the need to increase departmental productivity and make better use of its resources became more profound. In a relative sense, the Police Department was in a better condition to impose the managerial reforms demanded by the times than most other city agencies. To begin with, its personnel are among the most carefully trained. All members of the force are required to participate in programs at the Police Academy and many go on to pursue degrees in police science at the city's John Jay College of Criminal Justice. Moreover, there exists within the department a managerial-oriented leadership very much concerned with cultivating and protecting the professional image of their organization. At times the managerial orientation of the police brass has brought them into direct and open conflict with the Patrolman's Benevolent Association, the organized representative of all uniformed personnel below the rank of sergeant.[9]

Under the leadership of Commissioner Patrick Murphy, an Office of Programs and Policy was created within the department. This component, which draws on the analytical talent of both uniformed officers and civilian professionals, has primary responsibility for policy-oriented research, program monitoring, and advising the commissioner on issues of a technical nature. It was this group together with consultants from the New York City Rand Institute which was responsible for developing a new method of deploying manpower in 1972.

Method of Allocation. The New York City Police Department is organized into seven borough commands, fourteen divisional commands, and seventy-one neighborhood precincts. Patrolmen are deployed either in two-man radio cars or to foot patrols within a precinct sector.

The method by which patrolmen are assigned throughout neighborhood precincts is a significant matter of consideration from several perspectives. Most obviously, the more patrolmen there are in a precinct, the greater the availability of men to respond to the needs of a community. In addition to this, policemen are assigned to radio car or foot beats within a precinct in order to fulfill what police technicians refer to as a "preventive patrol" function. It is believed by these practitioners that the physical presence of uniformed policemen in a neighborhood works to deter individuals from committing crimes. In recent years this assumption has been brought into question by some experts. For example, a study of police patrol activities in Kansas City suggested that when patrol frequencies are low, this function may have little if any effect on crime.[10] From a more analytical perspective, Limring has argued that there is no empirically valid method to measure the amount of crimes which have not been committed as a result of police activity.[11]

An experiment conducted by the New York City Rand Institute in 1966 served to cast another interesting light on the subject, particularly from the perspective of the research concerns in the present study.[12] In the Rand experiment the number of police officers assigned to Manhattan's Twentieth Precinct was temporarily increased by 40 percent. According to the analysis made by James Press, its author, the intensified patrol was associated with two important outcomes. There was a significant decrease in outdoor crimes within the experimental precinct, most notably a 33 percent decrease in robberies and a 49 percent decrease in both grand larceny and auto theft. However, a partially compensating increase in such crimes occurred in neighboring precincts. Therefore, the net effect of the manpower change was to displace crime rather than prevent it. If the research in this experiment is reliable, then it can be claimed that an increase in the allocation of police personnel to a given precinct is not only an advantage to residents within that precinct, but a disadvantage to residents in neighboring precincts which do not receive similar increases. In this sense, the redeployment of police manpower becomes a meaningful issue in terms of both politics and equity.

Prior to 1973 the New York City Police Department utilized what is probably one of the more traditional and universal methods for allocating patrolmen. This technique, known as a "hazard rating formula," was originally developed by O. W. Wilson in the late nineteen-thirties.[13] With it a potential user would begin by identifying three types of variables which are believed to be pertinent to the relative needs for manpower among geographical districts: measures of crime (usually weighted according to severity), measures of activity (e.g., arrests or calls for services), and measures of implicit requirements (e.g., street miles, school crossings, number of playgrounds, etc.). The user would then attach an arbitrary weight to each variable corresponding to his subjective assessment of its importance in making decisions about manpower deployments. For example, the hazard rating formula used in New York prior to 1973 weighted variables as follows: crimes of personal violence 25 percent, other crimes 20 percent, juvenile delinquency 15 percent, accidents and aid 10 percent, total population 10 percent, miles of street 5 percent, business establishments and licensed premises 5 percent, school crossings, parks, and recreation areas 5 percent, and radio runs 5 percent. Once these values were determined, a hazard rating index was computed for each precinct within the city.

One of the greater advantages to using a hazard formula for deployment is its simplicity. Most calculations can be made by hand. Therefore, no highly trained technical staff or expensive equipment is needed for its adoption. The key disadvantage of this technique is that it depends upon a highly arbitrary system of weighting. While its goal is to equalize workloads among precincts, it does not include any provisions to maintain a standard level of performance throughout the city in terms either of minimizing response times for calls to service or of maintaining a prescribed level of preventive patrol. In fact, it does not even lead to an equalization of workload.

When hazard ratings are used, the reported crime rate usually becomes the most critical variable for determining manpower needs. For example, to take the New York system as a case in point, and its system was typical, 60 percent of the hazard index was reflective of crime. Crime is without doubt an important factor of consideration. However, when a particular precinct has a high responsibility for non-criminal activity—such as traffic control in mid-Manhattan or the protection of embassies in the United Nations area, manpower can become so absorbed that no preventive patrol is permitted and response times for emergencies are adversely affected.

In 1972 the New York City Rand Institute developed a more sophisticated computerized system which would allow a user to allocate manpower in a way consistent with citywide standards of performance. This system was particularly concerned with the allocation of policemen who were deployed in two-man patrol cars. The "patrol car allocation model," which in its later and refined form was dubbed PCAM (pronounced pe' kam),[14] could be used to designate citywide standards of performance in terms of average response times and preventive patrol levels. Response time standards are concerned with the amounts of time which elapse between a call for service, the dispatch of a radio car, and the arrival of policemen at the scene of an incident. The preventive patrol level is the proportion of time that an average patrol car is available for cruising in a sector.

The PCAM model makes use of historical data to estimate the projected needs and availability of police personnel in a given precinct. While crime data are still an important variable of consideration for this model, the range of information fed into the computer is wide and varied. It includes:

1. total calls for service, in order to assess demand for service
2. area within a command, for the purpose of estimating travel times
3. total response times, computed by adding dispatch times and travel times
4. average service times, which forecast the amount of time patrolmen are occupied with calls for service
5. parameters permitting one to compute how much duty time is spent on non-criminal activity such as traffic control

The use of historical data permitted police administrators to weigh need factors according to experience rather than on an arbitrary basis. The system could then be applied to answer two significant types of questions. How many men are needed to maintain a specific minimum level of performance across the city? What is the most effective way of deploying a fixed number of personnel?

Rand made the system available to the New York City Police Department in 1972. Police Commissioner Cawley adopted it in 1973 to institute Plan C, a new method of deployment, often referred to within the department as "Cawley's Cruiser Concept."[15] Plan C utilized a dual method of deployment which would allocate two-thirds of the department manpower to maintain citywide performance standards for patrol car operations and would then allocate the remaining one-third of the available men on the basis of a new hazard formula.

Plan C begins with the designation of a fixed standard of performance desired by the department throughout the city. This was defined in terms of response times and preventive patrol levels. For example, it was decided that all calls for service would be assigned to a priority category. Priority 1 calls, such as an assault in progress, would be allowed no delays from the time a call was received until the time a car was dispatched. Only 10 percent of all calls in which a fast response was preferable but which were not so urgent as a Priority 1 type were permitted to result in a queue from the moment a call was received until the dispatch of a radio car. An example of such a case would be a call concerning a disabled vehicle blocking traffic on a main highway. Finally, calls related to incidents where time was not a crucial issue would be held in queue until an adequate amount of manpower was available to maintain preventive patrol functions and remain available for high priority calls. An example of an incident left in queue would be a call concerning a burglary which had already occurred. Since the function of a policeman in such a case is primarily administrative, there is no need for a radio car to be rushed to the scene.

Once these standards were set, the Rand model was used to determine how many patrolmen would be needed in each precinct to insure that they were maintained all over the city. It was found that two-thirds of the department's manpower would be needed. Patrolmen were thus allocated according to the specific requirements of each precinct. The remaining one-third of police officers were placed in a "public safety pool" which was allocated according to a newly devised hazard formula. The new formula was based strictly on reported rates of crime. The heaviest weight (50 percent) was assigned to outside crimes of violence, including murder, non-negligent manslaughter, rape, sodomy, sex abuse, robbery, and felonious assault. The next weight (30 percent) was assigned to the same crimes listed in the first category but which were committed indoors. It also included non-personal crimes like burglary, auto theft, and grand larceny. The lowest weight was assigned to other crimes not included in the category above, such as narcotics felonies and mis-demeanors. The emphasis on outside crimes of personal violence in this system suggested a departmental priority to maximize the preventive patrol function in a way designed to protect people over property.

Since Plan C is, in effect, a combination of two allocation method-ologies in one, it can be expected that the deployment of New York City police personnel in 1973 was responsive to two kinds of environ-mental influences. The PCAM type which is concerned with controlling travel time and cruising rates for patrol cars, is particularly responsive to the geographic characteristics of precincts. While call rates and reported crime rates are indigenous to the system, such factors as traffic flow and precinct size weigh heavily in determining the length of time it takes to drive from one part of a precinct to another. These geographic factors also determine the number of policemen needed to insure a standard frequency in which a patrol car will pass through a sector.

In the case of the hazard type of system, where crime rate is the signifi-cant, or as in this case the only, criterion for deployment, geography plays no role in determining where patrolmen will be assigned. However, in an indirect rather than conscious way population factors become a critical variable for determining how manpower is allocated. This is true because, as we already know from past research, such population charac-teristics as low income, unemployment, and, most important for our purposes, a high proportion of minority residents are all associated with high crime rates.[16]

Patterns of Distribution. One of the basic determinants of the manpower needs in any police precinct is the size of the population which dwells within its boundaries. The more people who live in an area, the more likely it is that demands for service will be high. In order to control for the population variable in evaluating the equity of manpower allocations in this department, therefore, allocation data will be analyzed on a per capita basis in terms of the number of people residing in each precinct.[17]

It must also be noted, however, that given the peculiar characteristics of some precincts, in some cases the size of residential populations can be a misleading indicator of demands for service. There are several precincts in the city, for example, which serve large transient populations in comparison to the number of people who actually live within them. The most notable of these are the Midtown North and Midtown South precincts in Manhattan, and the First Precinct, which serves the city's financial district. While relatively few individuals live in these precincts, a large number of people frequent them daily for the purposes of business and recreation. Their low populations tend to exaggerate both per capita allocations and crime rates while at the same time they do not reflect the need for service resulting from the influx of a large number of people who are found in these areas daily.

For example, while the average population of these three precincts is 26,496, the average for all other precincts in the city is 115,472. These three precincts have an average allocation of 16.67 policemen per 1,000 residents and an average felony rate of 403.4 per 1,000 residents. All other precincts in the city average 2.00 policemen and 55.7 felonies per thousand people. We might add that while the average size of these three precincts is .96 square miles, the average for all others in the city is 4.19 square miles. Since these three precincts do not typify any others in the city and their residential populations are relatively low, we will exclude them from our composite analysis for racial groups. Including them within the group averages would skew the group data to such a great extent that it would not really reflect how residential communities with particular racial characteristics are served by their police department.

Keeping the overall citywide averages in mind (excluding the three precincts noted above), let us now consider the average data for the manpower allocations and the environmental characteristics of those precincts within each of the five racial groupings with which we are concerned. This information appears in table 5.1.

Reviewing the citywide data on the allocation of police manpower in 1973, one can detect a definite pattern in which the per capita deployment of policemen rises as the percentage of blacks and Puerto Ricans in a population increases. Except for the drop in manpower which takes place between groups 1 and 2, the pattern is almost constant. The sharpest rise in manpower takes place at two distinct points: the first as one goes from the white areas of group 1 (1.78) and 2 (1.53) to the integrated areas of group 3 (2.27); the second as one goes from group 3 to the minority areas of groups 4 (2.43) and 5 (2.57). Group 5, categorized here as highly segregated minority, which contains all precincts having populations that are 80 percent or more black and Puerto Rican, has the largest per capita allocation of policemen by far, with 2.57 for every 1,000 residents.

TABLE 5.1
NYC POLICE DEPARTMENT SERVICE DATA

Racial groups	Number of precincts	Average 1973 alloc. per 1,000	Average felonies per 1,000	Average size in sq. miles	Average population	Average 1972 alloc. per 1,000
1. highly segregated white	27	1.78	34.3	6.22	115,407	1.87
2. segregated white	13	1.53	45.8	5.28	142,155	1.59
3. integrated	9	2.27	67.7	2.07	106,792	2.45
4. segregated minority	7	2.43	66.6	1.98	95,629	2.57
5. highly segregated minority	12	2.57	81.8	1.31	104,799	2.77
Citywide average (68 precincts)		2.00	55.7	4.19	115,472	2.12

As we observe the felony rates for each of the five groups, it is apparent, as expected, that crime also increases as one goes from the whiter precincts in the city to those with larger portions of minority populations. Therefore, there does seem to be a relationship between the crime rate of a given area and the number of policemen per precinct. A closer examination of this relationship does, however, raise a couple of significant questions.

Let us first look at the relationship between group 1 (34.3 felonies per 1,000) and group 2 (45.8 felonies per 1,000). Here is one case in which the higher felony rate of the latter did not coincide with its lower manpower allocations. Does this mean that group 2 did not receive its fair share of police service? Not necessarily. The discrepancy can be explained by examining the kinds of demands made upon the precincts contained within the two groups. Group 1 contains four Manhattan precincts (6, 13, 17, 19), two Rockaway Beach precincts (100, 101), and that precinct covering the Coney Island–Brighton Beach areas of Brooklyn (61), in which a large number of policemen are needed for non–crime-related functions, particularly traffic control. Group 2 contains only two precincts of this type, both of which are located in Manhattan (10, 21). Therefore, group 1 can be expected to have a higher demand for non-crime-related services that are not reflected in the reported felony rates.

As one investigates the relationships between manpower allocations among racial groups and their respective crime rates, a more significant issue arises which remains to be addressed. It is particularly relevant to the overall purposes of this chapter. While Police Department allocations rise steadily with both the increased residency of minority group members and the higher incidence of crime, the fact remains that as we progress from groups 1 through 5 the crime rates rise at a more significant rate than does police manpower. While the crime rate per 1,000 population rises from 34.3 to 81.8, the allocation of manpower only increases from 1.78 to 2.57. Does this mean that although minority group members receive more police protection per capita, they do not receive a fair or equitable share of service with regard to their needs? At first glance the answer might appear to be yes, but further examination will cast a different light on the question.

In the last section it was explained that Plan C was a method of allocation which employed two distinct strategies in order to address two different types of needs. The hazard formula method by which one-third of the Police Department's manpower was deployed was designed to place more patrolmen in areas with severe crime problems. This strategy, supplemented by the fact that the PCAM model was also responsive to such factors as the number of calls for service and the crime rate in precincts, begins to explain why more policemen were placed in minority areas characterized by high crime rates. In order to address the question concerning why the increase in police manpower was not more proportional to the rising crime rate, we must once again consider the other need which Plan C, particularly the PCAM-oriented part of it, was designed to address. Plan C sought to regulate the amount of time it would take for a patrol car to respond to an emergency throughout all parts of the city. Therefore, larger precincts required more manpower.

If one examines the data on the average size per precinct within each of the five racial groups we have defined, he will discover that there is a significant decline in the average size per precinct as one goes from the whiter areas reflected in groups 1 (6.22 sq. mi.) and 2 (5.28 sq. mi.) to the more minority-occupied areas of groups 3 (2.07 sq. mi.), 4 (1.98 sq. mi.), and 5 (1.31 sq. mi.). The most significant drops in size occur at the points between groups 2 and 3 and between 4 and 5. Therefore, additional police personnel were needed in the white areas of the city to compensate for the much larger size of the precincts located within them. If manpower were allocated to the precincts in groups 4 and 5 solely on the basis of their crime rates, then service in the whiter areas would have dropped below the minimum standard defined by departmental officials for the whole city. In the final analysis, the allocation of police personnel in 1973 was a function of the deployment strategy which was adopted and the goals this strategy was designed to achieve.

A comparison between the manpower distribution in effect during 1973 with that of 1972 is particularly informative on this matter. It will be recalled that the Police Department operated strictly according to a hazard-based formula for reaching deployment decisions in 1972. While several other factors were built into the formula, a weight of 60 percent was attached to crime-related activity. Only a 5 percent level of significance was applied to precinct size, and no attempt was made to provide for minimum performance levels in terms of either response time or the preventive patrol function.

An analysis of the distribution data for 1972 and 1973 immediately points to the fact that there was less manpower available for all precincts within the city during 1973. Because of the hiring freeze imposed by the Mayor, the average per capita allocation per precinct in the city dropped from 2.12 per 1,000 to 2.00 per 1,000. Nevertheless, an examination of the relative distribution of manpower per racial group in 1972 at first reveals a similar pattern to that observed in the following year. There is a general per capita increase in policemen per precinct as one goes from group 1 to group 5, with the decrease from group 1 to group 2 again being the only break in the overall pattern.

A closer comparison of manpower distributions between the two years, however, does display the impact of a conversion from one type of deployment methodology to another. While the per capita allocation of manpower dropped for each of the five racial groups between 1972 and 1973, the most significant drops took place in groups 3 through 5. This point is better illustrated in graph A. It is indicative of the differential impact indigenous to a performance-based method of deployment as opposed to one which weighs more heavily on crime. If Plan C had relied entirely on the PCAM model to the total exclusion of the hazard-based system, we could have expected the difference between the two years to be more dramatic.

GRAPH A.
NYC Police Manpower Allocations, 1972, 1973

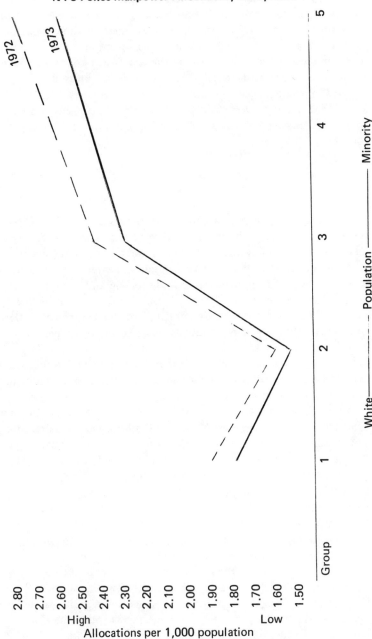

The most significant fact which emerges from our analysis of police allocations in 1972 and 1973 is that a larger proportion of manpower was deployed to black and Puerto Rican areas in both years. In order to compensate for their higher crime rates, these neighborhoods on the average contained more police precincts per square mile and more policemen per precinct than any others in the city. When police officials were faced with budget cuts which depleted their resources in 1973, they adopted a strategy which sought to continue compensating depressed areas for their more severe crime problems but at the same time attempted to provide some minimum standard of service for every citizen within the city.

FIRE

According to a legal mandate instituted as far back as 1864 and preserved in the City Charter, the duties of the New York Fire Department include the following: to extinguish fire; to protect life and property in the event of fire and disaster; to maintain and extend the fire alarm system; to prevent fire by education of the public and inspection for fire hazards; to investigate and determine causes of fire; and to enforce provisions of the Administrative Code relating to the department.[18] Despite this broad definition of responsibility, approximately 95 percent of the Fire Department's manpower is assigned to firefighting units. Thus, most fire officials in the city would agree that the primary responsibility of the department is to maintain a readiness to respond to emergencies in the fastest and most efficient way.

In the little more than a decade between 1960 and 1972, the annual demands made upon the New York City fire force increased dramatically. The number of initial alarms doubled, the total distance traveled by fire companies grew from 3 million miles to 5.2 million miles, and the incidence of false alarms multiplied fivefold. Despite this staggering increase in workload, the manpower strength of the department grew only 17 percent. Prior to 1968 city officials had attempted to respond to the increasing fire activity throughout the five boroughs with the addition of more firefighting companies. However, with an austere budget situation in later years, the prospect of adding more companies at a cost of $600,000 per company per year was becoming rather unlikely.

While the $2-million contract which the City signed with the Rand Corporation in 1968 was designed to upgrade the analytical and managerial capability of a number of agencies, it was within the Fire Department that Rand undertook its most significant efforts and made its greatest impact. Soon after Rand's arrival on the scene, the department began to assemble its own group of in-house professional analysts in its Division of Planning and Operations Research (PANDOR). This group, many of whom were civilian employees, was responsible for departmental planning, data collection, performance improvement, and strategic testing. In the years that ensued between 1968 and 1973, these Fire Department analysts worked more closely with the Rand consultants than did any other group within the city.[19] In addition to the development of a number of technological innovations, the joint effort resulted in the creation of several sophisticated techniques designed to achieve a more effective way to deploy and dispatch manpower.

Method of Allocation. In 1973 the Fire Department roster contained 11,000 uniformed men and 2,000 officers. This manpower was distributed over 5 borough commands, 14 divisions, 58 battalions, and 375 companies.[20] Except for the latter (companies) all of these organizational units are related to geographical subdivisions throughout the city.

There are two basic types of firefighting companies in a modern fire department. A ladder company which operates a large truck with aerial ladders is primarily responsible for lifesaving and rescue operations. An engine company which operates a smaller truck that can be hooked up to a hydrant and is capable of pumping water is primarily responsible for fire suppression. While some New York companies are quartered in their own house, most share a facility with another company of the other kind. This permits engine and ladder companies to complement each other's efforts when responding to the same emergency.

In 1972 a typical New York fire company of either type had a full complement of approximately twenty-five men excluding officers. Five members of the company would be on duty at a particular time, each playing a distinct, well-defined role within the lifesaving or fire suppression duties of his team. The highly essential role which each individual firefighter plays within his own work team is a determining factor which limits the flexibility of departmental officials in manpower deployment. Manpower is deployed on a company rather than an individual basis. While there are some exceptions that will be explained below, most decisions designed to reallocate or reduce resources come in the form of the relocation or the elimination of an entire fire company. Such decisions are not easily made in the highly volatile atmosphere of New York City politics.

The more apparent political implications of fire department deployment decisions greatly distinguish them from police decisions of the same type, where manpower can be reallocated by merely assigning more or fewer patrolmen to a precinct. The viability or existence of the neighborhood stationhouse is not usually threatened by such decisions. However, the disbandment of a fire company, which often results in the closing of a firehouse, has a highly visible and often dramatic impact upon a neighborhood. It is rarely done without a good share of political protest.

In addition to the political constraints within which he must function, the technology of fire protection also limits the range of choice which a fire administrator enjoys with regard to deployment decisions. While a police official has several criteria according to which he can act when allocating his manpower; e.g., reported crime rates, calls for service, preventive patrol frequency, response time, and a variety of non-crime-related activities, the options available within a fire command are more restricted. To begin with, the types of services a fire company provides are more limited in scope. The kinds of situations to which its personnel respond are—except for false alarms—almost always of an urgent nature. Therefore, the allocation strategy of a fire department must be designed to provide all locations of the city with the proximate availability of protection so that companies are within a "safe" distance for rapid response. In this sense, response time becomes a much more critical variable in the deployment of fire personnel.

The number of calls for service and the rate of fire incidence do play an important role in determining the number of companies a particular battalion should receive. But this is true only insofar as these factors affect the availability of fire companies in an area. Such factors are not criteria for deployment in and of themselves. They are important because they determine how many companies in an area are free to respond to situations. For example, if the number of fires in a particular battalion is so excessively high that a significant amount of manpower is always occupied, then that area may require additional companies to maintain a ready capability to respond to emergencies within a safe period of time. Nevertheless, response time does remain the critical variable.

Because of the heavy emphasis on rapid response in fire services, the fire dispatcher, unlike his counterpart in police, does not enjoy the luxury of queueing certain types of calls in order to leave personnel available for high priority services or other functions. All fire alarms must be responded to immediately. The only real flexibility which a fire dispatcher enjoys is in deciding how many and what kind of companies he should activate in initially responding to an alarm. Therefore, deployment decisions in the fire service can generally be divided among two types. One involves questions of initial dispatch; the other, more important for our purposes, addresses the question of where companies should be permanently located.

A history of the New York City Fire Department reveals that the deployment of fire companies began as an evolutionary incremental process which coincided with the slow but steady growth of the city over a period of two hundred years.[21] Fire companies originated as the city's population expanded from its original boundaries in lower Manhattan to the outer reaches of the Bronx, Brooklyn, Queens, and finally Staten Island. The method of deploying manpower was far from scientific. However, it tried to respond to the safety needs of the city as indicated by the influx of more people to its various regions and the experience of various fire commissioners in dealing with emergencies. The method was also guided, if not coerced, by the dictates of insurance underwriters who would not provide any building with financial protection unless it was within a "safe" distance from a fire company.[22] The concern of insurance underwriters continues to function as a tacit guarantee that no area of the city is allowed to exist without a minimum amount of fire protection.

By 1972 Fire Department analysts had devised a hazard rating system designed to evaluate the relative needs of fire protection for its fifty-eight geographically defined battalions throughout the city. This system categorized battalions according to two types of criteria: land use and fire risk. The city was first divided among commercial, industrial, hotel and theater, and residential districts. Then the residential areas were further divided according to their types of dwellings (private homes vs. apartment structures), fire protectiveness of their construction, and their rates of fire (high or low).

The need to categorize districts according to their land use is indicative of the different magnitude of responsibility imposed upon a fire department in comparison to the police. While police personnel are allocated according to the probability that people will be in an area, either as residents or transients, the fire department also has to maintain a capability to respond to areas where people neither live nor travel. An example of such regions is the warehouse areas on the West Side of Manhattan, or the industrial areas of Brooklyn and Queens, where few people live and relatively few people work. If the city does not maintain ample protection for these areas, then businesses within them are liable to lose their insurance. The city then runs the risk of having the firms move to another state and of losing needed revenue. Thus, a fire department must be more property or real estate conscious than a police department. This problem is also magnified by the fact that both business establishments and insurance companies are less likely to know how many policemen are stationed in a local precinct rather than how far a local fire company is in relation to a particular location.

The categorization of residential areas according to their type of dwellings is merely a quick and easy way of measuring population density. This serves as a means for estimating the relative demand for fire protection among battalions where people do in fact live. The designation of fire incidence categories serves as a similar demand indicator. Incidence rates, like considerations of population density, were formerly used as a proxy for determining how many fire companies were needed in an area to insure that one could respond to any emergency within a desirable period of time—the primary operational consideration of the department. These indicators were chosen because at the time of their use the department did not possess any more sophisticated techniques for analysis or prescription. Like the hazard ratings used in the Police Department prior to 1973, the hazard system of the Fire Department did not include any reliable or valid way for measuring or guaranteeing performance standards. It was this deficiency in the analytical capacity of the Fire Department that the Rand contract was meant to alleviate.

When the first group of Rand analysts came to the Fire Department in 1968, they found themselves in a fortunate position. The Fire Department had already key-punched an enormous amount of data on every fire which had occurred in the city since 1962. Therefore, the analysts had at their disposal a large data base for over one million alarms in computer-ready form. Computer card summaries included such information as the location, time, and type of each incident reported, in addition to information on the number of units responding to the incident and the amount of time it took to bring the matter under control.

In the initial phase of the Rand contract, city and fire officials in New York were concerned with addressing one particular problem: how could the Fire Department respond to the increasing demands being made upon it without supplementing its current manpower strength? By the beginning of 1969 the staggering increase in workload, particularly in high alarm areas such as the South Bronx, had become a key issue in a labor dispute between the Uniformed Fire Officers Association, its brother union the Uniformed Firefighters Association, and City negotiators.[23] The unions had been demanding the hiring of additional personnel in order to help alleviate the increasing demands that were being made upon the firefighting force. City officials, conscious of the ever-tightening budget situation, were reluctant to move in that direction at a very rapid pace.

Under pressure of the threat of job slowdowns and a possible strike, Fire Chief O'Hagan asked Rand to design a technique for defining the workload in the department and analyzing methods for its reduction. Rand had already been in the department for a year, and with the use of a simulation model was able to assess the probable impact of various proposals which were being circulated between the unions and agency officials. It was found that an increase in personnel, on the scale that was possible under the current budgetary restrictions, would not be an adequate means for alleviating the workload of those companies which were located in high alarm areas. Thus, the Rand analysts began to investigate the traditional dispatching policy of the department.

Until 1969 it had been a standard procedure in the Fire Department to dispatch three engine companies and two ladder companies to every alarm, whenever the amount of manpower available made it possible. However, an analysis completed by department officials had already shown that in 97 percent of all cases two engine companies and one ladder company would have been sufficient. If the standard number of companies dispatched to an alarm were reduced, then perhaps more companies would be available for service and the workload problems in high incidence areas could be addressed more effectively.

Rand utilized its simulation model to assess the probable impact of several alternative policies which might have been implemented. Through the use of several analytical models it began to formulate proposals which could be tested with the simulation. At the invitation of Chief O'Hagan, Rand's work became the basis for discussions taking place between department officials and the unions. In November of 1969 a settlement was finally reached. The City agreed to set up additional part-time companies in high incidence areas during peak alarm hours (3 p.m. to 1 a.m.). With the understanding that additional personnel would eventually be hired, the unions agreed to allow their members to man these Tactical Control Units on a voluntary basis.

A key ingredient of the 1969 settlement was the implementation of a new Adaptive Response system. Under Adaptive Response the standard dispatch policy was reduced to two engine companies and one ladder company. Coupled with the creation of Tactical Control Units, the implementation of Adaptive Response had the net impact of making more companies available to respond to alarms in high incidence areas and at the same time provided some relief for previously overworked personnel. The new system was initially tried on an experimental basis in the South Bronx. Later it was expanded to other high incidence areas in the city.

When Adaptive Response was inaugurated in 1969, it was hailed by many as a worthwhile innovation in municipal fire protection. Fire officials especially welcomed the idea that it might be possible to improve the performance of the department without a significant increase in expenditures. Moreover, through Adaptive Response the workload of heavy-duty companies could be alleviated without the necessity of relocating personnel from other areas in the city. Thereby city officials avoided the precarious type of decisions which make for political turmoil.

Unfortunately, however, Adaptive Response was only a temporary solution to the growing problems of fire protection in New York. Because of the poor financial situation which had developed, the City was unable to deliver on its promise to the unions to increase the manning level in the department. Thus, the unions, which felt duped, instructed their members to discontinue volunteering for duty in the Tactical Control Units. By the end of 1970 the TCUs were disbanded. Soon thereafter matters got even worse as the City had to face the imminent dilemma of actually reducing the number of fire companies remaining in operation. These decisions would require a basic analysis of allocation patterns throughout the city, and once again the Rand group was called upon for technical support.

Rand was asked to develop a model that would enable decision makers to know which performance levels could be achieved under any fixed amount of resources. The principal criterion for performance would be response time. It was hoped that with the use of the Rand model an allocation policy could be designed which would insure a minimum amount of protection for each location in the city and at the same time keep the overall average response time at a desirable level. A number of factors were analyzed, including:

1. travel distances
2. regional alarm rates
3. number of companies per region
4. service times of companies responding to different types of alarms

It was clear that the larger a region was, the more companies it would need to maintain safe response times. The busier that companies were in a demand region, the more would be needed to maintain an adequate availability of protection.

Through the efforts of Kenneth Rider, Rand constructed a Parametric Allocation Model.[24] This would enable Fire Department officials to accomplish a tradeoff between equalizing the average travel time and company workloads among battalions and keeping the citywide average travel time at a desired level. From the analysis of historical data on alarm rates and a consideration of the geographical characteristics of each region, the department was able to strike a balance between two types of demands for protection: the potential demands for service that were evident in all locations of the city and the actual demands for service that were evident in those areas where fire risks were the greatest.

As was the case with the PCAM system which was implemented in the Police Department, the design of a Parametric Allocation Model for fire services represented an attempt to utilize performance standards as a criterion for allocating agency manpower. Both systems were adopted as a technical means to help agency decision makers cope with a simultaneously increasing demand for services and decreasing resources. In November of 1972 the Fire Department announced that thirteen fire-fighting companies would be closed down. Seven of these would be relocated to other places in the city. Six would be permanently disbanded.

Patterns of Distribution. This section will begin with a presentation of 1973 data on the average per capita distribution of manpower and the average per capita rates of fire for battalions within each of the five racially defined categories being studied.[25] However, since response time is the key criterion of performance according to which fire companies are allocated, and the size of fire battalions in New York varies greatly (from .44 of a square mile to 27.37 square miles), manpower data and reported fire rates will be related to the area size of battalions. Therefore, the major part of the analysis in this section will focus on a comparison between the average number of personnel and the average number of reported fires per square mile among battalions in each population group.

As explained previously, it is the total number of available personnel per area rather than the number per resident which ultimately determines the amount of travel time which must be incurred before apparatus arrives at the scene of a fire. While population size may be used as a predictor of the demand for service in a given area, and therefore the availability of manpower within it, it is the total number of fires in an area which ultimately determines the probability that personnel will be free to respond to a given emergency.

Of the fifty-eight fire battalions that were in New York City in 1973, nine were classified by department analysts as non-residential. These comprise three battalions in lower Manhattan (1, 2, 5), four in the midtown area (6, 7, 8, 9), and two in the industrial areas of Long Island City, Queens (36, 45). Since this analysis is primarily concerned with the distribution of service among residential population groups, we will not include these nine battalions within the five categories being studied. To do so would only skew the average group data in misleading directions. For example, in 1973 the average residential battalion in the city had a manpower allocation of 33.67 firemen per square mile, a fire incidence rate of 433.55 fires per square mile, and an area of 5.97 square miles; the average non-residential battalion exhibited a manpower allocation of

82.87 per square mile, a fire incidence rate of 569.61 per square mile, and an average size of 1.81 square miles. These disparities between the residential and non-residential areas of the city raise some interesting questions in themselves, and they will be dealt with later in this section.

When one divides the forty-nine residential fire battalions according to their five population categories (see table 5.2), there is no readily discernible pattern among the racially defined groups with regard to per capita allocations of manpower, as was the case with police. A comparison of police and fire allocation data does reveal, however, that the range of per capita allocations among the groups is wider in the former than in the

TABLE 5.2
NYC FIRE DEPARTMENT SERVICE DATA 1

Racial groups	No. of batt.	Average 1973 alloc. per 1,000	Average fire rate per 1,000	Average pop. size	Average 1972 alloc. per 1,000
1. highly segregated white	20	1.23	11.09	184,012	1.24
2. segregated white	5	1.50	18.11	153,655	1.50
3. integrated	8	1.39	20.31	111,758	1.46
4. segregated minority	9	1.54	22.52	125,130	1.56
5. highly segregated minority	7	1.41	29.53	103,372	1.43
Citywide average (40 battalions)		1.37	18.04	146,782	1.39

latter. While average allocations of police personnel varied from 1.53 to 2.57 men per 1,000 population among the five groups, the range for fire manpower was merely 1.23 to 1.54 per 1,000. This appears to indicate that fire personnel were more evenly distributed among residential communities than were police, a finding which coincides with the stronger emphasis on balancing response times within fire protection services.

Further analysis of the per capita allocations in fire services does show a more favorable distribution of personnel among minority areas. Two of the three largest average deployments of manpower are found in group 4 (1.54 per 1,000) and group 5 (1.41 per 1,000), which have been categorized respectively as segregated minority and highly segregated minority districts. The lowest average per capita distribution of personnel (1.23 per 1,000) appears in group 1, which has been labeled highly segregated white.

An examination of the per capita rates of fire incidents in table 5.2 does show a clear pattern among the five racially defined groups. There is a steady increase in the average number of fires reported per 1,000 residents as one goes from the white areas of groups 1 and 2 (11.09 and 18.11, respectively) to the more minority-populated areas of groups 3, 4, and 5 (20.31, 22.52 and 29.53, respectively). These data are consistent with the results of a New York City Rand Institute study which shows a strong correlation between high incidence of fires and such

TABLE 5.3

NYC FIRE DEPARTMENT SERVICE DATA 2

Racial groups	No. of batt.	Average batt. size in sq. miles	Average 1973 alloc. per sq. miles	Average no. of fires per sq. miles	Average 1972 alloc. per sq. miles
1. highly segregated white	20	9.79	23.08	208.38	23.29
2. segregated white	5	6.16	37.34	451.79	37.34
3. integrated	8	2.23	69.51	1,017.94	73.09
4. segregated minority	9	2.52	76.59	1,118.26	77.38
5. highly segregated minority	7	1.44	101.39	2,119.44	102.78
Citywide average (49 battalions)		5.97	33.67	443.55	34.17
Non-residential (9 battalions)		1.81	82.87	569.61	88.95

environmental factors as population density, deteriorated housing, and minority group residence.[26] Thus, as is the case with police protection, black and Puerto Rican communities exhibit higher demands for fire service than do white communities.

Unlike the situation in the Police Department, however, this pattern of per capita demands for service is not reflected in terms of per capita allocations of manpower. This apparent disparity can be explained by the fact that personnel deployments in the fire service, which are more directly tied to the goal of reduced response times, are made in accordance with area needs rather than with the size of resident populations. An examination of the data in the first column of table 5.3 shows that the average size of fire battalions in the city steadily decreases as one goes from the white communities found in groups 1 (9.79 sq. mi.) and 2 (6.16 sq. mi.) to the minority communities in groups 4 (2.52 sq. mi.) and 5 (1.44 sq. mi.). Therefore, the average demands for service in terms of total area coverage and travel times is significantly less in the latter groups.

The actual linkage between the deployment of Fire Department man-power and the relative demands for fire service becomes most apparent when one compares the average data on manpower allocations and reported number of fires per square mile in the battalions found in each of our racially defined groups. As the data in table 5.3 indicate, there is a similar and consistent pattern on both counts. The average number of battalion personnel per square mile increases as one moves from groups 1 and 2 (23.08 and 37.34) through groups 3, 4, and 5 (69.51, 76.59, and 101.39). Likewise the number of reported fires per square mile increases as one goes from groups 1 and 2 (208.38 and 451.79) to groups 3, 4, and 5 (1,017.94, 1,118.26, and 2,119.44). Therefore, the data indicate that black and Puerto Rican communities in New York, which exhibit more severe demands for fire protection, also receive higher allocations of firefighting personnel per square mile.

Two significant questions remain to be addressed concerning the equity of resource allocations in the Fire Department. The first concerns how the forty-nine residential battalions in the city are served in comparison to the non-residential battalions. The second deals with the redistributive impact of the allocations which came about as a result of the cooperative effort between Rand and Fire Department analysts. The two issues are somewhat related.

In an earlier part of this section it was noted that the average non-residential battalion in the city was allocated 82.87 firefighting personnel per square mile, as opposed to a 33.67 allocation in residential battalions. The average rate of reported fires in non-residential battalions is 569.61 per square mile, while the average in residential battalions is 443.55. Despite the fact that the non-residential areas of New York's financial and commercial districts contain a large number of skyscrapers and other types of structures which have peculiar fire protection needs, it appears that they receive disproportionately high deployments of manpower in relation to their total number of fire occurrences.

Perhaps a further comparison of the data appearing in table 5.3 will put the matter in a more meaningful perspective. In analyzing the distribution patterns of residential battalions in the city, we have already observed a consistent increase in both manpower and fire rates per square mile as one moves from group 1 through group 5. When one compares the non-residential battalions in the city with these particular groups, the disparities become rather clear. The average manpower allocation of non-residential areas of the city (82.87) comes closest to that found in group 4 (76.59). However, while the average fire rate per square mile in group 4 is 1,118.26, that found among the non-residential battalions is merely 569.61.

Before attempting to explain this disparity, let us turn to the second question which has been posed: what was the distributive impact of the Rand-related reforms? This question can be most easily addressed by examining the allocation data for 1972, the period just prior to the deployment changes. The information appears in the final column of table 5.3. Insofar as the residential battalions of the city are concerned, the only one of our racially defined categories which endured an average reduction of more than one man per square mile was group 3. This group, which experienced an average reduction from 73.09 to 69.51 men per square mile, included all those battalions which were classified as integrated. Therefore, the reallocation of firefighting personnel which was announced at the end of 1972 did not appear to have penalized any particular racial community.

The largest reduction of manpower which occurred in 1973 took place in the non-residential districts of the city. These battalions suffered an overall average reduction from 88.95 to 82.87 men per square mile. The findings here are particularly significant in light of the disparities which were already observed between residential and non-residential battalions in 1973. They document the fact that such disparities were even more severe prior to the implementation of the Rand-related reforms. In this sense, the distributive decisions that were implemented seemed to have had a positive impact on the equitable allocation of fire protection services throughout the city. However, the question still remains as to why these redistributions were not carried even further.

The deployment technology developed by Rand in the early seventies provided fire officials in New York with the type of information required to make rational decisions concerning the efficient and effective utilization of their resources. However, in the final analysis such decisions are made in a highly complex organizational environment and therefore are not entirely of a technical nature. The distributive policy which emerged at the end of 1972 appears to have resulted in an equitable allocation of fire service among racial communities living in those battalions we have classified as residential. This policy also seems to have reduced a disparity of allocations we observed to exist between residential and non-residential districts in the city. However, from the information which we have analyzed, it appears that this disparity could have been reduced to a greater extent.

Although any explanation of these disparities is of a speculative nature, there is good reason to believe that at least part of the explanation is related to political considerations. As was noted in an earlier stage of this discussion, deployment decisions within the fire services remain among the most conspicuous and politically sensitive to be made in local government. By definition, the non-residential fire battalions in New York serve the needs of large commercial, financial, industrial, and entertainment establishments. These institutions not only provide a major source of revenue for the city, but together they represent some of the most influential business interests in the city.

At a time when deployment decisions in the Fire Department were made according to criteria set down in cruder, less sophisticated hazard rating systems, the latitude for political considerations in such decisions was significantly broader than it is today. It was these systems which led to the pre-1973 disparities. While the new technology of the seventies and the severe financial situation which led to its introduction provided public officials with a strong pressure to reduce that latitude, they may have been reluctant to move in a more drastic fashion than they did. Thus, the disparities remained, albeit in lesser magnitude, after 1973.

SANITATION

The New York City Sanitation Department is responsible for four major functions: the collection of residential solid waste; the disposal of residential, commercial, and industrial solid waste; street cleaning; and snow removal.[27] Seventy-five percent of its nearly ten-thousand-man uniformed force is employed in the Department's Bureau of Cleaning and Collection, which is concerned primarily with residential pickup and street sweeping services. In the 1972–73 fiscal year sanitation personnel collected 3,902,096 tons of refuse and swept 1,314,554 curb miles of street. While these figures represent a 41 percent increase in trash collection and a 78 percent increase in sweeping operations since 1960, the departmental workload had remained rather stable during the years immediately prior to the period studied.

The New York City Sanitation Department has been the beneficiary of a number of technological innovations which have brought about improvements in productivity. Among the more important are larger collection trucks, which increase collection time by requiring fewer trips to dumping areas, and mechanical broom trucks, which have virtually eliminated reliance on manual sweeping operations.

Despite these significant technological changes, managerial reform has often been a slow and difficult process within the Sanitation Department. Unlike police and fire personnel, who have been the beneficiaries of many training opportunities, a good deal of which were made available through federal funding, it is only recently that management-related training has received any form of priority in the Department of Sanitation.[28] Such manifestations of neglect have led to widespread feelings among members at all levels of this department that it is the last among equals of the three major uniformed services in the city. While a basic political dichotomy has often been observed between police and fire department managers and the organized members of their respective workforces, the career hierarchy in Sanitation has been known to share a strong sympathy with the attitudes and feelings of those men it manages.

In the late sixties and early seventies the Department of Sanitation did retain a group of in-house analysts in its Bureau of Industrial Engineers. However, the relationship between this small core of professionals and the operational hierarchy in the Bureau of Cleaning and Collection had always been rather tenuous. Career men spoke a different language from civilian analysts. Moreover, the career men were proud of the "street-wise" knowledge they had gained from many years of service on the force. They were reluctant to accept the managerial changes proposed by outsiders, who were often believed to be naive about the problems faced by the average "sanman." Many times carefully designed operational plans originating in the Bureau of Industrial Engineers were found stillborn in the Bureau of Cleaning and Collection. On one occasion a two-year engineering project intended to restructure broom routes throughout the city was never implemented into policy because operations chiefs did not feel they had played a significant enough role in its design.

By 1970 it was clear that no attempt at managerial reform would succeed within the Sanitation Department without the support and cooperation of those men who supervised the daily operations of the force. Therefore, when the management consulting firm of McKinsey and Company signed a contract with the City to devise methods for improving the productivity of the Sanitation Department, it adopted a strategy that would involve career men in both the design and implementation of the plan.

Method of Allocation. The Bureau of Cleaning and Collection, where 75 percent of the Sanitation Department's manpower is employed, is composed of 11 borough commands and 58 districts.[29] Approximately 80 percent of the man-hours in this bureau were dedicated to collection duties in 1972; 20 percent were associated with street cleaning functions. Thus, the major activity of this bureau and of the department was and still is residential trash pickups. The only diversion from this pattern occurs during the severe winter months when the Sanitation Department, and particularly the Bureau of Cleaning and Collection, assumes responsibility for removing snow and ice from the city streets.

Sanitation collections are usually carried out by three-man teams consisting of one driver and two loaders who man a compactor truck. The loaders are responsible for carrying trash containers from the curbside to the truck, loading the contents onto the truck, and returning the containers back to curbside. The driver takes the truck to the dumping areas when it is full. While loaders are supposed to assume manual street sweeping duties during the course of this trip, the fact remains that most street cleaning in the city is done by one-man operated mechanical broom trucks. These trucks cruise along curbsides and automatically remove any rubbish in their path. Sidewalk sweeping remains the responsibility of the public.

One of the distinguishing characteristics of sanitation technology is the easy measurability and predictability of the workload. Collection tasks can be measured in terms of tons of refuse to be collected; sweeping operations can be measured in terms of number of curb miles swept. The most reliable predictor of the demand for service in a particular district is its total population. The volume of solid waste which an area produces is directly related to the number of people who live there. Since commercial and industrial refuse is collected by private carters, the collection workload of the department is primarily responsive to the needs of residential populations.

Street sweeping operations do present an exception to this general rule, since this function is performed in all areas of the city. The demand for it tends to be relatively higher in several non-residential districts which are visited daily by large transient populations and require sweeping on a more frequent basis. One should be cautious, however, not to exaggerate the overall impact of this factor on the relative need for sanitation manpower throughout the city. It should be kept in mind that less than 20 percent of the total man-hours in the Bureau of Cleaning and Collection is devoted to the street cleaning function. Moreover, in those more numerous residential areas of the city where sweeping operations are conducted, population size continues to be the major indicator of the need for cleaning services. As one harried sanitation worker explained to this author, "It is people who litter the city streets. The more people there are in an area, the more likely it is that the streets will become dirty."

The next important factor for determining the need for sanitation manpower in a district is its actual geographic size. The total number of curb miles in a district directly affects both the distance and the time which collection or sweeping personnel must travel in order to complete their daily work tasks. Travel becomes an especially significant work factor in locations where population density is low and the families to be served are spread out over a large area. It is much more efficient on a per capita basis to serve a clientele which dwells in densely populated apartment structures than one which inhabits private or semi-private homes. In the former case, a sanitation crew can respond to the collection needs of a large number of families at a single stop; in the latter case travel time must be incurred between collections for each resident family. Therefore, while the absolute size of a population is directly related to the number of sanitation personnel it requires, population density (the number of people per block) is inversely related to the per capita manpower needs of a district so far as collection operations are concerned.

When the Department of Sanitation first contracted with McKinsey and Company in 1970 for the design of a productivity improvement project, it had already been struck with manpower reductions ordered from City Hall. It was decided at the time that the major part of the program would be concentrated on collection functions, where most of the department's resources are expended. Aware of the fate which befell previous reforms suggested by outsiders, the consultant staff took every precaution to assure that career personnel from the Bureau of Cleaning and Collection were involved in the project at the very outset. This strategy proved to be beneficial, for a good working relationship developed between the McKinsey people and the career men. As one of the original members of the project team elaborated to the author:

The McKinsey guys turned out to be pretty good. They had some good ideas, but they were also willing to listen to our suggestions. They asked questions and capitalized on our expertise. So we planned the project together. Once it was set up, then it became our baby. If you don't mind me saying so, I think it all worked very well.

The Productivity Improvement Project began with the appointment of a headquarters team from the Bureau of Cleaning and Collection. This team worked directly with the consultants in evaluating the current performance and procedures of the department and recommending change where it was deemed necessary. It consisted of an assistant chief of staff, an assistant borough superintendent, and a district foreman. All the team members were men with a minimum of fifteen years experience on the force who had literally worked their way up the ranks. Their participation in the project not only complemented the technical skills of hired analysts with street-wise knowhow, but it also provided the necessary departmental leadership required to inaugurate change. The basic formula carried out was to analyze, prescribe, and persuade. Thus, it may be said that the Productivity Improvement Project represented a human approach to management more than it did technological innovation.

The role of the headquarters team was to serve as a cadre for the selection and orientation of borough project teams in each of the department's eleven borough commands. A borough team would consist of an assistant borough superintendent and several district superintendents or foremen. Collectively the borough teams were assigned to evaluate the operations in each of the department's fifty-eight districts.

It was also stipulated in a project staff manual prepared by McKinsey consultants, in cooperation with the headquarters team, that borough team members would be chosen according to three specific criteria:

1. ability to gain confidence and respect of both officers and sanitationmen to sell their ideas

2. ability to act as self-starters

3. ability to solve problems on their own, yet be able to participate in the give and take of team discussions

Recruitment to a borough team might be considered a departmental reward. Selection was a recognition of one's leadership capability. Moreover, it provided an individual with an opportunity to work directly with men at the top of the departmental hierarchy, and successful participation in it might lead to further career advancement. One individual, who was a leader of the headquarters team, was eventually promoted to chief of staff, the highest position on the uniformed force.

The project was carried out by the eleven borough teams under the supervision of the headquarters team. Four distinct phases were implemented in each of the department's fifty-eight districts over a period of two years. These were:

1. statistical analysis of district performance

2. identification of productivity improvement opportunities from field observations

3. testing of assumptions and preliminary findings through experimental change

4. development and implementation of final recommendations

A borough team would spend approximately one month in each of the districts within its command. The first week would be spent reviewing daily and weekly records of operations that were kept in the district office. A number of factors were analyzed, including:

1. total tons of refuse collected

2. number of trucks used
3. tons collected per truck shift
4. number of full loads collected
5. number of partial loads collected
6. tons backlog
7. collections missed

The most important factors of consideration, however, were the total number of street miles in a district and a measure of "refuse density." Refuse density is a calculation of the number of tons collected per curb mile in a district. With the use of this concept the team would consider the volume of refuse collected in a district, its physical layout, and its population density. This permitted the team members to estimate more accurately the collection times and travel times of crews. The specified purpose of these measurements was to assist the team in establishing comparable performance standards for districts with similar characteristics.

Through an analysis of route structures and other work procedures, the borough team would begin to formulate its initial findings. These data would be discussed with the district superintendents and their foremen at the end of the first week. After this briefing the borough team would engage in a week of joint field observation with the district supervisors. The purpose of this exercise was to confirm or reject the initial findings. By the end of the second week specific recommendations would be jointly agreed upon concerning how operations in the district might be improved. Trucks were rerouted or reassigned in what was allegedly an attempt to equalize workloads for all districts and crews within the department.

During the third and fourth weeks the agreed upon suggestions would be implemented on a trial basis. At the conclusion of this period those experimental changes which proved successful were identified and implemented as permanent policy. Most of the route restructuring and reassignments took place within the boundaries of specific districts. Therefore, no major reallocations of manpower took place throughout the city as a result of the project. Yet, the methodology was indicative of the approach taken to resource allocations in the Sanitation Department.

It was hoped by the architects of the Productivity Improvement Project that their efforts would function to equalize performance standards among districts with similar service needs and in so doing improve the overall efficiency of the department. It took approximately two years to carry out the four-stage project among each of the fifty-eight districts within the city. The work which began in September of 1970 was finally completed on December 18, 1972. By July of 1973 some notable improvements were evident in the overall performance of collection services of the department. The tons of refuse collected per truck shift rose significantly from 8.7 to 10.3. The amount of missed collections, which was once about 10 percent of the total scheduled, was virtually eliminated.[30] The more efficient and effective utilization of manpower which evolved enabled the department to reduce the number of night collections from 15 percent to 4 percent of the total. The latter accomplishment not only reflected an improvement in the quality of service, with its substantial decrease in noise pollution during the evening hours, but it also led to a $1-million savings in night shift differential payments.[31]

It is difficult to ascertain the extent to which the productivity gains registered were directly related to the analytical and managerial efforts undertaken within the department. Part of the improvement might be accounted for by the introduction of new and better equipment. Some skeptics would argue that sanitation productivity automatically rises with personnel reductions because the total workload (in terms of tons of refuse to be collected) remains the same. These factors considered, however, the fact remains that within six months after the implementation of the Productivity Improvement Project, the City was receiving more work for a day's pay from sanitation workers than it had ever gotten before. These increases in productivity were also associated with observable and measurable improvements in the quality of service delivered to the public.

The basic questions still remain. Given the fact that the efficiency of sanitation collection services was improved, how were these services distributed throughout various parts of the city? Were these services responsive to the particular service needs of all the population groups with which this study is concerned?

Patterns of Distribution. As we have already explained in the prior section, total population is the most significant indicator for assessing the need for sanitation services in a given area. Therefore, our analysis of manpower distributions on a per capita basis (expressed in terms of sanitationmen per 1,000 residents) will provide us with a good starting point for measuring the equity of personnel allocations in the department.[32]

Since the City does not provide collection services to commercial and industrial establishments, sanitation services in the city on the whole remain very heavily a residential function in comparison to police or fire services.[33] Except for a few commercial areas in the city with peculiar demands for street cleaning activities, the non-residential responsibilities of the department do not tend to skew the per capita service needs among residential population groups. Therefore, it will not be necessary to exclude non-residential areas of the city from our analysis. In those cases where per capita service needs are skewed by peculiar demands for street sweeping operations, it will be noted.

It will be recalled that while population size tends to increase the total number of sanitationmen needed in an area, population density (the number of people per street mile) tends to decrease the per capita manpower requirements. The more densely situated a population group is, the less travel time there is accrued by a sanitation crew between residential pickups. In order to consider this factor in our analysis, the average per capita allocations for districts within each of the five racially defined groups will be compared to figures on population density. Population density will be expressed in terms of the average number of residents per street mile for districts in each group. This measure, which is a function of population and geographic size, will allow us to assess per capita manpower allocations in terms of per capita service needs.

Since population density tends to be higher in districts inhabited by blacks and Puerto Ricans, one might expect that the per capita sanitation requirements of these minorities is lower than that of whites. This expectation is supported by data which indicate that white middle class residents who buy more, eat more, and throw away more than poorer minorities tend to produce more refuse per capita than black and Puerto Rican families.[34] This general pattern of demand is somewhat modified by the fact that more densely populated areas of the city require and do receive more frequent street sweeping services. However, since less than 20 percent of the sanitationman's working hours are spent on sweeping operations, as opposed to collections, this factor cannot be expected to be significant enough to reverse the trend in total service needs.

At the time with which our study is concerned, manpower allocation data were reported in the Sanitation Department on the basis of a fiscal year. Since the Productivity Improvement Project was completed in December of 1972, this investigation of manpower distributions will focus on data for the 1973 fiscal year which encompasses the period from July of 1972 until June of 1973.

In FY 1973 the average sanitation district in New York had a manpower allocation of 1.20 personnel per 1,000 residents. It contained a total of 196 curb miles, a population of 135,551 residents, and a population density of 691.6 residents per street mile. As indicated in table 5.4, the average allocation of manpower among districts within the five racial groupings with which we are concerned ranged from a low of 1.04 to a high of 1.39 personnel per 1,000 population. This range was not nearly so wide as that observed within the police service (1.53 to

2.57), but slightly broader than that found in the fire services (1.23 to 1.54).

An analysis of the service data in table 5.4 does not reveal any such readily definable patterns of allocation or service needs among the five groups as those which were found within police or fire. For example, there is no constant trend in the per capita allocation of manpower as one moves from group 1 through group 5, nor is there a singular pattern of change in the population densities of the five groups. However, while the trend in neither variable is constant, the pattern of change for each variable tends to move in a similar direction. This is visually illustrated in the trend lines included in graph B.

TABLE 5.4
NYC SANITATION DEPARTMENT SERVICE DATA

Racial groups	No. of dists.	Average 1973 alloc. per 1,000	Average no. of street miles	Average pop.	Average pop. density*	Average 1971 alloc. per 1,000
1. highly segregrated white	32	1.23	232	127,596	549.9	1.31
2. segregated white	7	1.04	148	158,169	1,068.7	1.06
3. integrated	6	1.39	206	118,719	576.3	1.47
4. segregated minority	9	1.10	143	151,167	1,057.1	1.16
5. highly segregated minority	4	1.23	106	147,727	1,393.7	1.32
Citywide average (58 districts)		1.20	196	135,551	691.6	1.27

*Residents per street mile.

Graph B contains two superimposed scales. The ascending scale on the left side, which corresponds to the solid trend line, reflects the average manpower allocation per 1,000 residents in each of the five population groups. The descending scale on the right side, which corresponds to the broken trend line, refers to the average number of residents per street mile for each of the five population groups. The two scales are not meant to be proportionate, but are superimposed here to allow for comparison. A comparison of the two lines reveals some tendency whereby per capita allocations rise with a decrease in population density, but the pattern is

GRAPH B
NYC Manpower Allocations and Population Density in Sanitation Services

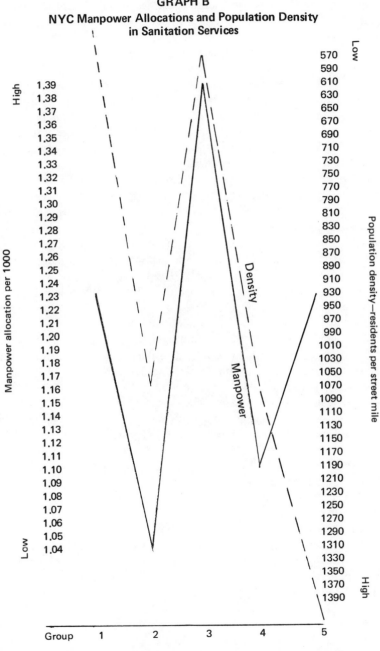

Manpower allocation per 1000

High

1.39
1.38
1.37
1.36
1.35
1.34
1.33
1.32
1.31
1.30
1.29
1.28
1.27
1.26
1.25
1.24
1.23
1.22
1.21
1.20
1.19
1.18
1.17
1.16
1.15
1.14
1.13
1.12
1.11
1.10
1.09
1.08
1.07
1.06
1.05
1.04

Low

Population density—residents per street mile

Low

570
590
610
630
650
670
690
710
730
750
770
790
810
830
850
870
890
910
930
950
970
990
1010
1030
1050
1070
1090
1110
1130
1150
1170
1190
1210
1230
1250
1270
1290
1310
1330
1350
1370
1390

High

Density

Manpower

Group   1   2   3   4   5

White ——————— Population ——————— Minority

not constant. The most significant break occurs with regard to group 5; a smaller break is evident in group 1. Let us consider the group data in more detail.

The population category which received the highest average per capita district manpower allocation of sanitationmen in February 1973 was group 3 (1.39 per 1,000). This group, which we have categorized as integrated, includes all districts which contain populations that are between 40 percent and 60 percent black or Puerto Rican (and conversely between 40 percent and 60 percent white). The large average size of its districts (206 street miles) leaves it with the second lowest average population density (576.3 residents per curb mile) of any group in the city. Group 3 contains a total of six districts. Of this total, three districts contain populations that are between 50 percent and 60 percent white; the other three contain populations which are between 40 percent and 50 percent white. When one compares the per capita allocations of its whiter and its more minority-based districts, it becomes apparent that the high average allocation figure of group 3 is really a function of large deployments in the three whiter districts. The average per capita allocation of these three districts is 1.64 per 1,000, significantly higher than the citywide average of 1.20 and the group average of 1.39. The average per capita allocation among the three minority-based districts is merely 1.13. These discrepancies can be explained, however, in terms of the per capita needs of the districts as related to their population densities. The average population density of the three whiter districts is 447.3; that of the minority areas is 734.6. These can again be compared to an overall group average of 576.3 and a citywide average of 691.6.

Those two groups with the lowest average per capita allocations in the city are group 2 (1.04 per 1,000) and group 4 (1.10 per 1,000). These groups, which are categorized as segregated white and segregated minority, respectively, have comparable need indicators which parallel their similarly small distributions of service personnel. Population density in group 2 is 1,068.7 residents per curb mile, while that for group 4 is 1,057.1.

The greatest disparity between sanitation district service needs and manpower allocations appears when one observes the data for groups 1 and 5. The districts within these groups display the same average per capita allocation of manpower (1.23). At that point, however, the similarity ends. Group 1 contains those districts with the highest average street mileage (232) and the lowest population density (549.9) of any in the city. In contrast, group 5 contains four districts with the lowest average street mileage (106) and highest population density (1,393.7) of any category.

Group 1 also includes three non-residential service districts with low populations and exceptionally heavy street sweeping responsibilities. These are District 1 in the downtown financial district of Manhattan and Districts 3 and 4 in the midtown area. The per capita allocations of manpower in these districts are especially high (1.71, 1.40, 2.16 per 1,000 respectively). Therefore, they tend to exaggerate slightly the average allocation of manpower in the residential white areas of their group.

A consideration of the data above indicates that group 1, which contains all districts which have 80 percent or more white populations, receives the lowest per capita allocation of manpower in terms of its measurable needs. While the average population density of its districts is the lowest among all the groups, their average per capita allocations of manpower are only slightly above the citywide average (1.20 per 1,000) and significantly lower than that of group 3 (1.39 per 1,000). This disparity between the indicator of need and the manpower allocation in group 1 is particularly significant in light of the fact that it contains thirty-two of the fifty-eight sanitation districts in the entire city.

There is little room for doubt that group 5, which comprises two districts from central Brooklyn (39, 40), a district in Harlem (10), and a district in the South Bronx (20), receives the highest per capita allocation of manpower in relation to its population density of any of the groups studied. While its districts contain the highest average population density of all the groups (1.393.7 per street mile), a factor which should drive the per capita allocation needs down, they receive the second highest per capita allocation of manpower (1.23 per 1,000 residents). Viewing these data from a comparative perspective, we find the most significant fact which emerges to be that, while the population group with the largest percentage of minority residents (group 5) displayed the disproportionately highest allocation of manpower, the group with the smallest percentage of minorities (group 1) displayed the disproportionately lowest allocation of manpower.

When asked about this apparent disparity between white and minority group areas, sanitation officials explained the matter in terms of a number of service-related factors. As was indicated before, areas with high population densities, such as those found in group 5, do have more severe per capita demands for street cleaning services than do low density areas. The higher concentration of people using the streets daily tends to cause these areas to accumulate more litter. Noting this factor, Sanitation Department officials pointed out that while low density areas in the city have their streets swept only once a week, high density areas received such services between three and five times per week in 1973.

The officials who were interviewed also explained the apparent disparities in manpower allocations in terms of the differing nature of the collection function in poorer minority areas. They asserted that while trash in middle class areas tends to be neatly packed, sometimes even bundled in plastic bags, which makes it easier for handling, waste containers in poorer areas are usually in a dilapidated state or may not exist at all. Therefore, the task of having to haul away unpackaged or poorly packaged refuse in the latter cases tends to increase the workload of crews in these areas. As one twenty-year veteran of the force explained it:

Working a collection route in a poor neighborhood is an altogether different kettle of fish. Many times you can't tell the difference between street litter and the garbage that people put out for collection. The cans are so broken down that more of the stuff winds up on the street than in the container. So you don't cart it, you pick it up with a broom and shovel.

Of course every landlord is supposed to supply his tenants with the proper containers. We have health codes which require it. But most of the landlords don't live in the buildings, so it's hard to enforce these laws. People have to dispose of their garbage somehow. Once they get it on the street, it's our duty to take it away no matter how it's put out.

We try to keep every neighborhood in the city clean, no matter what condition it is in when we find it. If we don't, the newspapers blame the department, not the negligent landlords. Then we hear it from the commissioner, and the flack comes all the way down the line.

What the sanitation officers are saying here is that there are qualitative differences in the workloads among districts which are not reflected in our quantitative assessment of service need (as indicated by population density). While there are no reliable data available to substantiate or reject these claims, they do seem reasonable. Thus, the testimony above provides at least a partial explanation to the disparities we have observed with regard to groups 1 and 5.

A comparison of the manpower data for the periods immediately prior to and following the implementation of the Productivity Improvement Project reveals that the most significant change to occur in the intervening years was a general reduction of the workforce. The average allocation of personnel to districts throughout the city was reduced from 1.27 per 1,000 residents in FY 1971 to 1.20 per 1,000 residents in FY 1973. A further analysis of these manpower reductions according to our five racial categories (see graph C) reveals an across-the-board cut for all groups, with higher reductions for those originally containing more personnel. Thus, as was expected, the Productivity Improvement Project did not result in any major reallocations of manpower among racial communities in the city.

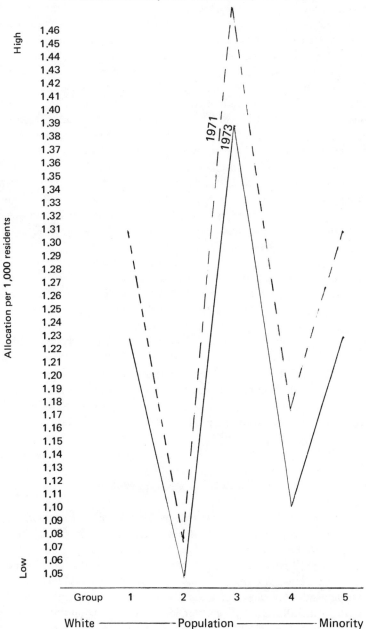

GRAPH C

NYC Sanitation Manpower Allocations, 1971, 1973

The Productivity Improvement Project carried out in the Sanitation Department represents a classic case of organizational cooptation. City officials, faced with an austere budgetary situation, sought to enact a program which would result in a better utilization of agency resources. By making career personnel a party to the change, its architects hoped to mitigate the level of resistance that could have been expected. The managerial and operational reforms which ensued came about as the product of a cooperative activity, perhaps a series of agreements, between high ranking career civil servants and their on-line supervisors.

The ultimate criteria by which the program must be judged concern whether it resulted in a sufficient amount of change to improve the effective utilization of manpower so as to improve productivity, and at the same time provide for an equitable distribution of service for the public. The data we have analyzed in this section seem to indicate that the project succeeded on both counts. The performance data on the operations of the department speak for themselves. They record a significant improvement in both the quantity and quality of service over the two-year period when the reforms were originally implemented.

On the final count, the data above also indicate that black and Puerto Rican districts in the city did receive an adequate share of sanitation manpower to address their service needs. This pattern was found to exist both prior to and subsequent to the productivity-related reforms. The key point of contention with regard to the equity issue revolves around the question of whether minorities received an excessively high allocation of manpower at the expense of the white neighborhoods in the city. Given the strong role which district superintendents and their foremen played in the development and implementation of the project, it is difficult to believe that any of these front-line supervisors would have accepted a complement of men which was not suitable for the service responsibilities of his jurisdiction.

SUMMARY AND ANALYSIS

The three case studies in this chapter have given us an opportunity to examine decision making in three traditionally organized public bureaucracies. We have analyzed how service needs are defined, where resources are allocated, and why allocations are not always made in direct response to needs. All three agencies we have studied were faced with urgent demands to perform their functions in a more efficient way at the time with which this study is concerned. Therefore, the allocation strategies which were carried out in each of these organizations were designed to a large extent to fulfill the traditional administrative goal of operational efficiency.

Despite efforts by agency officials to utilize their resources more effectively, these case studies serve to illustrate some of the institutional factors which restrain both the rationality and the efficiency with which things get done in a public bureaucracy. Contrary to the hopes of Wilsonian theorists, the cases show in varying ways that politics cannot be completely separated from the administrative process. As Simon has pointed out, rationality and efficiency are goals which public bureaucracies can only hope to approximate, some perhaps more than others, but rarely to the extent that the governmental organization is capable of accomplishing its service mission to an agreed upon "best way."

The case studies in this chapter are illustrative of three types of decision making environments which permitted agency officials to approximate the rational ideal with varying degrees of success. Their outcomes provide us with an empirical basis for judging whether traditionally organized hierarchic structures are capable of addressing the service needs of politically disadvantaged racial minorities in a fair and equitable manner.

The three types of decision making environments with which we are concerned may be classified as follows:

1. classical bureaucratic type in which decisions are hierarchically determined and implemented without interference or input from the lower echelons of the organization or the clientele being served

2. client-responsive type in which decisions at the top of an organizational hierarchy are influenced by considerations of the preferences of the clientele being served

3. labor-responsive type in which decisions made at the top of an organizational hierarchy are sensitive to the wants, needs, and preferences of individuals at the operational levels of the organization

The classical bureaucratic type of decision making environment is epitomized by the way deployment policy was formed in the Police Department. While in many cases the New York Police Department exhibits the characteristics of a labor-responsive type of system, as do all agencies with strong unions, those characteristics were not manifested in this case. The classical bureaucratic approach to deployment decisions was made possible by the fact that information on the relative distribution of manpower was limited to but a few officials who sat at the top of the police hierarchy. These individuals, therefore, allocated manpower as they saw fit with little or no interference from anyone else from either inside or outside of the organization.

The client-responsive type of decision making environment is most clearly illustrated by the way deployment decisions are made in the

Fire Department. Because the allocation of fire companies is a policy output which is easily observable, these decisions are among the most politically sensitive. Therefore, the outcome suggests that they seem to have been made with particular attention to the interests of the more politically powerful among the client population.

The labor-responsive type of decision making environment was represented in two cases. It is most clear in the Sanitation Department, where executive, middle, and first line managerial and supervisory personnel all participated in the planning and implementation of the operational reforms that were carried out. The labor-responsive type of environment was also evident in the Fire Department, for it was the workload issue that was raised by the unions which finally led to a reexamination of the dispatching and deployment policies of the department.

It should be emphasized that, while the decision making environments in the Sanitation and Fire departments seemed to have allowed for a consideration of the policy preferences of either or both of the internal workforce and the external clientele, in neither case did the upper level of the organizational hierarchy lose control of the decision making process. Ultimately the decision making prerogative remained in the hands of the established organizational hierarchy in each of the agencies we have observed. There was not even any clear evidence of direct client participation in the distributive decisions of the Fire Department. In this sense, the three organizational environments we have analyzed all fit rather easily into the institutional classification we have identified with the old public administration.

An examination of manpower allocations among residential districts in all three departments has revealed a discernible pattern in which black and Puerto Rican neighborhoods received larger distributions per person and per square mile than did white communities. These distributions can generally be associated with similar allocations of large capital equipment such as patrol cars for policemen, ladder and pumper trucks for firemen, and collection trucks and mechanical sweepers for sanitationmen. The more favorable distributions to minority areas were generally consistent with quantifiable indicators of more intense service needs, although the relationship between allocations and needs appeared to be closer in the emergency services than in sanitation.

This compensatory allocation policy towards minorities was most apparent in the Police Department, which we have classified as a classical bureaucratic type. The police actually utilized two types of deployment methodologies, one designed to provide all citizens with a minimal and safe standard of service, the other meant to meet the particular needs of high-crime precincts. This latter group of high-crime precincts was found predominantly in minority areas of the city.

There appeared to be a similar compensatory policy among residential districts in the Fire Department which resulted in more firefighting personnel per square mile in areas with higher alarm rates. However, a comparison between residential and non-residential districts in this client-responsive organizational environment has shown that the more influential business districts of the city have managed to receive better protection than residential ones. This finding illuminates the core of the difference between classical bureaucratic decision making environments and those we have classified as client-responsive. The more political the process of resource distribution becomes, the more likely it is to favor those who already possess political influence.

One of the most interesting developments which emerges from the case studies in this chapter concerns the role which labor, in its organized and operational forms, plays in determining the outcome of distributive decisions. It is directly relevant to the equity issue and the predicament of our minority populations whose service needs are the most severe and whose political influence tends to be wanting.

We have seen that the equalization of workloads was a key factor in the deployment strategies which were carried out in each of the services that were studied. More ostensibly, it was the officers' and firefighters' unions in the Fire Department which demanded an increase in manning levels in order to alleviate the intense workload of companies in the South Bronx and other troubled areas. It was in the labor-responsive environ-ment of the Sanitation Department that minorities appeared to have received the highest allocation of agency resources in terms of the quantitative measures of service need that were available. By continuing to demand equalities in workload, labor may emerge, although in an indirect and unconscious way, as a major force in favor of the equitable distribution of service-related resources to minority areas where demands for service tend to be so exacting. Such a development would also have serious implications for the prospects of decentralized government in New York. We will consider these implications in the next chapter.

6

BUREAUCRACY AND REPRESENTATIVE GOVERNMENT
The Research Findings

The fundamental issue posed in the foregoing study involves the capability of traditional bureaucratic institutions to fulfill the normative ideal of representativeness. The particular focus of the research dealt with an investigation of the degree of representation which was provided to black and Puerto Rican minorities in New York City during the years of the Lindsay administration.

In an introductory discussion appearing in the first chapter, it was explained that the concept of representation may be understood at three distinct levels of analysis:

1. formal representation, which is related to the criteria by which public officials are selected

2. descriptive representation, which is concerned with the degree to which the social composition of the government reflects that of the general population

3. interest representation, which concerns whether the government acts according to the wants and needs (interests) of the citizenry which it serves

The manner in which individuals are selected for public service is significant from the perspective of the representative norm because it determines the prospects which each individual or group enjoys of having its potential advocates chosen for positions within the government. From a seemingly more practical perspective it is significant because it determines the level of employment opportunity which individuals are afforded within the public service.

In recent years we have witnessed a growing commitment on the part of the federal government and the courts to insure that the formal mechanisms by which individuals are recruited for public service are fair and not unjustly discriminatory. However, we have also seen that, because of the difficulty involved in evaluating the validity of merit examinations and other criteria for qualification, those responsible for protecting the right of equal employment opportunity have become increasingly reliant upon investigating the level of descriptive representation found within public agencies as a means of assessing the formal system of selection. Thus, an investigation of the descriptive representation within public agencies is important on two counts. While it most directly provides one with a barometer for determining whether the social composition of the government is similar to that of the public being served, tests for descriptive representation are also used as a basis for assessing the fairness of formal recruitment practices.

Even in those cases where descriptive representation is found to exist within a government or its agencies, there is no guarantee that the "interests" of the entire citizenry will be protected. Interest representation is more primarily concerned with the products of the policy process than with the identity or characteristics of the participants in that process. Therefore, its existence is most easily tested by analyzing the manner in which public goods and services are distributed among people.

The research in the present study was carried out in two distinct parts. The first was concerned with ascertaining the level of descriptive representation which has been afforded black and Puerto Rican minorities in New York City government as a result of a recruitment policy based upon the traditional merit system. The second was concerned with analyzing the allocation of service-related resources among the same groups by three traditionally structured bureaucratic organizations (the Police, Fire, and Sanitation departments).

It was hypothesized that blacks and Puerto Ricans in New York do enjoy descriptive representation within the local government bureaucracy and receive an equitable share of service-related resources from city agencies. Descriptive representation was defined as a situation in which the racial composition of the civil service workforce proportionately resembles that of the city population as a whole. An equitable distribution of service-related resources was defined as one in which allocations are made on the basis of relative community needs.

EMPLOYMENT

Making use of an employment census which was completed by the City Commission on Human Rights in 1971, the descriptive representation of minorities in New York has been analyzed on several levels. These include the general representation of minorities across the entire workforce and representation by agency, occupational level, and salary range. A comparison was also made of the general representation which was found to exist in 1971 with that which was made evident in a previous employment census completed by the Human Rights Commission in 1963. The latter comparison is significant in light of the fact that the Lindsay administration had implemented a number of social and reform programs, many of which were federally supported, in the years which elapsed between the two censuses. These programs were designed to increase the local employment opportunities for minorities and to sensitize the merit system of recruitment to the particular circumstances of the socially and culturally disadvantaged.

General Representation. On the whole, minorities were found to be well represented in the local civil service, holding a slightly higher percentage of city jobs than would have been required for proportional representation. These data are particularly significant given the fact that the proportion of minorities who are of working age was found to be lower than that of whites. On the whole, minorities in New York also tend to be less educated than whites, which puts them at a competitive disadvantage insofar as merit qualification is concerned.

When the representation of minorities was analyzed in more detail, it was found that while blacks were somewhat overrepresented in the citywide workforce, Puerto Ricans were underrepresented. This pattern is similar to a national pattern that became evident from a review of the research literature. It is usually associated with the fact that Puerto Rican Americans, like Mexican Americans, suffer from severe educational and language barriers that serve to distinguish them even from other minority groups.

When the employment data for 1971 were compared with those of 1963, it was found that the representation of minorities in the local civil service had improved both absolutely and in comparison to their general representation in the citywide population. While no direct connection can be made between these improvements and the variety of employment programs and reforms that were conducted during the intervening years, it is fairly safe to conclude that these federally financed and locally initiated efforts did exert a positive impact on the situation of minorities.

Representation by Agency. The 1971 data did document a tendency on the part of minorities to cluster within those agencies which are particularly concerned with servicing the needs of their own people. Even Puerto

Ricans, for example, who were underrepresented in the City workforce on the whole, were found to be overrepresented in housing-related services. Blacks were more concentrated in the health and social welfare fields. The underrepresentation of minorities was found to be most severe in the field of education and in the uniformed services (e.g., police, fire, and sanitation).

The tendency of minority civil servants in New York to cluster within agencies that are particularly concerned with disadvantaged clientele is consistent with a national pattern which was evident from the research literature. This pattern may be indicative of a strong social consciousness on the part of minorities who enter the public service. While some critics of the merit system have claimed that such concentrations are the result of discriminatory and unfair hiring practices in white-dominated public agencies, there is not sufficient data available from the present research either to confirm or reject these allegations.

Representation by Occupational Level. The one finding in the New York City research which greatly distinguishes it from the national trend is that which concerns the distribution of minorities by occupational levels. Despite the facts that minorities on the whole are less educated and less likely to be of working age than whites, they were proportionately well represented at the higher occupational levels of the City workforce. This was particularly true at the official, administrator, and technician categories but somewhat less so in the professional classification.

The one exception to the general rule among minorities was the case of Puerto Ricans, who were found to be concentrated at the lower levels of the occupational hierarchy. This latter finding once again appeared to be a function of the educational and language deficiencies suffered by many Puerto Ricans in the city. It ran in striking contrast to the situation observed among better educated non-Puerto Rican Hispanics and Asians who were found to be overrepresented by 100 percent in professional level jobs.

Representation by Salary Range. The most negative finding of the research is that concerned with the representation of minorities at better pay grades. Despite the facts that minorities were found to be well represented in the city government on the whole and well represented at the higher occupational levels, they have fared rather poorly with regard to the level of compensation they receive for their work. The only exception to this rule was the case of that group which was categorized as other minorities, who were found to be significantly overrepresented in the professional classification.

This poor showing of minorities with regard to salary might be seen as a counterweight to the more positive results that were indicated by the other findings. For example, while the representation of minorities at the higher occupational levels of the local civil service may serve to enhance the influence which these groups enjoy within city government, their failure to match occupational status with monetary compensation may function to decrease the role which public employment plays as a vehicle for social mobility.

The analysis in chapter 4 suggests that such disparities in pay grade are less related to the civil service system than they are to the collective bargaining practices which have become commonplace in New York. Minorities do not do well in this process because the unions where they are most strongly represented have failed to gain the degree of local influence that has been enjoyed by those collective bargaining units which are the stronghold of the city's older ethnic groups. In this sense, the salary predicament of minorities appears to be more a function of their social and political status in the city than it is of the formal civil service.

DEPLOYMENT

The second part of the research performed in this study involved an examination of manpower allocations in the Police, Fire, and Sanitation departments of the city. While manpower constitutes only one service-related resource, the manpower distributions which were studied can generally be associated with similar allocations of large capital equipment such as patrol cars, engine and ladder trucks, sanitation collection trucks, and mechanical sweepers.

The distributive policies which are carried out in the Police, Fire, and Sanitation departments in the city are a significant matter of consideration from at least two perspectives. To begin with, all three of these departments are responsible for the delivery of essential local services to the public. Second, and more important for the purposes of this study, all three are ones in which the descriptive representation of minorities was found to be low. Thus, an analysis of the allocations in these three departments will allow us to determine whether a public agency which lacks descriptive representation is capable of representing the interests of all groups which are dependent upon its services.

General Patterns of Distribution. An examination of the deployment strategies followed in the three agencies studied showed that there was a general commitment on the part of decision makers in each of them to allocate resources on the basis of clearly defined indicators of service need. While the designated purpose of this approach was to achieve a more efficient utilization of agency resources, this approach was also supported by a labor-oriented demand for the equalization of workloads among personnel. This strategy also resulted in a rather equitable distribution of service-related resources among population groups throughout the city.

The pattern of distribution tended to favor minority areas where service needs were found to be the most severe. This pattern was even found to persist within the Sanitation Department, where the more pronounced service needs of minorities was less apparent according to the quantitative data. Therefore, it can be said that although minorities did not enjoy descriptive representation in these three agencies, their interests were well represented in terms of the responsiveness which was shown for their service wants and needs.

Police Distributions. The most straightforward policy of deployment observed in the three agencies studied was that found within the Police Department. The decision making environment in that agency was classified as classical bureaucratic. While the deployment strategy which was carried out was designed to equalize the workload among personnel and respond to the peculiar service needs of each community, deployment decisions were made in a hierarchic, almost "corporate" fashion with no evident input or interference from the lower echelon of the organizational structure or outside client groups. In accordance with the standard of equity which has been defined, the policy which emerged insured a minimum level of police protection for all locations in the city and provided supplementary protection to those areas where the needs were more severe. While the reallocation of resources which was carried out in 1973 functioned to redistribute some manpower out of the high-crime precincts, the final pattern of distribution continued to favor this latter group.

Fire Distributions. The decision making environment in the Fire Department has been described here as client-responsive. While citizen groups did not directly participate in the deployment decisions that were made in this case, the environment of the department is client-responsive in the sense that the impact of its distributive policies is more apparent to the public and therefore more likely to spark a community reaction when disfavorable to any particular group. Therefore, fire officials must be more alert to the anticipated responses of community groups when making decisions concerning "who gets what" in terms of protection.

As was the case in the Police Department, the deployment policy in the Fire Department was designed to provide each residential area in the city with a minimum level of protection needed and to compensate the high incidence residential areas with more personnel per square mile. In this sense, the Fire Department policy seemed to be fair, equitable, and responsive to the peculiar service needs of minority neighborhoods. However, when a comparison was made between the deployments in residential areas with those in non-residential areas, it was found that the latter were receiving disproportionately high allocations in terms of their rates of fire incidence. This disparity was somewhat reduced as a result of the productivity-related reforms implemented at the end of 1972. Yet, the redistribution which was then brought about was not as drastic as what could have measurably been absorbed by the non-residential areas of the city.

Sanitation Distributions. The decision making environment in the Sanitation Department has been described as labor-responsive. This designation stems from the fact that the distribution of manpower which came about under the Productivity Improvement Project was the result of cooperative agreements made between career executives and middle and lower level line managers. It should be emphasized, however, that the process by which personnel were deployed in the department was not a wholly subjective one. The designated purpose of the Productivity Improvement Project was to increase the efficiency of operations in the department and to establish similar performance standards for districts with comparable service needs. The measurable increases in departmental productivity which were observed at the completion of the project speak for themselves.

During the course of the project personnel were assigned and collection routes restructured on the basis of quantitative calculations of refuse density. In accordance with the methodology which was adopted, population density became the most reliable predictor of per capita allocations among service districts. While there was no clear-cut pattern of association between the racial identity of district populations and manpower allocations, as was the case in the emergency services, a certain disparity was found in favor of minorities. Departmental officials explained the disparity in terms of qualitative differences in service needs among the racially defined population groups.

One cannot overestimate the role which concerns for equalized workloads had in determining the final outcome of deployment patterns within the labor-responsive environment of the Sanitation Department. It is interesting to note that, of the three services studied, the Sanitation

Department was the one in which districts with a high proportion of minority populations received a greater allocation of manpower than the quantitative indicators of service need would have required. This pattern serves to underline a certain commonality of interest between labor's concern for equalized workloads among personnel and minority group concerns for service equity. This commonality of interest was also clearly illustrated in the workload dispute which emerged in the Fire Department as a result of the intense demands being made upon firefighting personnel in the South Bronx and other high incidence neighborhoods of the city.

THE COMMON THREAD:
EMPLOYMENT AND DEPLOYMENT DISTRIBUTIONS

The research summarized in the preceding pages serves to support the two-point hypothesis which has been proposed concerning the condition of minorities in New York City:

1. Under a formal system of recruitment based upon the merit system, minorities were provided with a proportionate share of jobs within the local civil service.

2. Under a hierarchic system of organization operating according to predetermined standards of efficiency, minorities received an equitable share of public service in accordance with their peculiar service needs. Thus, it may be concluded that, on the whole, minority groups enjoyed both descriptive representation and interest representation within the traditional bureaucratic institutions of the city government during the years of the Lindsay administration.

The research has also shown that there were certain discontinuities from the general patterns of representation which were found to exist in the local bureaucracy. These discontinuities which were observed are interesting in and of themselves, for they serve to emphasize an underlying theme which is basic to the lesson to be drawn from the present study: the greatest disparities in the allocation of both jobs and services are those which were associated with those aspects of the bureaucratic system which were most sensitive to political considerations and the forces of local influence.

Insofar as the employment research is concerned, the one level of the local bureaucracy where minorities were found to be underrepresented was at the higher pay scales. The foregoing analysis suggests that this outcome was less related to the formal structure of the civil service than it was to the highly politicized process of collective bargaining in the city. With regard to the deployment research, the greatest disparity between quantitative indicators of service need and resource allocations was found in the Fire Department, where the environment was described as client-responsive. While the distributive outcome there did not penalize minorities in particular, it worked to the advantage of the more influential business interests of the city and to the loss of all residential population groups.

The point to be made here can be stated rather simply: contrary to the claims of many contemporary reformers who would further politicize the administrative process through decentralization, there seems to be a practical affinity between the traditional bureaucratic goal of political neutrality and the normative ideal of social equity.

IMPLICATIONS FOR DECENTRALIZED GOVERNMENT

There is no sure way of predicting what form the decentralized governments of the near or distant future will take in American cities. There are some indications in the existing research literature that decentralized government has resulted in increased satisfaction with the quality of local services. Yet, despite the hope for more representative administrative institutions, citizen participation in community elections has been excessively low. There have also been some serious questions raised concerning how representative of their communities participants in these local contests have actually been. If decentralization is going to be a successful venture from the point of view of the representative norm, its architects will need to overcome a long history of voter apathy towards local government elections and an endemic feeling of alienation within poor and minority neighborhoods.

The history of decentralized government in New York City has not been an altogether encouraging one. For example, while participation in federal anti-poverty program elections has been extremely low, both the Community Action and Model Cities experiments have served as catalysts for bitter rivalry and discord among black and Puerto Rican residents of the affected areas. In attempting to implement a plan for decentralized government, former Mayor John Lindsay met such formidable local resistance from established interests that he was forced to retreat from his original program of reform. Yet in 1975 the voters of New York approved a new City Charter which will bring about a moderate form of decentralized government in their city.

The most direct consequence of the new institutional arrangement to be established is a changeover in the decision making environment from one which is basically bureaucratic to one which is more client-responsive.

The major difference between the present institutional arrangement and the client-responsive institutions of the future is that in the latter community groups will be provided with a direct channel of access to the decision making process of government. According to the new City Charter, community boards have been granted advisory power on matters relating to land use, budgeting, and service monitoring. The extent and manner in which local boards will be allowed to utilize this advisory power remain to be seen. In the long run, however, the success of this experiment in community government must be measured in terms of the comparative merits of the present institutional arrangement. The research appearing in the preceding pages indicates that such criteria for success will not make for an easy task.

One of the greatest dangers inherent in the recent mandated charter reforms is the potential for a further politicalization of the administrative process manifest by a conversion of the distributive process from a technical operational procedure to a contest of local influence. Such a development might work to the disadvantage of the poor, who currently appear to enjoy an equitable distribution of services which is responsive to their social needs but who may not possess the local political influence to maintain that state of affairs.

As information on resource allocations becomes a matter of public knowledge, it is conceivable that representatives of more influential middle class communities will begin to demand a more equal distribution of service benefits throughout the city. In the long run, the participation of communities in decisions concerning the distribution of public services may result in a reallocation of resources in favor of the middle class, while black and Puerto Rican communities are told that they will have to do with less, regardless of their needs. It is an unfortunate but undeniable fact of political life that those who enter political contests with greater social resources usually end up with the greater rewards. Our own research has shown that the most severe inequities of the current distributive process, in terms of both jobs and services, are those associated with the political aspects of local decision making.

The present study also suggests, however, a commonality of interest between communities with severe service needs and the public employees who are required to address those needs. Both have a stake in insuring that adequate public resources are made available so that services can be delivered in a manner which protects the welfare and safety of the civil servant and community resident alike. This common interest may become more apparent as the distributive process and its outcomes become more open and subject to public scrutiny. Perhaps, therefore, the demand by public employees and their unions for a fair distribution of work responsibilities will provide the necessary leverage to maintain an equity in the distribution of public services.

In the final analysis, however, the only true safeguard of social equity under the administrative reforms that are anticipated will be found in the design of the distributive process itself. Hence, the ultimate responsibility will lie with those public officials who are charged with implementing the newly decentralized system that is mandated under the broad guidelines of the City Charter. It will be their responsibility to insure that community government is not allowed to degenerate into a contest of "who gets what" for shouting the loudest. It will be their responsibility to maintain objective standards of service need, such as those which are currently in existence, so that public goods and services are allocated in an efficient, economical, and equitable manner.

One of the great advantages of decentralized government is that it provides a channel of communication whereby citizens are able to articulate their peculiar service preferences. However, these preferences must be evaluated within the parameters of fixed formulas of service need. These formulas should be designed to provide a minimum level of service for all citizens throughout the city and additional service for those communities with extraordinary needs. Under such an arrangement it will be possible to reap the benefits of both a centralized and decentralized system of administration, combining rational technical planning with an awareness of the service priorities of the citizenry being served.

7

BUREAUCRACY AND SOCIAL
JUSTICE
A Conclusion

John Rawls has proposed a theory of justice which calls for a system in which social and economic inequalities are arranged so that (1) the greatest benefits are given to the least advantaged, and (2) they are attached to offices and positions open to all under fair equality of opportunity.[1] In the latter part of his prescription Rawls comes out in favor of a system of selecting public officials on the basis of some form of merit. In this sense, he is in accord with the general principles of selection by which individuals are currently chosen for the civil service. However, Rawls goes beyond the career open to talent principle of the traditional merit system in that he fixes upon the privilege of public office the responsibility of not turning it into a private benefit. Thus, his first priority calls for a form of distribution which allocates public goods and services to the benefit of the socially disadvantaged.

Rawls's system of distribution has been found here to contain several positive attributes that are both within and beyond the realm of ethics. It is rational in the sense that it leads to a direct fulfillment of the normative ideals of the liberal democratic society he describes. It is economically efficient in the sense that it utilizes public resources where they can exert the greatest impact. It is "non-political" in the sense that it calls for an allocation of goods and services on the basis of social need rather than social influence.

The present study has been concerned with the feasibility of applying Rawls's ethical system to a particular social environment, the administrative branch of government. In a previous discussion it was noted that there does exist a logical tension between the equal opportunity principle and a competitive merit system of recruitment. The traditional merit system is, in reality, one which provides equal opportunity for all those who have the technical qualifications for office. Thus, the socially deprived are placed at a competitive disadvantage within the process of selection. As is the case in the Rawlsian system, the civil service system of merit recruitment can be used to deny the disadvantaged descriptive representation within the government. A review of the literature on public employment in the United States has illustrated this quite clearly. It shows that, on the whole, minorities have been unable to successfully compete for positions within the higher civil service. While the results of the present New York study were more positive concerning minorities in general, the competitive disadvantage of the poor was manifest by the weak showing made by Puerto Ricans, the most depressed minority group in the city.

Rawls's system of justice would compensate the poor for their competitive disadvantage in the recruitment process with a distributive process which works in their favor. Given the fact that politics basically involves a contest between self-serving parties, the key issue concerning the application of Rawls's system in an administrative environment relates to the capability of our bureaucratic institutions to make allocations in the same way. Thus, the question was posed: does a formal system of recruitment which may deny descriptive representation to some groups possess the capability to represent the interests of the entire citizenry?

If the traditional literature of public administration that has been reviewed here is to be taken seriously, then, at least on a theoretical level, our bureaucratic institutions are capable of replicating the distributive formula of Rawls's system. We have been told by some of our more eminent scholars that bureaucracy provides us with an institutional means for the rational pursuit of social ends. These ends have been defined in terms of the democratic ideals of representativeness and social justice. We have been told by the same thinkers that bureaucratic institutions are capable of achieving high levels of operational efficiency. This efficiency has been defined in terms of the economical and effective utilization of public resources. Finally, we would be led to believe that there is an aspect of bureaucratic activity which proceeds in an objective and politically neutral fashion. Hence we may appropriately inquire, "How well has the distributive process within bureaucracy served our disadvantaged communities?"

The research in the present study has shown that there is an aspect of bureaucratic decision making which is rational, efficient, and largely removed from the political process. Such decision making has resulted in a distribution of public goods and services that is responsive to the needs of the poor. Thus, the traditional principles of public administration are not only attainable in the real world of government, but they may also serve as a vehicle for the attainment of social equity within the bureaucratic process of distribution. Given the fact that the three public agencies chosen for our distributive analysis were all ones in which minorities did not enjoy proportional representation, it may also be concluded that bureaucratic institutions which lack descriptive representation are capable of representing the interests of all people.

Lest the positive findings of the present study be exaggerated, certain qualifications are in order as we move from the specifics of these particular cases to a more general proposition concerning bureaucracy and social justice. It is not the intention here to suggest that all bureaucratic institutions allocate their goods and services in an equitable manner. Therefore, a question remains concerning the circumstances that led to the policy outcomes found. Moreover, it is important to recognize the present limits of bureaucratic institutions in attaining our normative ethical ideals. Such a recognition will provide us with more realistic expectations concerning the performance of these institutions and a more concrete basis for their improvement.

THE CONDITIONS OF A JUST BUREAUCRACY

We have seen that there are those students of the subject who would ably argue that bureaucracy is merely an extension of the normal political process. Thereby they would deny the validity of the supposed politics-administration dichotomy. For example, Freeman, Rourke, Wildavsky, and others have demonstrated that public bureaucracies often find themselves reliant upon powerful interest groups for support in order to maintain their own viability within the political and governmental process.[2] Thus, it is often the case that these institutions are not capable of allocating their resources without catering to the needs of those clientele who make their appeals for service from a powerful political vantage point. The evidence of these studies notwithstanding, the preceding case studies have shown that some public bureaucracies are capable of making distributive decisions on an objective basis which addresses the needs of those who are not influential. Thus, the obvious question which arises is: what were the conditions which made the latter developments possible?

One characteristic which the three city agencies shared is that each delivered such a vital service to all the residents of the city that none was ever in a position where its political viability or support was seriously threatened. While some groups dispute the manner in which things get done in these departments, the existence of a police, fire, or sanitation department in the city is rarely challenged. Because of the general public acceptance of their functions, none of these agencies was ever reliant upon a particular client group for political or institutional support. Thus, decision makers within these organizations acted in a relatively interference-free political environment.

In the latter sense, it may be said that managers in the three city agencies were, to a large extent, able to proceed in a businesslike fashion in accordance with the efficient pursuit of their operational objectives. Janowitz has observed a similar decision making environment in the military,[3] where reliance upon outside group support for survival is limited because of the general acceptance of the defense function. Likewise James R. Schlesinger has explained the successful implementation of new management systems in the Defense Department in accordance with the advantageous degree of autonomy and freedom which that agency enjoys for operating without interference from outside parties.[4] Thus, one of the preconditions for the efficient operation of a public bureaucracy appears to be that its organizational goals address such a vital public function that it is not reliant upon any specific client group for institutional support.

The favorable situation of performance-oriented managers in the city agencies was further augmented by the fact that their operational objectives were consistent with the concerns expressed by their own personnel. Allocating service-related resources on the basis of community need allowed these organization managers to distribute the day-to-day workload among personnel evenly. Therefore, their operational decisions did not receive any internal organizational resistance.

Henceforth, it may be concluded that there are two conditions which allowed the three city agencies to allocate their resources in a rational, efficient, and equitable manner:

1. Each was responsible for providing such an essential public function that it was not reliant upon any specific client group for support;

2. Each had managed to carry out its operational objectives with relatively little or no internal organizational resistance.

These conditions have significant implications insofar as the general capacity of local administrative institutions are concerned. Local governments are involved in the delivery of a wide variety of essential services to the entire public, and in this sense are less specialized than federal agencies in the clienteles which they serve. Moreover, while local labor groups have generally enjoyed more leverage in policy making than have federal workers, the results of this study suggest rather strongly that labor does have an interest, albeit an indirect one, in the efficient and equitable allocation of service-related resources.

THE LIMITS OF BUREAUCRACY

By tying the distributive process to the operational goal of efficiency, I have, in effect, staked the normative ideal of social equity on the proposition that public agencies are capable of making distributive decisions in a rational and objective manner. While the research findings of this study support that proposition, the operational proficiency of public bureaucracy must be understood within limits. These boundaries have already been defined in terms of Herbert Simon's important work.[5] They are also apparent within the context of the present case studies.

The Limits of Rationality. According to Simon's "satisficing" notion, total rationality is impossible within an administrative setting, because the decision maker does not have all the information required to determine his total range of alternatives or their likely consequences. Thus, the exercise of discretion is somewhat arbitrary and, for the sake of minimizing risk, policy outcomes tend to result in incremental rather than drastic changes from what has been done before.

While the development of modern managerial techniques such as systems analysis has functioned to better inform decision makers of their policy options and the relative benefits of each, these techniques have only somewhat narrowed the realm of human judgment in the decision process. Moreover, the distilled wisdom which is provided us from the most sophisticated managerial systems is only as keen as the information with which we supply it, and often this information is rather deficient.

Such technological deficiencies can be illustrated by a critical analysis of the deployment strategies which were described in the present case studies. While there seemed to be a serious commitment on the part of agency executives to deploy manpower on the basis of objective indicators of service need, their managerial systems were ultimately reliant upon an arbitrary weighting of service priorities. In addition to this, the information utilized within these systems was not always the most appropriate. We may briefly consider some of the components of these systems here; however, it should be stressed that this analysis is meant to be exemplary rather than exhaustive.

While the PCAM model developed for the Police Department by Rand represented a significant improvement over the hazard type of system that had been previously used, police officials were still left with the responsibility of selecting service priorities among an assortment of functions. The range of choice was wide and varied, including such activities as crime prevention, criminal apprehension, and non–crime-related activities like traffic control, domestic disputes, and accidents. Thus, it was necessary for police officials to categorize different types of crimes according to some notion of severity; a standard was chosen which defined what constituted a "safe" response time throughout the city; and a determination was made concerning what calls for service should be allowed to remain in queue.

A large part of the problem of defining service needs within police work stems from the fact that there is little agreement among experts regarding what the extent and priorities of a policeman's role actually are.[6] Even when such a determination is reached by a police administrator, he does not always have at his disposal the most relevant information for measuring relative demands for service. This type of deficiency is most apparent in New York with the heavy reliance upon reported crime rates as an indicator for actual criminal activity. The work of a number of criminologists has shown that such data in fact lead to an underestimation of criminal activity, and this is particularly true within minority areas where victims are less likely to report offenses.[7]

While the variety of functions performed by a fire department is less overwhelming than in the case of the police, the problem of selecting service priorities is nevertheless a real one. The two major functions carried out by a fire department generally include fire suppression (which also involves rescue operations) and fire prevention. The latter includes a variety of activities ranging from building inspections and code enforcement to public information campaigns. While experts such as Herbert Simon and his colleagues had recognized the significance of the prevention function as far back as 1943,[8] the fact remains that most departments in the nation have placed an inordinate priority on suppression activities. New York is no exception, and in this sense the deployment strategy of its Fire Department suffers from a severe error of omission.

While one should not undermine the importance of the suppression function, an overemphasis of it at the neglect of preventive activities represents a symptomatic approach to the problem of fire protection. The neglect of the latter type of activity can be partially explained in terms of the ignorance on the part of fire officials regarding its overall effectiveness. As several experts in the field have recently noted, there is a conspicuous lack of reliable information on the relative costs and benefits between the performance of suppression and prevention functions.[9] Notwithstanding the significant strides made within the fire service as a result of the Rand research, New York is only one of many cities which would benefit from the availability of additional information on how it might better utilize its firefighting manpower among a variety of protective services.

Sanitation services remain among the most clearly definable and easily measurable of all local government functions. Yet, the problem of manpower and resource deployments within this service is not entirely a simple one. While the Productivity Improvement Project provided sanitation officials in the city with an effective means for measuring the demand for collection services and allocating manpower accordingly, the overall effectiveness of the program seemed to have been weakened by the lack of a similar technique with regard to street cleaning operations. Part of this may again have been due to a lack of suitable information. The demand for street cleaning services is, on the whole, more difficult to assess than that for collection services. However, since the inauguration of the Productivity Improvement Project significant strides have been made in the art of monitoring street cleaning operations, and the New York Sanitation Department is in a rather fortunate position to take advantage of these advances.

In 1972 the Urban Institute began to develop a rather reliable technique for measuring and comparing the cleanliness of city streets.[10] The project was first implemented in Washington, D.C. Subsequently, the Fund for the City of New York in cooperation with the City Sanitation Department developed a similar system for New York.[11] Since 1975 the City Sanitation Department has been using this system as a technique for monitoring the effectiveness of street cleaning activities in the city. Sanitation officials would be well advised to utilize this technique as an instrument for measuring the demand for street sweeping services. Coupled with the allocation techniques which are also available for collection activities, a more sophisticated method can be developed for the effective deployment of manpower between and within both functions.

Despite the significant advances recently made in the art of measuring and improving local government productivity, much work needs to be done. City officials are still forced to rely on inadequate information for making decisions, and often the choices made regarding how one might best use agency resources are highly arbitrary.

Given the fact that a multitude of deficiencies has been identified within the deployment strategies of the city agencies studied, one might rightfully ask: what was rational, efficient, objective, and equitable about the allocation of services in New York? The deployment strategies implemented were rational in the sense that they permitted agency managers to utilize the best information which was available at the time for the effective performance of service functions. These strategies were efficient in the sense that they permitted the agencies to get a better return on the dollar for resources invested than they had received previously. The strategies were objective in the sense that they were generally politically neutral and did not intentionally favor any particular client group. Most important of all, they were equitable in the sense that they represented a conscious effort to distribute public goods and services on the basis of community need.

The point to be made by the foregoing critical analysis is that, as Simon would have us believe, however well intentioned the objectives or however sophisticated the techniques of administrative decision makers, there is a limit to the degree of rationality, objectivity, and efficiency which is attainable within a human organization. Thereby it might be said that there is also a limit to the level of equity which can be reached in the distribution of local government services.

The Problem of Implementation. Once an organizational strategy is selected by the decision maker, the next order of business is to translate that strategy into an operable policy. Simon identified two potential sources of resistance which might serve as an obstacle to the successful implementation of administrative programs. In so doing he recognized the fact that in the process of mitigating such resistance the organizational executive might have to be content with a less than optimal operation of his most carefully thought out plans. Thus, it may be said that, in addition to the informational problems that have been discussed, the rational and efficient pursuit of organizational objectives may be adversely affected by the human element within the process of administration.

The two potential sources of resistance with which Simon was concerned included internal organizational membership and external clientele. Both types played significant roles in determining the way in which deployment policies were implemented in the New York City agencies. The former (internal) was most apparent within the Sanitation Department. The latter (clientele) was most apparent in the Fire Department. While neither presented unsurmountable obstacles to the successful utilization of the deployment strategies, both seemed to undercut the maximum utilization of the information which was available to agency managers.

While the position taken by agency personnel in Sanitation could hardly be described as one of internal resistance, the determination of departmental officials to involve lower level supervisors in the implementation of the Productivity Improvement Project can certainly be interpreted as a tactic to offset the development of such resistance. Unlike the situation in the Police Department, where deployment decisions were the direct outcome of statistical calculations, the situation which emerged in the Sanitation Department was a bargaining one.[12] Thus, the deployment policy which resulted was the product of a compromise. In this way it cannot be said that the distributive process within the Sanitation Department was a totally rational one that was entirely based upon the objective information that was available.

The decision making environment in the Fire Department, which has been described as client-responsive, proved even more difficult from the point of view of the performance-conscious manager. While client groups did not directly participate in the decision making process there, the nature of the policies being determined was such that the anticipated reactions of the public were a serious matter for consideration. Moreover, while management and personnel in the Department eventually took a common approach to the issue of deployment, the operational goals of fire officials and the interests of more influential clientele were not entirely consistent. Thus, the redistribution of agency resources which took place within the Fire Department was less drastic than the available objective information would have required.

The lessons to be drawn from the latter two case studies serve to illustrate Simon's notion of administrative implementation rather well. One cannot realistically expect the human organization to operate in the rigid fashion of an inanimate mechanical structure. Because of the human element both within and outside the organizational environment, public managers will often have to settle with a less than optimal utilization of the resources at their command. However, such constraints need not necessarily work towards a total undermining of an organization's operational objectives. Thus, the ideals of a rational, objective, and efficient approach to public administration are, in fact, achievable.

It was to the credit of officials in both the Sanitation and Fire departments that, despite the potential and real sources of resistance with which they had to deal, they were able to bring about a generally success-ful implementation of the deployment strategies which were conceived. The increased productivity of sanitation personnel and the reallocation of fire companies worked to improve the overall quality of management in the city. Most important of all, the distribution of sanitation and fire services among residential population groups was found to be equitable.

The Opportunity Dilemma. While the general findings of the employment-related research that have been presented here have also been favorable, something remains to be said about some of the evident weaknesses in the bureaucracy's capacity to provide equal opportunity for the poor. Al-though the overall descriptive representation of minorities within the local civil service was found to be proportionate to their numbers in the population, and that of blacks was particularly high, this was not the case with Puerto Ricans, the city's most depressed minority.

The problem here relates to the fact, already mentioned several times before, that there is a basic tension between the equal opportunity principle and the competitive merit system of recruitment. Thus, while the public service has provided a means of employment, social mobility, and community influence for many minorities before, it has not been entirely effective in reaching the most desperately disadvantaged.

The fiscal crisis which became apparent in New York during 1975, and which similarly threatens other large municipalities, has not served to improve the situation for minorities. Because of a recent emphasis on economy in local government spending, New York has found it necessary to reduce the size of its labor force by nearly 20 percent. Although part of these reductions has been absorbed through ordinary attritions resulting from retirements and voluntary terminations, a greater part has been brought about through across-the-board layoffs. Because of a seniority system which dictates that the last hired must be the first fired, minorities have already borne a disproportionate share of these recently imposed austerity measures. As such fiscal restraints continue to require cities like New York to decrease the size of their labor forces, the prospect of using local government as an employer of last resort for the most disadvantaged may become even more dim.

The infusion of federal monies to localities through the Comprehensive Employment and Training Act (CETA) has to some degree assisted municipalities like New York in mitigating the problems of the chronically unemployed while at the same time enduring cutbacks in their own budgets. However, in the long run local governments themselves will have to assume the responsibility of constructively employing the poor and maintaining a career civil service which is reflective of the client populations being served. Therefore, the successful implementation of employment programs and civil service reforms we have witnessed in New York during the late sixties and early seventies serves to emphasize the need for similar efforts in the future. Job programs must be supplemented by training, and a constant reevaluation of the merit system must be made in order to insure that civil service examinations do not erect an unfair barrier to the culturally disadvantaged. Moreover, because of the austere fiscal situation which exists, it is now time to raise some new and serious questions concerning how manpower reductions can be absorbed in a way which does not penalize minorities and the poor.

On the one hand, it may be necessary to consider the possibility of providing incentives for early retirements as an alternative to removing those who are recently hired. On the other hand, it also seems appropriate to reevaluate the long-standing criterion of reversed seniority when selecting those who will be released from government service because of budgetary restraints. Since the exercise of such options, particularly the latter, run contrary to an entire national tradition in both public and private employment, it is not likely that they will be implemented with either great facility or great speed. However, under the present circumstances, the serious consideration of these policies would signify an essential step in the right direction.

PROSPECTS FOR THE FUTURE

Assuming that the types of civil service reforms which have been suggested are not imminent in the near future, the fundamental question concerning the capability of institutions which lack descriptive representation to respond to the interests of the entire citizenry has become more relevant today than it was during the years of the Lindsay administration. Given the fact that the austere budgetary situation which plagues American cities today will continue to persist for some time, the underlying issue concerning the relationship between the operational goal of efficiency and the normative ideal for social equity becomes even more profound.

The brief review of history appearing in the present volume has documented the political viability of programs designed to extract a better quantity and quality of service for the public dollars being spent. We have seen that it was the appeal for economy and efficiency in government which finally broadened the political base of early twentieth-century reform movements. We have seen a reform-minded New York mayor attempt to cultivate the public favor with the promise of increased productivity in the local service delivery system. Anyone who has witnessed recent mayoral electoral campaigns, in either New York or any other large American city, would be hard put to find a candidate who ran on a platform which did not include a public management plank. Thus, the demand for increased efficiency in government has proved to be a politically feasible and acceptable one, and this is encouraging.

The current fiscal situation in American cities has done more than just increase the urgency of efficient government. In a large way it has changed the stakes of government administration. It will require that municipalities in the process of reducing their expenditures do so without degrading the level of service to such an extent that they adversely affect the quality of urban life. Moreover, it will require, in those cases where resource appropriations must be cut back, that such actions will be carried out in a fair and equitable manner which continues to respond to the peculiar service needs of all communities.

With the emergence of decentralization, we might also expect that the process of administration will undergo some change. With the politics of retrenchment upon us the basic question of political life may be altered from the proverbial "Who gets what?" to a more controversial "Who gets less?" The research in the preceding pages has demonstrated that bureaucratic institutions are capable of allocating their services in a fair, efficient and equitable manner. The basic challenge which lies ahead is to insure that, in those cases where such a desirable outcome exists, it is allowed to continue, within the confines of both fiscal restraint and the highly visible arena of community government.

As contemporary advocates of decentralization have declared, the responsiveness of bureaucratic institutions could be enhanced with the creation of new channels of communication between their leaders and the clients they serve. However, the future of local government, and its capacity to respond to the needs of the poor, lies in the successful integration of the more positive features of older and newer types of institutions. The basic right of the citizen to be provided with direct access to government is undeniable. Yet, if the normative ideals which have been associated with the New Public Administration are to be attained, a conscious effort must be made to keep the process of distribution, and one might add retrenchment, outside the purview of local politics.

NOTES

PREFACE

1. Joseph P. Viteritti, *Police, Politics and Pluralism in New York City.*
2. Wallace Sayre and Herbert Kaufman, *Governing New York City.*
3. See Frank Marini, ed., *Toward a New Public Administration.*
4. See, for example, Wallace Sayre, *Proceedings of the Academy of Political Science* (May 1974); Herbert Kaufman, "Administrative Decentralization and Political Power," *Public Administration Review* 29 (January-February 1969).
5. Joseph P. Viteritti, "Politics, Science and Public Policy."
6. John Rawls, *A Theory of Justice;* Hanna Pitkin, *The Concept of Representation* (Berkeley: University of California Press, 1967).

1. INTRODUCTION

1. Herbert Kaufman, "Emerging Conflicts in the Doctrines of Public Administration," *American Political Science Review* 50 (December 1956): 1057-73.
2. Ibid., p. 1067.
3. H. George Frederickson, "Toward a New Public Administration," in Frank Marini, ed., *Toward a New Public Administration* (Scranton: Chandler, 1971), p. 311.
4. Richard Cole, *Citizen Participation and the Urban Policy Process,* p. 134; John Strange, "The Impact of Citizen Participation on Public Administration," *Public Administration Review* 32 (September 1972); George J. Washnis, *Neighborhood Facilities and Municipal Decentralization* (Washington: Center for Governmental Studies, 1971); Neil Gilbert, *Clients and Constituents* (San Francisco: Josey-Bass, 1970); Willis Sutten, "Differential Perceptions of Impact of a Rural Anti-Poverty Campaign," *Social Science Quarterly* 50 (December 1969); Peter Rossi, "No Good Idea Goes Unpublished," *Social Science Quarterly* 50 (December 1969); James J. Vanceko, "Community Organization and Institutional Change," *Social Science Quarterly* 50 (December 1969).
5. Sanford Kravitz, "The Community Action Program in Perspective," in Warner Bloomberg and Henry Schmandt, eds., *Power, Poverty and Urban Policy* (Beverly Hills: Sage Publications, 1968); Richard Cloward, "The War on Poverty: Are the Poor Left Out?" in Chaim Waxman, ed., *Poverty, Power and Politics* (New York: Grosset & Dunlap, 1969).

6. Robert K. Yin and Douglas Yates, *Street-Level Governments* (Lexington, Massachusetts: D. C. Heath & Company, 1975), pp. 50–56.
7. Ibid., p. 180.
8. Douglas Yates, *Neighborhood Democracy;* Norman Fainstein and Susan Fainstein, "The Future of Community Control," p. 912.
9. New York City Charter, amended to June 1, 1977.
10. H. H. Gerth and C. Wright Mills, eds., *From Max Weber: Essays in Sociology* (New York: Oxford University Press, 1946), pp. 196–244; A. M. Henderson and Talcott Parsons, eds., *Max Weber: The Theory of Social and Economic Organization* (New York: Free Press, 1947), pp. 329–41.
11. Woodrow Wilson, "The Study of Public Administration."
12. Herbert Simon, *Administrative Behavior.*
13. Alan Altshuler, *Community Control*, pp. 64–65.
14. For another analysis of the political model, see Milton Kotler, *Neighborhood Government.*
15. See, for example, Charles Silberman, *Crisis in Black and White* (New York: Random House, 1964); Marion K. Sanders, *The Professional Radical: Conversations with Saul Alinsky* (New York: Harper & Row, 1970).
16. See, for example, Peter M. Blau, *Bureaucracy in Modern Society,* pp. 27–36.
17. Hanna Pitkin, *The Concept of Representation* (Berkeley: University of California Press, 1967).
18. A. M. Henderson and Talcott Parsons, p. 339.
19. John Scharr, "Equality of Opportunity and Beyond," *Nomos IX Equality* (New York: Atherton, 1967).
20. *Griggs v. Duke Power Company*, 401 U.S. 424, 433 (1973).
21. See David Rosenbloom and Carole Cassler Obuchowski, "Public Personnel Examinations and the Constitution."
22. Cited in David Rosenbloom, "The Civil Service Commission's Decision to Authorize the Use of Goals and Timetables in the Federal Equal Employment Opportunity Program."
23. *Regents of the University of California v. Allan Bakke,* 46 U.S.L.W. 4896 (1978).
24. Harold D. Lasswell, *Politics: Who Gets What, When, How* (New York: World, 1936).
25. David Easton, *A Systems Analysis of Political Life* (New York: John Wiley, 1965), pp. 343–57.
26. Pitkin, p. 155.
27. *Hawkins v. Shaw,* 424 F. 2d 1286 (5th Cir., 1971).
28. *Beal v. Lindsay,* 468 F. 2d 287 (2nd Cir., 1972).
29. *Serrano v. Priest,* 5 Cal. 3d 584 (1971).
30. *Van Dusartz v. Hatfield,* 334 F. Supp. 870, D. Minn. (1971); *Rodriguez v. San Antonio Independent School District,* 337 F. Supp. 280, W. D. Texas (1972); *Milliken v. Green,* 389 Mich. 1 (1972); *Robinson v. Cahill,* 62 N.J. 473 (1973).
31. *Rodriguez v. San Antonio Independent School District,* 337 F. Supp. 280, W. D. Texas (1972), reversed 93 S. Ct. 1278 (1973).
32. *Robinson v. Cahill,* 62 N.J. 473, (1973).
33. *Levittown v. Nyquist,* New York Supreme Court, June 23, 1978.
34. See Frank J. Macchiarola, "Constitutional and Legal Dimensions of Public School Financing," *Municipal Yearbook* (Washington: International City Managers' Association, 1974), pp. 17–23.
35. For a discussion on the various definitions of service equity, refer to: Stephen Chitwood, "Social Equity and Social Service Productivity"; Alan Campbell, "Approaches to Defining, Measuring and Achieving Equity in the Public Sector"; William H. Lucy, Dennis Gilbert, and Guthrie Birkhead, "Equality and Local Service Distribution," *Public Administration Review* 37 (November-December 1977).

36. John Rawls, *A Theory of Justice*, p. 302.
37. Ibid., p. 303.
38. Ibid., p. 302.
39. Ibid., p. 62.
40. John W. Chapman, "Rawls's Theory of Justice," *American Political Science Review* 69 (June 1975): 591-92.
41. See, for example, Yehezkel Dror, "Policy Analyst: A New Professional Role in Government," *Public Administration Review* 27 (September 1967): 200; Ralph Huitt, "Political Feasibility," in Austin Ranney, ed., *Political Science and Public Policy*, pp. 263-76.
42. Charles L. Schultz, *The Politics and Economics of Public Spending* (Washington: Brookings Institution, 1968), p. 9.
43. Arnold J. Meltsner, "Political Feasibility and Policy Analysis," *Public Administration Review* 32 (November-December 1972): 859-67.
44. Robert Lane, *Political Life* (Glencoe, Ill.: Free Press, 1959), ch. 16; Lester Milbrath, *Political Participation* (Chicago: Rand McNally, 1963), ch. 5; Austin Ranney, "Turnout and Representation in Presidential Primary Elections," *American Political Science Review* 66 (March 1972).
45. Donald Matthews and James Prothro, *Negroes and the New Southern Politics* (New York: Harcourt, Brace & World, 1967).
46. I have illustrated this point in *Police, Politics and Pluralism in New York City.*
47. This definition is based on the discussion of the concept appearing in Herbert Simon, Donald Smithberg, and Victor Thompson, *Public Administration*, pp. 488-512.
48. J. Donald Kingsley, *Representative Bureaucracy.*
49. Norton Long, "Bureaucracy and Constitutionalism."
50. Camilo Marquez, *Municipal Expenditures by Neighborhood.*
51. John Weicher, "The Allocation of Police Protection by Income Class," *Urban Studies* 8 (1971); John Bollens, ed., *Exploring the Metropolitan Community*, ch. 14; Charles Benson and Peter Lund, *Neighborhood Distribution of Local Government Services*, ch. 3.
52. Benson and Lund.
53. Frank Levy et al., *Urban Outcomes.*
54. Robert Lineberry, *Equality and Urban Policy*, p. 183.
55. Ibid., p. 184.

2. AMERICAN PUBLIC ADMINISTRATION

1. Paul Van Riper, *History of the U.S. Civil Service*, p. 554.
2. Frederick C. Mosher, *Democracy and the Public Service*, pp. 55-61.
3. According to Sidney Aronson, the changes in the composition of the higher civil service in the United States were only moderate between the administrations of Adams, Jefferson, and Jackson. The percentages of employees at these ranks drawn from the upper class were 70%, 60%, and 53%, respectively, according to his findings in *Status and Kinship in the Higher Civil Service*, p. 61.
4. For example, Richard P. Nathan has shown that many of the political and governmental abuses which led to "Watergate" were originally carried out and justified by the Nixon administration as administrative reforms designed to increase the efficient operation of the executive branch. See Richard P. Nathan, *The Plot That Failed: Nixon and the Administrative Presidency* (New York: John Wiley, 1975).
5. Allen Schick, "The Trauma of Politics: Public Administration in the Sixties," in Frederick C. Mosher, ed. *American Public Administration*, pp. 142-80.

6. While Vincent Ostrom traces the formulation of the classical model in America to Woodrow Wilson, he rightfully compares this model to the ideal type model of bureaucracy described by Weber. See *The Intellectual Crisis in American Public Administration*, pp. 29–33.

7. Lincoln Steffens, *The Shame of the Cities* (St. Louis: S. S. McClure, 1902).

8. Van Riper, p. 85.

9. A compendium of Taylor's essays on management appears in Frederick Taylor, *The Principles of Scientific Management*.

10. Woodrow Wilson, "The Study of Public Administration."

11. Ibid., p. 190.

12. Ibid., p. 202.

13. Ibid., p. 197.

14. Dwight Waldo, *The Administrative State,* chs. 3 and 9.

15. W. H. Allen, *Efficient Democracy* (New York: Dodd, Mead, 1907), p. vii, cited in Waldo, p. 193.

16. M. L. Cook, "The Spirit and Social Significance of Scientific Management," *Journal of Political Economy* 21 (June 1913): 493, cited in Waldo, p. 52.

17. Leonard D. White and T. V. Smith, *Politics and Public Service* (New York: Harper, 1939), pp. 7–8, cited in Waldo, p. 196.

18. Frank J. Goodnow, *Politics and Administration* (New York: Macmillan, 1900); W. F. Willoughby, *Principles of Public Administration* (Washington: Brookings Institution, 1927).

19. Van Riper, p. 320.

20. United States President's Committee on Administrative Management, *Report with Studies* (Washington: U.S. Government Printing Office, 1937).

21. Luther Gulick, "Politics, Administration and the New Deal," *Annals of the American Academy of Political and Social Science* (September 1933), p. 55.

22. Luther Gulick, "Science, Values and Public Administration," in Luther Gulick and Lyndall Urwick, eds., *Papers on the Science of Administration*, p. 192.

23. Luther Gulick, "Notes on the Theory of Organization," in Gulick and Urwick, eds., p. 10.

24. W. F. Willoughby, "The Science of Public Administration," in J. Mathews and James Hart, eds., *Essays in Political Science* (Baltimore: Johns Hopkins University Press, 1939).

25. Leonard D. White, *Introduction to the Study of Public Administration.*

26. The first Hoover Commission was appointed by Congress in 1947. The second was set up by President Eisenhower in 1953. It is important to point out, however, that the latter commission was more oriented to the decentralization of power in the national government.

27. David Lilienthal, *The TVA: An Experiment in the "Grass Roots" Administration of Federal Functions* (Knoxville: Harper & Brothers, 1939); Orday Tead, *New Adventures in Democracy* (New York: McGraw-Hill, 1939); Schuyler Wallace, *Federal Departmentalization* (New York: Columbia University Press, 1941).

28. Marshal Dimock, *Modern Politics and Administration* (New York: American Books, 1937).

29. Amitai Etzioni, *Modern Organizations* (Englewood Cliffs: Prentice-Hall, 1965).

30. William Foote Whyte, "An Interaction Approach to the Theory of Organization," in Mason Haire, ed., *Modern Organization Theory* (New York: John Wiley, 1959), pp. 154–84.

31. Robert Merton, "The Unanticipated Consequences of Purposive Social Action," *American Sociological Review* 1 (1936).

32. Robert Merton, "Bureaucratic Structure and Personality," *Social Forces* 18 (1940).

33. Chester Barnard, *The Functions of the Executive.*

34. Herbert Simon, *Administrative Behavior.*

35. Ibid., p. 121.
36. Ibid., p. 122.
37. Ibid., pp. 110–42.
38. See James March and Herbert Simon, *Organizations.*
39. Philip Selznick, *TVA and the Grass Roots* (Berkeley: University of California Press, 1949).
40. J. Leiper Freeman, *The Political Process* (New York: Random House, 1955).
41. Charles Lindblom, "The Science of Muddling Through." See also David Braybrooke and Charles Lindblom, *A Strategy for Decision.*
42. Aaron Wildavsky, *The Politics of the Budgetary Process* (Boston: Little, Brown, 1964).
43. Francis E. Rourke, *Bureaucracy, Politics, and Public Policy;* John Rehfuss, *Public Administration As a Political Process* (New York: Scribner, 1973).
44. For a history of the U.S. Civil Service Commission's effort in this area, see Samuel Krislov, *The Negro in Federal Employment;* David Rosenbloom, *The U.S. Civil Service Commission's Role in the Federal Equal Employment Opportunity Program 1965-1970* (Washington: U.S. Civil Service Commission, December, 1970).
45. For a comparative analysis of these two programs, refer to David Rosenbloom, "The Civil Service Commission's Decision to Authorize the Use of Goals and Timetables in the Federal Equal Employment Opportunity Program."
46. Cited in Rosenbloom, "The Civil Service Commission's Decision to Authorize the Use of Goals and Timetables in the Federal Equal Employment Opportunity Program," p. 247.
47. E. S. Quade, introduction to E. S. Quade, ed., *Analysis for Military Decisions,* p. 4.
48. Allen Schick has appropriately pointed out that the main goal of program budgeting is to rationalize policy making by providing (1) "data on the costs and benefits of alternative ways of attaining proposed public objectives, and (2) output measurements to facilitate the effective attainment of chosen objectives." Allen Schick, "The Road to PPB," pp. 250–51.
49. See Charles Hitch and Roland McKean, *The Economics of Defense in a Nuclear Age;* Charles Hitch, *Decision Making for Defense.*
50. James R. Schlesinger, *Systems Analysis and the Political Process,* pp. 14–17.
51. See, for example, Alice Rivlin's account of the application of systems analysis in civilian agencies, in *Systematic Thinking for Social Action.*
52. Ida Hoos, *Systems Analysis in Public Policy,* p. 10.
53. Frank Marini, "The Minnowbrook Perspective and the Future of Public Administration Education," in Frank Marini, ed., *Toward a New Public Administration,* p. 354.
54. H. George Frederickson, "Toward a New Public Administration," in Marini, ed., p. 324.
55. Orion White, "Social Change and Administrative Adaptation," in Marini, ed., pp. 79–83.
56. W. Henry Lambright, "The Minnowbrook Perspective and the Future of Public Affairs," in Marini, ed., p. 341.
57. Robert P. Biller, "Some Implications of Adaption Capacity for Organizational and Political Development," in Marini, ed., pp. 108–9. See also Michael Harmon, "Normative Theory and Public Administration: Some Suggestions for a Redefinition of Administrative Responsibility," in Marini, ed., pp. 172–85.
58. Frederickson, p. 315.
59. Sheldon Wolin, "Political Theory As a Vocation," *American Political Science Review* 63 (December 1969).
60. Theodore Lowi, "American Business, Public Policy, Case Studies and Political Theory"; Austin Ranney, ed., *Political Science and Public Policy;* Ira Sharkansky, ed., *Policy Analysis in Political Science.*
61. Frederickson, p. 319.

62. Stokely Carmichael and Charles V. Hamilton, *Black Power*.

63. Frances Fox Piven and Richard Cloward, *Regulating the Poor*, p. 261.

64. Among the more influential of these were Paul Ylvisaker, a political scientist from the Ford Foundation; Richard Cloward, Paul Ohlin, and Sanford Kravitz, who were recruited from Schools of Social Work; Leonard Cuttrell, a sociologist from the Russell Sage Foundation; and the economist Robert Lampman.

65. These include the Advisory Commission on Governmental Relations (1967), the National Commission on Urban Problems (1968), and the National Advisory Commission on Civil Disorders (1968).

66. John Donovan, *The Politics of Poverty*, ch. 7.

67. See James Sundquist, *Making Federalism Work: A Study of Program Coordination at the Community Level* (Washington: Brookings Institution, 1969).

68. Sar Levitan, *The Great Society's Poor Law*, p. 114; Daniel P. Moynihan, *Maximum Feasible Misunderstanding*, p. 137.

69. Neil Gilbert, *Clients and Constituents* (San Francisco: Josey-Bass, 1970), p. 150; Walter Grace and Herbert Costner, "Organizing the Poor: An Evaluation of a Strategy," *Social Science Quarterly* 50 (December 1969): 643-57.

70. Moynihan, pp. xxix-xxxvi, 167-203.

71. Theodore Lowi, *The End of Liberalism*.

72. Sanford Kravitz, "The Community Action Program; Past, Present and its Future," in James Sundquist, ed., *On Fighting Poverty*, pp. 52-70; Richard Cloward, "The War on Poverty: Are the Poor Left Out?" in Chaim Waxman, ed., *Poverty, Power and Politics* (New York: Grosset & Dunlap, 1968), pp. 159-70; Brandeis University Study, "Community Representation in 20 Cities," in Edgar Kahn and Barry Passett, eds., *Citizen Participation* (Trenton, N.J., Community Action Training Institute, 1970), p. 130; Howard Hallman, "The Community Action Program: An Interpretative Analysis," in Warner Bloomberg and Henry Schmandt, eds., *Power, Poverty and Urban Policy* (Beverly Hills: Sage Publications, 1968); Richard A. Cloward and Francis Fox Piven, eds., *The Politics of Turmoil* (New York: Pantheon Books, 1965). A similar analysis is presented on the Model Cities program in Sherry Arnstein, "Maximum Feasible Manipulation," *Public Administration Review* 32 (September 1972): 377-90.

73. See Irving Kirstol, "Decentralization for What?"; Carl Stenberg, "Citizens and the Administrative State: From Participation to Power," *Public Administration Review* 32 (May-June 1972): 194; Joseph Zimmerman, *The Federated City*, p. 16; Henry Schmandt, "Municipal Decentralization," p. 571.

74. Eugene McGregor, "Social Equity and the Public Service," p. 18.

3. ADMINISTRATIVE REFORM

1. In line with its broader national perspective, the Bureau of Municipal Research now operates under the name Institute of Public Administration.

2. Wallace Sayre and Herbert Kaufman, *Governing New York City*, pp. 657-58.

3. John V. Lindsay, *The City*, p. 25.

4. James Q. Wilson, *The Amateur Democrat* (Chicago: University of Chicago Press, 1962), pp. 32-64, 258-78.

5. Sterling Spero and John Capozzola, *The Urban Community and Its Unionized Bureaucracies*, pp. 62-65.

6. Oliver Pilat, *Lindsay's Campaign* (Boston: Beacon, 1968).

7. Nat Hentoff, *A Political Life*, p. 123.

8. Raymond D. Horton, *Municipal Labor Relations in New York City*, pp. 91-116.

9. David A. Grossman, private interview held at Nova Institute, New York City, August 4, 1977. See also David A. Grossman, "The Lindsay Administration: A Partisan Appraisal," *City Almanac* 8 (October 1973).

10. City of New York, Municipal Civil Service Commission and the Department of Personnel, *Annual Report*, 1954, p. 5.
11. David Stanley, *Professional Personnel for the City of New York.*
12. City of New York, Civil Service Commission and Department of Personnel, *Annual Report, 1963*, p. 22.
13. Ibid., *1965*, p. 45.
14. Frank Arricale II, private interview held at New York City Board of Education, Brooklyn, N.Y., September 21, 1977.
15. See, for example, E. S. Savas and Sigmund E. Ginsberg, "The Civil Service," pp. 70–85.
16. City of New York, Civil Service Commission and Department of Personnel, *Annual Report, 1967*, p. 13.
17. Ibid., p. 15.
18. City of New York, Civil Service Commission and Department of Personnel, *Annual Report, 1966*, p. 36.
19. Frank Arricale II, private interview held at the New York City Board of Education, Brooklyn, N.Y., September 21, 1977.
20. Daniel P. Moynihan, *Maximum Feasible Misunderstanding*, p. 147.
21. Richard A. Cloward and Lloyd E. Ohlin, *Delinquency and Opportunity.*
22. Moynihan, p. 44.
23. Stephen M. David, "Welfare: The Community Action Program Controversy," in Jewel Bellush and Stephen M. David, eds., *Race and Politics in New York City*, pp. 30–40.
24. Ibid.
25. Study prepared for the state Charter Revision Commission for New York City, *The Community Action Experience*, November 1973, p. 72.
26. These three areas included Harlem, Bedford-Stuyvesant, and the South Bronx in New York.
27. Study prepared by the staff of the state Charter Revision Commission for New York City, *Report On Model Cities*, November 1973, p. 6. See also pp. 34–69.
28. Marilyn Gittell, *Participants and Participation;* David Rogers, 110 Livingston Street.
29. Study prepared for the state Charter Revision Commission for New York City, *The Impact of School Decentralization in New York City on Municipal Decentralization*, June, 1974, p. 23.
30. Report of the Mayor's Advisory Panel on Decentralization of New York City Schools, *Recommendations for Learning: A Community School System for New York City Schools*, 1967.
31. Diane Ravitch, *The Great School Wars*, chs. 31–33.
32. Louis Harris Associates, news release, January 1969.
33. David A. Grossman, private interview held at the Nova Institute, New York City, August 4, 1977.
34. *Impact of School Decentralization*, p. 66.
35. Ibid., p. 77.
36. Ibid., p. 119.
37. Ibid., p. 118.
38. Ibid.
39. Ibid.
40. Report of the State Education Commission on School Financing, vol. 3.
41. Local Laws of the City of New York for the Year 1969, no. 39.
42. John V. Lindsay, "Plan for Neighborhood Government for New York City," June 1970.
43. Frederick O'R. Hayes, "From Inside the System," in Alvin W. Drake et al., eds., *Analysis of Public Systems*, p. 8.
44. Ibid.

45. Martin Greenberger, et al., *Models in the Policy Process*, p. 238.

46. Ibid., pp. 287-93.

47. Frederick O'R. Hayes, *Productivity in Local Government*, pp. 105-6.

48. Warren Walker, private interview held at the Urban Academy, New York City, September 16, 1977. This position is corroborated by Greenberger, Crenson, and Crissey in their analysis of the fire project, pp. 231-35.

49. Hayes, *Productivity*, p. 103.

50. Edward V. Hamilton, "Productivity," p. 787.

51. See, for example, Jerome Mark, "Meanings and Measures of Productivity," p. 748; John P. Ross and Jesse Burkhead, *Productivity in the Local Government Sector*, p. 5.

52. City of New York, Office of Mayor, *First Quarter Progress Report-Comprehensive Productivity Program*, December 30, 1973, p. 1.

53. See Harry P. Hatry, "Issues in Productivity Measurement in Local Government," pp. 776-83; Ross and Burkhead, pp. 35-58.

54. See Herbert Haber, "New York City Productivity Bargaining," *Labor Management Relations Newsletter* 4; Chester Newland, "Personnel Concerns in Productivity Improvement," *Public Administration Review* 32 (November-December 1972), pp. 807-15; George Brooks, "Negotiating for Productivity in Sanitation," *Labor Management Relations Service*, June 1973.

55. Hayes, *Productivity*, pp. 99-100.

56. Raymond D. Horton, "Productivity and Productivity Bargaining in Government," pp. 407-14.

57. See Joseph P. Viteritti, "New York's Management Plan and Reporting System."

4. MINORITY EMPLOYMENT

1. City Commission on Human Rights, "The Ethnic Survey: A Report on the Number and Distribution of Negroes, Puerto Ricans and Others Employed by the City of New York," 1964.

2. City Commission on Human Rights, "The Employment of Minorities, Women, and the Handicapped in City Government," 1973.

3. Rheinhard Bendix, *Higher Civil Servants in American Society;* W. Lloyd Warner et al., *The American Federal Executive*.

4. Franklin Kilpatrick et al., *The Image of the Federal Executive* (Washington: Brookings Institution, 1964); V. Subramaniam, "Representative Bureaucracy."

5. Milton Cummings et al., "Federal and Non-Federal Employees."

6. Don Hellriegel and Larry Short, "Equal Employment Opportunity in the Federal Government."

7. David Nachmias and David Rosenbloom, "Measuring Bureaucratic Representation and Integration."

8. Those other agencies where high integration was found included the Government Printing Office, the Civil Service Commission, the Veterans Administration, and the Department of State.

9. Kenneth J. Meier, "Representative Bureaucracy."

10. Harry Kranz, *The Participatory Bureaucracy*.

11. In accordance with the more recent concern for sexual discrimination, Kranz's data also included information on the status of women in government.

12. Kranz, p. 194.

13. Ibid., p. 155.

14. Unless otherwise stated, employment data in this section are derived from the New York City Commission on Human Rights employment surveys of 1963 and 1971 which are cited in notes 1 and 2 of this chapter.

15.   Those non-mayoral agencies not cooperating included: the Transit Authority, the Judicial Conference, the City Council, the Board of Elections, the Brooklyn and Richmond offices of the borough president, the Kings County Office of the District Attorney, the Brooklyn and Queensborough public libraries, and the Bureau of Retirement and Pension. The Board of Higher Education was completing its own census at the time for the U.S. Department of Health, Education and Welfare.

16.   Those agencies not participating in 1963 were the Board of Higher Education (instructional personnel only); the Bureau of Water Supply; the Department of Industry; the Brooklyn, New York, and Richmond offices of the district attorney; the Civil Court; the Criminal Court; the Family Court; the Law Department; the Police Department; the Probation Department; the Transit Authority; and the Youth Counsel Bureau.

17.   New York did not have a significant non-Puerto Rican Hispanic community until after 1965, when an amendment to the immigration law resulted in a rapid influx of Latin Americans into the city who were not of Puerto Rican origin.

18.   See table 4.3, n. 1.

19.   See note 14.

20.   Daniel P. Moynihan and Nathan Glazer, *Beyond the Melting Pot* (Cambridge: M.I.T. Press, 1963).

21.   Raymond D. Horton, *Municipal Labor Relations in New York City*, pp. 94–98. According to Horton's data, the base salary for patrolmen and firemen in 1972 was $12,800. The parity agreement with the sanitationmen's union was set at 90% of the two other uniformed forces. Ibid., p. 95.

22.   According to Horton's data, the minimum starting salary for teachers in 1972 was $9,400. Ibid., p. 99.

23.   New York City Commission on Human Rights, "The Employment of Minorities, Women and Handicapped in City Government," 1973, p. 35.

24.   Here Horton's data show that the average base pay for members of D. C. 37 in 1972 was $7,500. Op. cit., p. 101.

25.   New York City Commission on Human Rights, pp. 34–35.

5. ALLOCATION OF SERVICES

1.   Clarence E. Ridley and Herbert A. Simon, *Measuring Municipal Activities.*

2.   Henry Schmandt and G. Ross Stephens, "Measuring Municipal Output," *National Tax Journal* 13 (December 1960).

3.   D. F. Bradford, R. A. Malt, and W. E. Oates, "The Rising Cost of Local Public Services: Some Evidence and Reflections," *National Tax Journal* 22 (June 1969).

4.   Urban Institute, and International City Management Association, *The Challenge of Productivity Diversity* (Washington: Urban Institute, 1972). See also Urban Institute, and International City Management Association, *Measuring the Effectiveness of Basic Municipal Services* (Washington: Urban Institute, 1974); *How Effective Are Your Community Services?* (Washington: Urban Institute, 1977).

5.   An excellent review of the literature is contained in John P. Ross and Jesse Burkhead, *Productivity in the Local Government Sector.*

6.   See, for example, Kenneth Webb and Harry Hatry, *Obtaining Citizen Feedback: The Application of Citizen Surveys to Local Governments* (Washington: Urban Institute, 1973); B. Stipak, *Citizen Evaluations and Municipal Services in Los Angeles County* (Los Angeles: Institute of Government and Public Affairs, UCLA, 1974); Harry Hatry and Louis Blair, "Citizen Surveys for Local Governments," *Policy and Politics* 4 (June 1976).

7. John Weicher, "The Allocation of Police Protection by Income Class," *Urban Studies* 9 (1971); John Bollens, *Exploring the Metropolitan Community*, 14; Charles Benson and Peter Lund, *Neighborhood Distribution of Local Government Services*, ch. 3; Frank Levy et al., *Urban Outcomes*.

8. New York City Charter, effective 1963, amended June 1, 1977; ch. 18, sec. 435.

9. This point is illustrated in Joseph Viteritti, *Police, Politics and Pluralism in New York City*, pp. 18–23, 35–40. See also Arthur Niederhoffer, *Behind the Shield* (New York: Doubleday, 1969), pp. 16–23.

10. George Kelling, Tony Pate, Duane Durkman, and Charles Brown, *The Kansas City Preventive Patrol Experiment* (Washington: Police Foundation, 1975).

11. Franklin Limring, *Perspectives on Deterrence* (Washington: National Institute of Mental Health, Center for the Study of Crime and Delinquency, 1971). See also M. D. Maltz, *Evaluation of Crime Control Programs* (Washington: National Institute of Law Enforcement and Criminal Justice, 1972).

12. S. James Press, *Some Effects of an Increase in Police Manpower in the 20th Precinct in New York City* (New York: New York City Rand Institute, R-704, October 1971). The displacement impact of crime control activities has also been documented in a study of the New York City Transit Authority: see Jan Chaiken, Michael Lawless, and Kenneth Stevenson, *The Impact of Police Activity on Crime: Robberies on the New York City Subway System* (New York: New York City Rand Institute, R-1424, January 1974).

13. O. W. Wilson, *Police Administration* (New York: McGraw-Hill, 1963), pp. 227–81.

14. This model was based on several systems which preceded it. The most notable are Richard Larson, *Urban Police Patrol Analysis* (Cambridge: M.I.T. Press, 1972), and International Business Machines, "LEMRAS Application Description Manual," document H20-629. For a complete description see Jan Chaiken, *Patrol Car Allocation Methodology for Police Departments* (New York: New York City Rand Institute, R-1852-1, 2, 3, 1975).

15. This analysis of Plan C is based on documentary information made available by the Office of Programs and Policy (N.Y.P.D.). I am particularly indebted to Inspector Patrick Murphy, Joseph Eiss, Aaron Wilner, and Sergeant James Devine for their help and cooperation.

16. A study completed jointly by the *New York Times* and the Rand Institute in 1973 found high homicide and burglary rates to be associated with neighborhoods with high proportions of people who were black or Hispanic and had lower incomes. For example, the ten precincts in the city with the highest homicide rates were found to be 54% black and 28% Hispanic. The ten precincts with the lowest homicide rates were found to be 2% black and 6% Hispanic. *New York Times*, July 30, 1973. Similar patterns of racial characteristics and crime were found to exist on a national level by the President's Commission on Law Enforcement and the Administration of Justice, *The Challenge of Crime in a Free Society* (Washington: U.S. Government Printing Office, 1967), pp. 136–37.

17. Manpower allocation data in this section are based on New York City Police Department, *Field Force Reports* for 1972 and 1973. Crime statistics for 1972 were obtained from New York City Police Department, *Annual Statistical Report, 1973*. Information on the size of precincts was made available by the New York City Police Department's Cartography Division.

18. New York City Charter, effective 1963, amended 1977, ch. 19, secs. 487–91.

19. An account of the joint project undertaken by the New York City Fire Department and the Rand Institute appears in Edward H. Blum, "The New York City Fire Project," in Alvin W. Drake et al., eds., *Analysis of Public Systems.*

20. This description of the deployment and dispatching methodology utilized by the New York City Fire Department is based on Edward Ignall et al., *Improving the Deployment of New York City Fire Companies* (New York: New York City Rand Institute, P-5280, July 1974). It also draws heavily upon discussions which the author had with Warren Walker and Edward Ignall, who were both members of the Rand Fire Project staff.

21. Lowell M. Limpus, *History of the New York Fire Department* (New York: Dutton, 1940).

22. Ibid.

23. For a more detailed analysis of the workload dispute and its outcome, see Martin Greenberger et al., *Models in the Policy Process*, pp. 263–79.

24. Kenneth L. Rider, *A Parametric Model for the Allocation of Fire Companies* (Santa Monica: Rand Corporation, R-1646, August 1975).

25. Allocation data in this section are based on New York City Fire Department rosters for 1972 and 1973. Data on incidence of fire are taken from New York City Fire Department, *Annual Reports* for 1972 and 1973. Information on the size of fire battalions has been provided by the New York City Fire Department Division of Planning and Operations Research (PANDOR). The author is particularly indebted to Marc Leopold of PANDOR for his assistance on each of these matters.

26. Edward Blum, *Urban Fire Protection: Studying the Operations of the New York City Fire Department* (New York: New York City Rand Institute, January 1971).

27. New York City Charter, effective 1963, amended June 1, 1977; ch. 31, sec. 753.

28. Joseph P. Viteritti, "Implementing Change through Training."

29. Information in this section on the New York City Sanitation Department productivity project is based on "Improving Collection Productivity: The Project Team Manual," New York City Department of Sanitation, 1970.

30. Citizens' Budget Commission, "New York City's Productivity Program: The Department of Sanitation" (New York: Citizens' Budget Commission, 1973), pp. 11–12.

31. Frederick O'R. Hayes, *Productivity in Local Government*, p. 101.

32. Information in this section on manpower allocations and the size of sanitation districts is based upon the *Annual Progress Report and Statistical Review*, New York City Sanitation Department, 1971, 1973.

33. It should be pointed out that the department does provide collection services for hospitals, schools, churches, and other nonprofit institutions. However, these demands for service do not generally skew the demand patterns that are manifest by resident population groups.

34. Louis Blair, *The Challenge of Productivity Diversity: Improving the Measurement and Evaluation of Local Governments*, part 2 (Washington: Urban Institute, 1972).

7. BUREAUCRACY AND SOCIAL JUSTICE

1. John Rawls, *A Theory of Justice*, p. 302.

2. J. Leiper Freeman, *The Political Process* (New York: Random House, 1955); Francis E. Rourke, *Bureaucracy, Politics and Public Policy;* Aaron Wildavsky, *The Politics of the Budgetary Process* (Boston: Little, Brown, 1964).

3. Morris Janowitz, *The Professional Soldier* (New York: Free Press, 1960).

4. James R. Schlesinger, *Systems Analysis and the Political Process*, pp. 14–17.

5. Herbert Simon, *Administrative Behavior.*

6. See, for example, Gary Hirsch and Lucius Riccio, "Measuring and Improving the Productivity of Police Patrol," *Journal of Police Science and Administration* 2 (1974); National Commission on Productivity and Work Quality, *Opportunities for Improving Productivity in Police Services* (Washington: National Commission on Productivity and Work Quality, 1973).

7. Albert Biderman, "Social Indicators and Goals," in Raymond Bauer, ed., *Social Indicators* (Cambridge: M.I.T. Press, 1966), pp. 111–28; M. D. Maltz, *Evaluation of Crime Control Programs* (Washington: National Institute of Law Enforcement and Criminal Justice, April 1972).

8. Herbert Simon, R. W. Shephard, and F. W. Sharp, *Fire Losses and Fire Risks* (Berkeley: Bureau of Public Administration, University of California, 1943).

9. Phil Schaenman and Joe Schwartz, *Measuring Fire Protection Productivity in Local Government* (Boston: National Fire Protection Association, 1974); Urban Institute and National Fire Protection Association, *Measuring the Effectiveness of Basic Municipal Services* (Washington: Urban Institute, 1976).

10. Louis Blair and Alfred Schwartz, *How Clean Is Our City?* (Washington: Urban Institute, 1972).

11. Stan Altman, P. Nowrocki, and F. Potter, *Institutional Framework for Evaluating Municipal Services* (New York: Fund for the City of New York, 1974); Gregory Farrell, *Designing, Testing and Measuring the Performance of Selected City Services* (New York: Fund for the City of New York, 1975).

12. For a comparison of a "computational" and a "bargaining" type of decision making structure, one might refer to James D. Thompson and Arthur Tuden, "Strategies, Structures and Processes of Organizational Decision," in James D. Thompson and Arthur Tuden, eds., *Comparative Studies in Administration* (Pittsburgh: University of Pittsburgh Press, 1959).

BIBLIOGRAPHY

1. PUBLIC ADMINISTRATION AND ORGANIZATION THEORY

Barnard, Chester. *The Functions of the Executive.* Cambridge: Harvard University Press, 1938.

Blau, Peter. *Bureaucracy in Modern Society.* New York: Random House, 1956.

Braybrooke, David and Charles Lindblom. *A Strategy for Decision.* New York: Free Press, 1963.

Downs, Anthony. *Inside Bureaucracy.* Boston: Little, Brown, 1966.

Gortner, Harold F. *Administration in the Public Sector.* New York: John Wiley, 1977.

Gulick, Luther, and Lyndall Urwick, eds. *Papers on the Science of Administration.* New York: Institute of Public Administration, 1937.

Lindblom, Charles. "The Science of Muddling Through." *Public Administration Review* 19 (spring 1959).

March, James, and Herbert Simon. *Organizations.* New York: John Wiley, 1958.

Marini, Frank, ed. *Toward a New Public Administration.* Scranton: Chandler, 1971.

McGregor, Douglas. *The Human Side of Enterprise.* New York: McGraw-Hill, 1960.

Merton, Robert, ed. *Social Theory and Social Structure.* New York: Free Press, 1949.

Morrow, William. *Public Administration.* New York: Random House, 1975.

Mosher, Frederick C. *Democracy and the Public Service.* New York: Oxford University Press, 1968.

Mosher, Frederick C., ed. *American Public Administration: Past, Present, Future.* University, Ala.: University of Alabama Press, 1975.

Nigro, Felix, and Lloyd Nigro. *Modern Public Administration.* New York: Harper & Row, 1965.

Ostrom, Vincent. *The Intellectual Crisis in American Public Administration.* University, Ala.: University of Alabama Press, 1974.

Rourke, Francis E. *Bureaucracy, Politics and Public Policy.* Boston: Little, Brown, 1969.

Simon, Herbert. *Administrative Behavior.* New York: Collier-Macmillan, 1945.

Simon, Herbert, Donald Smithberg, and Victor Thompson. *Public Administration.* New York: Knopf, 1950.

Taylor, Frederick. *The Principles of Scientific Management*. New York: Harper, 1911.

Waldo, Dwight. *The Administrative State*. New York: Ronald Press, 1948.

Waldo, Dwight. "The Administrative State Revisited." *Public Administration Review* 25 (March 1965).

Waldo, Dwight, ed. *Public Administration in a Time of Turbulence*. Scranton: Chandler, 1971.

Weber, Max. "Bureaucracy." *From Max Weber: Essays in Sociology*. Edited by H. H. Gerth and C. Wright Mills. New York: Oxford University Press, 1946.

White, Leonard D. *Introduction to the Study of Public Administration*. New York: Macmillan, 1939.

Wilson, Woodrow. "The Study of Public Administration." *Political Science Quarterly* 2 (June 1887).

Woll, Peter. *American Bureaucracy*. New York: W. W. Norton, 1963.

2. THE CIVIL SERVICE AND MINORITY EMPLOYMENT

Aronson, Sidney. *Status and Kinship in the Higher Civil Service*. Cambridge: Harvard University Press, 1964.

Bendix, Reinhard. *Higher Civil Servants in American Society*. Denver: University of Colorado Press, 1949.

Campbell, Alan K. "Civil Service Reform: A New Commitment," *Public Administration Review* 38 (March-April 1978).

Cummings, Milton, M. Kent Jennings, and Franklin Kilpatrick. "Federal and Non-Federal Employees: A Comparative Social-Occupational Analysis." *Public Administration Review* 27 (December 1967).

Hellriegel, Don, and Larry Short. "Equal Employment Opportunity in the Federal Government: A Comparative Analysis." *Public Administration Review* 32 (November-December 1972).

Hoogenboom, Ari. *Outlawing the Spoils*. Urbana: University of Illinois Press, 1961.

Kingsley, J. Donald. *Representative Bureaucracy*. Yellow Springs, Ohio: Antioch Press, 1944.

Krislov, Samuel. *The Negro in Federal Employment*. Minneapolis: University of Minnesota Press, 1967.

Krislov, Samuel. *Representative Bureaucracy*. Englewood Cliffs: Prentice-Hall, 1974.

Kranz, Harry. *The Participatory Bureaucracy*. Lexington, Mass.: D. C. Heath, 1976.

Long, Norton. "Bureaucracy and Constitutionalism." *American Political Science Review* 46 (September 1952).

Meier, Kenneth J. "Representative Bureaucracy: An Empirical Analysis." *American Political Science Review* 69 (June 1975).

Nachmias, David, and David Rosenbloom. "Measuring Bureaucratic Representation and Integration." *Public Administration Review* 33 (November-December 1973).

Rosenbloom, David. "The Civil Service Commission's Decision to Authorize the Use of Goals and Timetables in Federal Equal Employment Opportunity Program." *Western Political Quarterly* 26 (June 1973).

Rosenbloom, David, and Carole Cassler Obuchowski. "Public Personnel Examinations and the Constitution: Emergent Trends." *Public Administration Review* 37 (January-February 1977).

Savas, E. S., and Sigmund Ginsberg. "The Civil Service: A Meritless System." *Public Interest* (summer 1973).

Stahl, O. Glenn. *Public Personnel Administration*. New York: Harper & Row, 1971.

Subramaniam, V. "Representative Bureaucracy: A Reassessment." *American Political Science Review* 61 (December 1967).

Van Riper, Paul. *History of the United States Civil Service.* New York: Row Peterson, 1958.
Warner, W. Lloyd, et al. *The American Federal Executive.* New Haven: Yale University Press, 1963.

3. PARTICIPATION, POWER AND POLITICS IN THE CITY

Altshuler, Alan. *Community Control.* New York: Pegasus, 1970.
Bachrach, Peter. *The Theory of Democratic Elitism.* Boston: Little, Brown, 1967.
Banfield, Edward. *The Unheavenly City.* Boston: Little, Brown, 1968.
Banfield, Edward, and James Q. Wilson. *City Politics.* New York: Vintage Books, 1963.
Carmichael, Stokely and Charles V. Hamilton. *Black Power: The Politics of Liberation in America.* New York: Vintage Books, 1967.
Cloward, Richard, and Lloyd Ohlin. *Delinquency and Opportunity: A Theory of Delinquent Gangs.* New York: Free Press, 1960.
Cole, Richard. *Citizen Participation and the Urban Policy Process.* Lexington, Mass.: D. C. Heath, 1974.
Dahl, Robert. *A Preface to Democratic Theory.* New Haven: Yale University Press, 1956.
Dahl, Robert. *Who Governs?* New Haven: Yale University Press, 1966.
Donovan, John. *The Politics of Poverty.* New York: Pegasus, 1967.
Fantini, Mario, and Marilyn Gittell. *Decentralization: Achieving Reform.* New York: Praeger, 1973.
Kotler, Milton. *Neighborhood Government.* Indianapolis: Bobbs-Merril, 1969.
Kristol, Irving. "Decentralization for What?" *Public Interest* 11 (spring 1968).
Levitan, Sar. *The Great Society's Poor Law.* Baltimore: Johns Hopkins University Press, 1969.
Lowi, Theodore J. *The End of Liberalism.* New York: Norton, 1969.
Moynihan, Daniel P. *Maximum Feasible Misunderstanding.* New York: Free Press, 1969.
Piven, Frances Fox, and Richard Cloward. *Regulating the Poor.* New York: Vintage Books, 1971.
Polsby, Nelson. *Community Power and Political Theory.* New Haven: Yale University Press, 1967.
Schmandt, Henry. "Municipal Decentralization: An Overview." *Public Administration Review* 32 (October 1972).
Sundquist, James, ed. *On Fighting Poverty.* New York: Basic Books, 1968.
Yates, Douglas. *Neighborhood Democracy.* Lexington, Mass.: D. C. Heath, 1973.
Yin, Robert, and Douglas Yates. *Street-Level Governments.* Lexington, Mass.: D. C. Heath, 1975.
Zimmerman, Joseph. *The Federated City.* New York: St. Martin's Press, 1972.

4. NEW YORK CITY GOVERNMENT AND POLITICS

Bell, Daniel, and Virginia Held. "The Community Revolution." *The Public Interest* 16 (summer 1969).
Bellush, Jewel, and Stephen M. David, eds. *Race and Politics in New York City.* New York: Praeger, 1971.
Dahlbert, Jane. *The New York Bureau of Municipal Research.* New York: New York University Press, 1966.
Fainstein, Norman, and Susan Fainstein. "The Future of Community Control." *American Political Science Review* 70 (September 1976).

Gittell, Marilyn. *Participants and Participation: A Study of School Policy in New York City*. New York: Praeger, 1967.

Gordon, Diana. *City Limits*. New York: Charter House, 1973.

Greenberger, Martin, Matthew Crenson, and Brian Crissey. *Models in the Policy Process*. New York: Russell Sage Foundation, 1976.

Hamilton, Edward V. "Productivity: The New York Approach." *Public Administration Review* 32 (November-December 1972).

Hayes, Frederick O'R. *Productivity in Local Government*. Lexington, Mass.: D. C. Heath, 1977. Ch. 6.

Hentoff, Nat. *A Political Life: The Education of John V. Lindsay*. New York: Knopf, 1969.

Horton, Raymond D. *Municipal Labor Relations in New York City: Lessons of the Lindsay-Wagner Years*. New York: Praeger, 1973.

Horton, Raymond D. "Productivity and Productivity Bargaining: A Critical Analysis." *Public Administration Review* 36 (July-August 1976).

Lindsay, John V. *The City*. New York: Norton, 1969.

Marquez, Camilo. *Municipal Expenditures by Neighborhood*. New York: Office of the Mayor, 1970.

Moynihan, Daniel P., and Nathan Glazer. *Beyond the Melting Pot*. Cambridge: M.I.T. Press, 1963.

Ravitch, Diane. *The Great School Wars*. New York: Basic Books, 1974.

Rogers, David. *110 Livingston Street*. New York: Random House, 1968.

Rogers, David. *Can Business Management Save the Cities?* New York: Free Press, 1978.

Sayre, Wallace and Herbert Kaufman. *Governing New York City*. New York: Russell Sage Foundation, 1960.

Spero, Sterling, and John Capozzola. *The Urban Community and Its Unionized Bureaucracies*. New York: Dunellen, 1973.

Stanley, David. *Professional Personnel for the City of New York*. Washington: Brookings Institution, 1963.

Sviridoff, Mitchell. *Developing New York's Human Resources*. New York: Institute of Public Administration, 1966.

Temporary Commission on City Finances. Final Report: *The City in Transition*. New York: Arno Press, 1978.

Viteritti, Joseph P. *Police, Politics and Pluralism in New York City: A Comparative Case Study*. Beverly Hills: Sage Publications, 1973.

Viteritti, Joseph P. "New York's Management Plan and Reporting System: A Descriptive Analysis." *Public Administration Review* 38 (July-August 1978).

Viteritti, Joseph P. "Implementing Change through Training: A Case Study," *Public Administration Review* 38 (September-October 1978).

5. POLICY ANALYSIS AND SOCIAL EQUITY

Balk, Walter, ed. "Symposium on Productivity in Government." *Public Administration Review* 38 (January-February 1978).

Benson, Charles, and Peter Lund. *Neighborhood Distribution of Local Government Services*. Berkeley: University of California Press, 1969.

Bollens, John C. *Exploring the Metropolitan Community*. Berkeley: University of California Press, 1961.

Campbell, Alan. "Approaches to Defining, Measuring and Achieving Equity in the Public Service." *Public Administration Review* 36 (September-October 1976).

Chitwood, Stephen. "Social Equity and Social Service Productivity." *Public Administration Review* 34 (January-February 1974).

Dror, Yehezkel. *Public Policymaking Re-examined*. New York: Chandler, 1968.

Dror, Yehezkel. *Design for Policy Sciences.* New York: Elsevier, 1971.

Frederickson, H. George, and Charles Wise, eds. *Public Administration and Public Policy.* Lexington, Mass.: D. C. Heath, 1977.

Lasswell, Harold D. *The Future of Political Science.* New York: Atherton, 1963.

Hatry, Harry. "Issues in Productivity Measurement in Local Government." *Public Administration Review* 32 (November-December 1972).

Levy, Frank, Arnold Meltsner, and Aaron Wildavsky. *Urban Outcomes.* Berkeley: University of California Press, 1974.

Lineberry, Robert L. *Equality and Urban Policy.* Beverly Hills: Sage Publications, 1977.

Lowi, Theodore. "American Business, Public Policy, Case Studies and Political Theory." *World Politics* 16 (June 1964).

Mark, Jerome. "Meanings and Measures of Productivity." *Public Administration Review* 32 (November-December 1972).

McGregor, Eugene. "Social Equity and the Public Service." *Public Administration Review* 34 (January 1974).

Meltsner, Arnold. *Policy Analysts in the Bureaucracy.* Berkeley: University of California Press, 1976.

Ranney, Austin, ed. *Political Science and Public Policy.* Chicago: Markham, 1968.

Rawls, John. *A Theory of Justice.* Cambridge: Harvard University Press, 1971.

Ridley, Clarence E., and Herbert A. Simon. *Measuring Municipal Activities.* Chicago: International City Managers' Association, 1938.

Ross, John P., and Jesse Burkhead. *Productivity in the Local Government Sector.* Lexington, Mass.: D. C. Heath, 1974.

Scioli, Frank P., and Thomas J. Cook, eds. *Methodologies for Analyzing Public Policies.* Lexington, Mass.: D. C. Heath, 1975.

Sharkansky, Ira, ed. *Policy Analysis in Political Science.* Chicago: Markham, 1969.

The Urban Institute. *How Effective Are Your Community Services?* Washington: Urban Institute, 1977.

Viteritti, Joseph P. "Politics, Science and Public Policy: An Essay on the Use and Abuse of Behavioral Theory." *Journal of Political Science* 3 (spring 1976).

6. SYSTEMS ANALYSIS AND THE NEW SCIENCE OF MANAGEMENT

Drake, Alvin W, Ralph L. Keeney, and Philip M. Morse, eds. *Analysis of Public Systems.* Cambridge: M.I.T. Press, 1972.

Greenberger, Martin, Matthew Crenson, and Brian L. Crissey. *Models in the Policy Process.* New York: Russell Sage Foundation, 1976.

Hitch, Charles. *Decision Making for Defense.* Berkeley: University of California Press, 1965.

Hitch, Charles, and Roland McKean. *The Economics of Defense in a Nuclear Age.* Cambridge: Harvard University Press, 1960.

Hoos, Ida. *Systems Analysis in Public Policy: A Critical Analysis.* Berkeley: University of California Press, 1972.

Quade, E. S., ed. *Analysis for Military Decisions.* Chicago: Rand McNally, 1967.

Quade, E. S. *Analysis for Public Decisions.* New York: Elsevier, 1975.

Rivlin, Alice. *Systematic Thinking for Social Action.* Washington: Brookings Institution, 1971.

Schick, Allen. "The Road to PPB: The Stages of Budget Reform." *Public Administration Review* 26 (December 1966).

Schiesl, Martin. *The Politics of Efficiency.* Berkeley: University of California Press, 1977.

Schlesinger, James R. *Systems Analysis and the Political Process.* Santa Monica: Rand Corporation, P-3464, 1967.

White, Michael, Michael Radnor, and David Tonsik. *Management and Policy Science in American Government.* Lexington, Mass.: D. C. Heath, 1975.

INDEX